The Law Commission

(LAW COM No 246)

SHAREHOLDER REMEDIES

Report on a Reference under section 3(1)(e) of the Law Commissions Act 1965

Presented to Parliament by the Lord High Chancellor by Command of Her Majesty October 1997

Cm 3769

£18.20

The Law Commission was set up by section 1 of the Law Commissions Act 1965 for the purpose of promoting the reform of the law.

The Commissioners are:

> The Honourable Mrs Justice Arden DBE, *Chairman*
> Professor Andrew Burrows
> Miss Diana Faber
> Mr Charles Harpum
> Mr Stephen Silber QC

The Secretary of the Law Commission is Mr Michael Sayers and its offices are at Conquest House, 37-38 John Street, Theobalds Road, London, WC1N 2BQ.

The terms of this report were agreed on 11 September 1997.

The text of this report is available on the Internet at:

> http://www.gtnet.gov.uk/lawcomm/homepage.htm

EXECUTIVE SUMMARY

WHY SHAREHOLDER REMEDIES?

1. This report recommends law reform designed to make shareholder remedies more affordable and more appropriate in modern conditions.

2. There are three main shareholder remedies:

   ♦ the "unfair prejudice" remedy, in which a member seeks redress for action by the company which injures his interest as a member

   ♦ the derivative action, in which a member seeks to enforce a claim belonging to his company

   ♦ action to enforce the company's constitution.

3. The unfair prejudice remedy and the derivative action are specialist remedies, and the former is far more common than the latter.

4. The unfair prejudice remedy is most commonly used by private companies of which, as at 3 August 1997, there were some 1,080,671[1] in Great Britain. We recommend statutory and other changes to simplify the remedy, and help reduce its high cost to litigant[2] and taxpayer alike.[3]

5. The derivative action is not common but it is an important mechanism of shareholder control of corporate wrongs. The current law is archaic. Our principal recommendation is for a new rule of court which would set out in a modern and accessible form the circumstances in which the courts will permit the derivative action to be brought. The underlying policy, which is restrictive of the circumstances in which a derivative action may be brought, is not affected.[4]

6. Prevention is better than cure. Litigation is time-consuming and costly. In order to minimise reliance on shareholder remedies, we recommend that a new article is added to Table A, which is the statutory model form of a company's articles of association. This contains a basic dispute resolution mechanism, and will encourage shareholders in future to have pre-agreed routes to resolve disputes without litigation.

THE WAY AHEAD

7. It is for the Government, Parliament and the new Civil Procedure Rule Committee to decide whether to implement our recommendations.

---

[1] Unaudited figure supplied by Companies House.

[2] See para 1.6.

[3] See para 1.6.

[4] The Scottish Law Commission's discussion and recommendations relating to the position under Scots law as respects the shareholder's action - the equivalent to the derivative action under English law - is contained in Appendix D to this report.

8.	By our principal recommendations we seek

- in relation to unfair prejudice, new primary legislation

- in relation to the derivative action, new primary legislation[5] and a new rule of court

- in relation to Table A, the insertion of a new regulation by statutory instrument.

9.	Implementation of the new rule of court for the derivative action and the new regulation in Table A does not depend on Parliamentary time.

[5]	For Scotland, primary and subordinate legislation would be required.

LAW COMMISSION

SHAREHOLDER REMEDIES

CONTENTS

PART 4: OTHER REFORMS RELATING TO PROCEEDINGS UNDER SECTIONS 459-461

PART 5: ARTICLES OF ASSOCIATION

PART 6: A NEW DERIVATIVE ACTION

GLOSSARY OF ABBREVIATIONS

In this report the following terms and expressions are used for the sake of brevity:

ADR	Alternative dispute resolution
CCR	the County Court Rules
Draft Civil Proceedings Rules	*Access to Justice, Draft Civil Proceedings Rules* (July 1996)
DTI	Department of Trade and Industry
LCD Working Paper on Judicial Case Management	Lord Chancellor's Department, *Access to Justice, Judicial Case Management, the Fast Track and Multi-track, A working paper* (July 1997)
the 1990 Practice Direction	Practice Direction (Ch D) Companies Court: Contributory's Petition) [1990] 1 WLR 590
RSC	the Rules of the Supreme Court
the 1986 Rules	Companies (Unfair Prejudice Applications) Proceedings Rules 1986 (SI 1986 No 2000)
Woolf Interim Report	*Access to Justice, Interim Report to the Lord Chancellor on the Civil Justice System in England and Wales* (June 1995)
Woolf Report	*Access to Justice, The Final Report to the Lord Chancellor on the Civil Justice System in England and Wales* (July 1996)

CASES

Ebrahimi	*Ebrahimi v Westbourne Galleries Ltd* [1973] AC 360
Prudential	*Prudential Assurance Co Ltd v Newman Industries Ltd (No 2)* [1982] Ch 204
Saul D Harrison	*Re Saul D Harrison & Sons plc* [1992] BCLC 724 (Ch D); [1995] 1 BCLC 14 (CA)

LIST OF CASES REFERRED TO IN THIS REPORT

PART 1
INTRODUCTION

Terms of reference

1.1 In February 1995, the Lord Chancellor and the President of the Board of Trade requested us, in consultation with the Scottish Law Commission:

> ... to carry out a review of shareholder remedies with particular reference to:- the rule in *Foss v Harbottle* (1843) 2 Hare 461 and its exceptions; sections 459 to 461 of the Companies Act 1985; and the enforcement of the rights of shareholders under the articles of association; and to make recommendations.[1]

1.2 The focus of the project was on the *remedies* available to a minority shareholder[2] who is dissatisfied with the manner in which the company of which he is a member is run. This may be because there has been a breach of duty by the directors; or it may be because of the way in which the majority shareholders have used their voting power to cause the company to act in a manner which unfairly prejudices the interests of the minority shareholder; or it may simply be that the requirements of the company's constitution have not been properly complied with. We were not able, in the context of our limited terms of reference, to undertake a wider review of company law as a number of commentators have suggested would be desirable.[3]

1.3 So far as directors' duties are concerned, we explained in the consultation paper[4] that the project is concerned only with the machinery by which the duties owed in

---

[1] The original terms of reference continued: "**The review is to be conducted under the present law and under proposals to be made by the Department of Trade and Industry as to the reform of the law relating to duties of the directors of companies and as to Part X of the Companies Act**". The Department of Trade and Industry's ("DTI") work on directors' duties was, however, delayed and our review was conducted only under the present law.

[2] Ie one or more members not holding the majority of voting rights capable of being cast at general meetings. A shareholder who holds a majority of the voting rights will not usually need to resort to the remedies under consideration in this project, although he may be able to claim to have been unfairly prejudiced; see the comments of Knox J in *Re Baltic Real Estate Ltd (No 1)* [1993] BCLC 498, 501, and in *Re Baltic Real Estate Ltd (No 2)* [1993] BCLC 503, 506-507.

[3] See Rees, "Shareholder Remedies" [1997] 5 ICCLR 155. See also John Lowry, "Restructuring Shareholder Actions: A response to the Law Commission's Consultation Paper: Shareholder Remedies"; C A Riley, "The Law Commission Consultation Paper on Shareholder Remedies: Problems, Principles and Evidence"; and David Sugarman, "Enhancing Access to Justice, or Rouge on the Unacceptable Face of Capitalism". All three papers were delivered to a joint workshop on Consultation Paper No 142, under the joint auspices of the SPTL Company Law Section and the Institute of Advanced Legal Studies Centre for Corporate Law and Practice, 13 December 1996.

[4] See Consultation Paper No 142, para 1.5.

law can be enforced. The content of those duties is outside the scope of the project, as is the accountability of directors to shareholders in listed companies.[5]

Problems identified in the consultation paper

1.4   In the consultation paper we identified two main problems. The first is the obscurity and complexity of the law relating to the ability of a shareholder to bring proceedings on behalf of his company. He may wish to do so to enforce liability for a breach by one of the directors of his duties to the company.[6] Generally it is for the company itself, acting in accordance with the will of the majority of its members, to bring any such proceedings. This is as a result of principles commonly known as the rule in *Foss v Harbottle*. However, if the wrongdoing director(s) control the majority of votes they may prevent legal proceedings being brought. There are therefore exceptions to the rule which enable a minority shareholder to bring an action to enforce the company's rights. But our provisional view was that the law relating to these exceptions is rigid, old fashioned and unclear.[7] We pointed out that it is inaccessible save to lawyers specialising in this field because, to obtain a proper understanding of it, it is necessary to examine numerous reported cases decided over a period of 150 years. We also explained that the procedure is lengthy and costly, involving a preliminary stage which in one case took 18 days of court time to resolve.[8]

1.5   The second main problem which we identified in the consultation paper relates to the efficiency and cost of the remedy which is most widely used by minority shareholders to obtain some personal remedy in the event of unsatisfactory conduct of a company's business. This is the remedy for unfairly prejudicial conduct contained in sections 459-461 of the Companies Act 1985. Although the remedy can be used in companies of any size and for unfairly prejudicial conduct of any kind,[9] we pointed out[10] that it is often used where there is a breakdown in relations between the owner-managers of small private companies and one of them is prevented from taking part in management. The dissatisfied shareholder can obtain a variety of types of relief but the most popular is a court order requiring the majority shareholder(s) to purchase his shares. As at 3 August 1997, there were some 1,080,671 private companies in Great Britain.[11] Our statistical

---

[5]   In this connection, the Hampel Committee is carrying forward the work of the Cadbury Committee on the Financial Aspects of Corporate Governance and the Greenbury Committee on Director's Remuneration. The Hampel Committee published an interim report on 5 August (*Committee on Corporate Governance, Preliminary Report* (August 1997)) and intends to publish a final report in December 1997.

[6]   These duties include fiduciary duties of loyalty and good faith, which mean that directors are obliged to act honestly and in good faith in the interests of the company, to exercise their powers for a proper purpose and not to place themselves in a position where their interests conflict with their duties to the company. They also include duties of skill and care in relation to the management of the company's business.

[7]   See Consultation Paper No 142, paras 1.6 and 14.1-14.4.

[8]   *Smith v Croft (No 2)* [1988] Ch 114.

[9]   Including breaches of directors' duties.

[10]   See Consultation Paper No 142, para 1.7.

[11]   Unaudited figure supplied by Companies House.

2

survey of petitions filed under section 459 at the High Court in London[12] has indicated that 97% of petitions related to private companies and 93% of petitions related to companies with 10 or fewer members. 76% of petitions involved companies where all or most of the shareholders were involved in the management, and 64% of petitions included an allegation of exclusion from management.

1.6   Our provisional view was that proceedings under section 459 are costly and cumbersome. Unfair prejudice cases which go to trial often last weeks rather than days,[13] and the costs of the litigation can be substantial.[14] There is also a significant cost on the tax payer.[15]

[12]   See Appendix J, and see para 3.13 below. The statistics related to petitions filed between January 1994 and December 1996. A total of 254 petitions were recorded as presented during this period, of which 233 section 459 petitions were inspected.

[13]   We have examined the cases reported in Butterworth's Company Law Cases for the last ten years (1988-1997). Fourteen cases were shown to have gone to a full trial and the average length of the hearing was just over three weeks (16 days). One of the most extreme examples of lengthy trials to which we drew attention in the consultation paper was the unreported case of *Re Freudiana Music Co Ltd* 24 March 1993 (unreported, Jonathan Parker J) where the hearing lasted for a year and extended over some 165 court days.

[14]   There is little information available about the costs of section 459 proceedings. However, in *Re Elgindata Ltd* [1991] BCLC 959 the hearing lasted 43 days, costs totalled £320,000 and the shares, originally purchased for £40,000, were finally valued at only £24,600. In *Re Macro (Ipswich) Ltd* [1994] 2 BCLC 354 the hearing of s 459 proceedings and a related action lasted 27 days at first instance alone. The parties subsequently claimed that they were entitled to recover total costs of £725,000 under orders of the court; see *Re Macro (Ipswich) Ltd* [1996] 1 WLR 145, 148. This did not include the costs of the subsequent appeal hearing: *Re Macro (Ipswich) Ltd* 22 May 1996 (unreported, CA).

Some research has been done on costs in civil litigation in connection with Lord Woolf's Inquiry into *Access to Justice* (see paras 1.28-1.30 below). This research was based on a survey of the costs allowed to the winning party in a sample of 673 cases of various types submitted to the Supreme Court Taxing Office (SCTO) in 1994/5. These cases had terminated at various stages in the litigation. No figures are available for s 459 cases alone. The survey contained a number of findings. For instance, the survey showed that the average costs allowed to the winning party in cases where the value of the claim was between £50,000 and £100,000 was £23,760 (with the lowest allowed being £4,667 and the highest costs allowed being £121,545 (*Access to Justice, Interim Report to the Lord Chancellor on the Civil Justice System in England and Wales* (June 1995), Annex III)). Later research was done on a sample of 2,184 cases submitted to SCTO between 1990 and 1995. The sample was analysed according to case type, weight and claim value (where applicable). There was no specific type for s 459 cases. For the Bankruptcy/Companies Court case type the median costs allowed to the winning party for claims having a value between £50,000 and £100,000 was £9,015, but this calculation included cases of different weight, duration and claim value. The median costs allowed for the heaviest and lightest weight of cases where any value was claimed were £170,129 and £5,559 respectively. Median costs in the Bankruptcy/Companies Court case type where the amount claimed was between £50,000 and £100,000 was 15% (*Access to Justice, The Final Report to the Lord Chancellor on the Civil Justice System in England and Wales* (July 1996), Annex III). The figures in the annexes to Lord Woolf's reports were based on the costs of the winning party submitted to taxation. The total costs of all parties would be substantially higher.

[15]   A working figure for the cost to the taxpayer of a day in the High Court is about £2,000 (figure provided by the Court Service, based on costs for 1995-6). This figure does not take into account the cost of providing Legal Aid where that is available and is granted.

1.7   We expressed the view that small owner-managed companies are particularly affected by this problem.[16] This is because the case law on section 459 enables members of those types of companies to resort to this remedy more easily than members of other types of companies; and because the consequent delays and lost management time are particularly detrimental to such companies. While the dispute between the shareholders is continuing, the companies business can be brought to a standstill.

1.8   A third problem which we examined in the consultation paper is the enforcement of shareholders' contractual rights under the articles of association. This includes the extent to which a shareholder can insist on the affairs of the company being conducted in accordance with the articles of association. However, our provisional view was that no hardship was being caused by any difficulty in identifying personal rights conferred by the articles.[17]

Guiding principles

1.9   In the consultation paper we set out six guiding principles for our proposals in relation to the reform of the law and procedure relating to shareholder remedies. These were as follows:

(i) Proper plaintiff

Normally the company should be the only party entitled to enforce a cause of action belonging to it. Accordingly, a member should be able to maintain proceedings about wrongs done to the company only in exceptional circumstances.

(ii) Internal management

An individual member should not be able to pursue proceedings on behalf of a company about matters of internal management, that is, matters which the majority are entitled to regulate by ordinary resolution.

(iii) Commercial decisions

The court should continue to have regard to the decision of the directors on commercial matters if the decision was made in good faith, on proper information and in the light of the relevant considerations, and appears to be a reasonable decision for the directors to have taken.[18] In those circumstances the court should not substitute its own judgment for that of the directors.

---

[16]   See Consultation Paper No 142, paras 1.7 and 14.5; see also para 1.5 above.

[17]   *Ibid*, at para 14.9.

[18]   See generally *Howard Smith v Ampol Petroleum Ltd* [1974] AC 821 (PC) at pp 832-835. The requirement that directors should have acted reasonably can be seen, for example, in the judgment of Slade J in *Re Burton & Deakin Ltd* [1977] 1 WLR 390, 397; in *Smith v Croft (No 2)* [1988] Ch 114, 189, *per* Knox J and in *Re D'Jan of London Ltd* [1994] 1 BCLC 561, 563, *per* Hoffmann LJ (sitting as an Additional Judge of the High Court). Section 727(1) of the Companies Act 1985 provides a defence for directors who are sued for breach of duty as follows:

(iv) Sanctity of contract

A member is taken to have agreed to the terms of the memorandum and articles of association when he became a member, whether or not he appreciated what they meant at the time. The law should continue to treat him as so bound unless he shows that the parties have come to some other agreement or understanding which is not reflected in the articles or memorandum.[19] Failure to do so will create unacceptable commercial uncertainty. The corollary of this is that the best protection for a shareholder is appropriate protection in the articles themselves.

(v) Freedom from unnecessary shareholder interference

Shareholders should not be able to involve the company in litigation without good cause, or where they intend to cause the company or the other shareholders embarrassment or harm rather than genuinely pursue the relief claimed. Otherwise the company may be "killed by kindness",[20] or waste money and management time in dealing with unwarranted proceedings. The importance of this principle increases if the circumstances in which the individual shareholders can bring derivative actions are enlarged. Nuisance or other litigation of this nature has to be identified on a case by case basis. This means that the requisite control has to be exercised by the courts, with increased powers if necessary.

(vi) Efficiency and cost effectiveness

All shareholder remedies should be made as efficient and cost effective as can be achieved in the circumstances. This is largely a matter for the courts and the report prepared by Lord Woolf on the civil justice system in England and Wales,[21] but it has to be considered whether any additional powers are needed in the case of shareholder litigation.

1.10   We went on to say that we provisionally considered that all save the first two of these principles were applicable to all kinds of shareholder remedies. The first two were relevant only to derivative actions.[22] The fifth had only limited relevance to proceedings under section 459, since, in general, such proceedings do not require the company to take an active role (although, in small owner-managed companies,

> If in any proceedings for negligence, default, breach of duty or breach of trust against an officer of a company ... it appears to the court hearing the case that that officer ... is or may be liable in respect of the negligence, default, breach of duty or breach of trust, but that he has acted honestly and reasonably, and that having regard to all the circumstances of the case, ... he ought fairly to be excused ... that court may relieve him, either wholly or partly, from his liability ... .

---

[19]   In some situations this principle may have to give way to the jurisdiction under s 459.

[20]   *Prudential Assurance Co Ltd v Newman Industries Ltd (No 2)* [1982] Ch 204, 221.

[21]   *Access to Justice, The Final Report to the Lord Chancellor on the Civil Justice System in England and Wales* (July 1996). See paras 1.28-1.30 below.

[22]   However, there may be some overlap between the second principle and the approach of the court under s 459 to trivial or technical infringements of the articles; see *Re Saul D Harrison & Sons plc* [1995] 1 BCLC 14, 18, *per* Hoffmann LJ.

section 459 proceedings may well result in lost management time). However, if a member seeks a winding up order as an alternative to relief under section 459 in circumstances in which this is unjustified, then the relevance of the fifth principle was increased.

1.11   Applying these principles, we reached three basic provisional conclusions. The first of these was that, within proper bounds, the rule in *Foss v Harbottle*[23] should be replaced by a simpler and more modern procedure if a satisfactory procedure could be devised. The second was that the court must have all necessary powers to streamline minority shareholder litigation so that it is less costly and complicated. The third was that we should provide a "self-help" remedy (or range of remedies) to avoid the need for shareholders to resort to the court to resolve disputes.

1.12   There was virtually unanimous support for these principles from those who commented on consultation. (Indeed, perhaps not surprisingly, consultees were unanimous in approving the sixth principle). In the light of this clear expression of opinion we have applied these principles in framing our recommendations in this report. Thus a key feature of the new structure for shareholder remedies recommended in this report is strong judicial control. In some contexts, the control consists of the exercise of a discretion (or residual discretion) conferred by procedural rules or statute which for good reason has to be open-textured to deal with the variety of cases that come within it.[24] In other contexts in the field of shareholder remedies, such as the derivative action, we have so far as we can specifically pointed the court to the relevant considerations which are derived from the guiding principles as set out above. One of the advantages in controlling the derivative action by a rule of court is that the form of the rule can be strengthened, extended or clarified if that proves necessary to achieve the policy behind the guiding principles.[25] Again, in the light of this strong expression of opinion, we have it in mind that, in so far as the court is free to decide how to exercise its control over shareholder actions, it too would apply the same policy.

Provisional recommendations

1.13   In the light of the principles and conclusions set out above,[26] we proposed three main approaches in the consultation paper to deal with the problems identified. First, we proposed that there should be a new derivative action governed by rules

---

[23]   As restated in *Prudential Assurance Co Ltd v Newman Industries Ltd (No 2)* [1982] Ch 204; see para 6.2 below.

[24]   See, for example, the discussion at paras 4.3-4.15 below.

[25]   It is particularly important in derivative actions in public companies that the procedure should not facilitate litigation brought either to obtain a personal benefit for the claimant or to establish a point of principle rather than obtain redress for a wrong. Moreover, if shareholder remedies are too readily available in those companies, this may lead directors to favour a course which provides benefits to shareholders rather than make a more balanced judgment and take a decision which they would otherwise feel free to take. In the larger companies, the derivative action has to be seen in the context of a complex web of control mechanisms, which include regulatory action, institutional investor attitudes, DTI inquiries, and so on.

[26]   Paras 1.9-1.11.

of court which would replace the main exception to the rule in *Foss v Harbottle*.[27] More modern, flexible and accessible criteria for leave to bring a derivative action would replace the current "fraud on the minority" exception.[28] It was suggested that not only would this be desirable in itself, in simplifying and modernising the derivative action, but it may also encourage members to bring this claim rather than the wide-ranging proceedings under section 459 in appropriate cases.[29] The proposal for a new derivative action is also in line with international developments, notably in Australia, Canada, Hong Kong, Japan, South Africa and New Zealand.[30]

1.14   Secondly, we proposed that the courts should be given all necessary powers to streamline shareholder litigation so that it is less costly and complicated.[31] A range of case management techniques was put forward. Some of these involved new powers drawn from the reforms recommended in the Woolf Report; others involved greater use of existing powers. Although this approach is clearly relevant to all shareholder proceedings, it is in dealing with the often cumbersome and factually complex claims which are brought under section 459 that we considered that effective case management would be of particular benefit.

1.15   One option which we canvassed to assist in streamlining shareholder litigation (although no provisional recommendation was made) was the introduction of a new remedy for small owner-managed companies. This would be directed at the situation where a shareholder entitled to management participation is wrongly excluded,[32] and provide a more focused alternative to proceedings under section 459.

1.16   Thirdly, we proposed a "self-help" approach which would seek to avoid the need to bring legal proceedings at all.[33] Three draft regulations were set out in the consultation paper[34] which we suggested could be inserted into Table A: a shareholders' exit article for smaller private companies; an arbitration article; and a valuation procedure article.

1.17   A number of other suggestions for reform were also canvassed.[35]

---

[27]   Consultation Paper No 142, paras 14.13 and 15.2-15.3.

[28]   *Ibid*, at paras 4.7-4.18, and see paras 6.4-6.6 below.

[29]   *Ibid*, at para 15.5.

[30]   See paras 6.8-6.9 below.

[31]   See Consultation Paper No 142, paras 14.13 and 15.5.

[32]   Which our statistical analysis showed to be the most common allegation in unfair prejudice cases; see Consultation Paper No 142, para 18.6, and see para 1.5 above.

[33]   See Consultation Paper No 142, paras 14.13 and 15.6.

[34]   *Ibid*, at Appendix H.

[35]   See *ibid*, Part 20.

Response to consultation and summary of main recommendations

1.18   We received 109 responses to the consultation paper. The vast majority of these agreed with our identification of the two main problems, and our approach to reform. In particular, there was widespread support for the increased use of effective case management techniques to deal with the length and cost of proceedings under section 459, and the introduction of new articles of association to try to avoid disputes arising which have to be brought before the courts.[36]

1.19   The proposals for a new unfair prejudice remedy for smaller companies[37] received a mixed response and, as explained below,[38] we do not favour the introduction of such a remedy. However, we do recommend the introduction into sections 459-461 of presumptions that, in certain circumstances, there has been unfairly prejudicial conduct and that, where a purchase order is made, the shares should be valued on a pro rata basis.[39] Although this is a rather different approach, we consider that it can achieve much the same as the proposed new remedy without some of the disadvantages.[40]

1.20   A number of other reforms canvassed in respect of proceedings under section 459 received support from respondents, notably proposals for a limitation period and for the addition of winding up to the remedies available to the court on a finding of unfairly prejudicial conduct.

1.21   The vast majority of respondents agreed that the operation of the rule in *Foss v Harbottle* is unsatisfactory. Some concerns were expressed about the proposals for a new derivative action, and in particular whether they were really necessary when derivative actions are brought so rarely in practice. Nevertheless, for the reasons given below,[41] we still consider that it would be desirable for a new derivative procedure to be introduced along the lines of the provisional recommendations. However, in the light of the responses received, we do recommend some changes to the proposals put forward in the consultation paper.

1.22   Respondents agreed with the provisional view that no hardship is being caused by difficulties in identifying personal rights conferred by the articles and we maintain our view that no reform is necessary in this respect.

1.23   Accordingly, our main final recommendations are as follows:

---

[36]   Although, the draft arbitration article which we provisionally suggested was not so well received. As we explain below (paras 5.34-5.48), we no longer recommend that the draft arbitration and valuation procedure articles should be included in Table A.

[37]   Which we did not recommend, but merely put forward for discussion.

[38]   See para 3.19-3.25.

[39]   See para 3.8 below for a brief explanation of the difference between a "discounted" and "pro rata" basis of valuation.

[40]   See paras 3.28-3.29 below.

[41]   See paras 6.4 and 6.8-6.14 below.

(i)   the problems of the excessive length and cost of many proceedings brought under section 459 should be dealt with primarily by active case management by the courts;

(ii)   there should be presumptions in proceedings under section 459 that in certain circumstances (a) conduct will be presumed to be unfairly prejudicial, and (b) where the court grants a purchase order in favour of the petitioner the shares will be valued on a pro rata basis;

(iii)   a number of other amendments should be made to proceedings under section 459, notably that there should be a limitation period in respect of claims under the section and that winding up should be added to the remedies available;

(iv)   a draft regulation should be included in Table A to encourage parties to sort out areas of potential dispute at the outset so as to avoid the need to bring legal proceedings;

(v)   there should be a new derivative procedure with more modern, flexible and accessible criteria for determining whether a shareholder should be able to pursue the action;

(vi)   there is no need for reform in relation to the enforcement of the rights of shareholders under the articles of association.

Scottish Law Commission

1.24   We have continued to act in consultation with the Scottish Law Commission which agrees with the content of this report.

1.25   Copies of the consultation paper were circulated in Scotland by the Scottish Law Commission. Six responses were received by the Scottish Law Commission and these also broadly supported the approach to reform and the provisional recommendations. The consultation identified the need for a different mechanism for Scotland to achieve a similar practical result to that proposed for England and Wales in the new derivative procedure. We are informed by the Scottish Law Commission that under Scots law, there is no recognised representative or derivative action; the shareholder's right to seek a remedy for the company is conferred by substantive law and not by procedural rules. Amendment of the law relating to that right requires separate legislative provision to fit with the substantive rules of Scots law relating to title and interest to sue. The Scottish Law Commission's consideration of the shareholder's action to seek a remedy for the company, and their recommendations which parallel our recommendations contained in Part 6 of this report, are set out in Appendix D.

1.26   As regards section 459 proceedings, consultation supported, and the Scottish Law Commission agrees, that active case management is a matter for rules of court to be drawn up by the appropriate authority. Where appropriate, the power of the Secretary of State under section 411 of the Insolvency Act 1986 to make rules, so far as it relates to a winding up petition, is also available to a petition under section 459.[42] In so far as matters which we discuss in this report might appropriately be matters for rules of court for Scotland, any further consultation required in that regard will be a matter for the appropriate rule-making authority.

Northern Ireland

1.27 The Law Reform Advisory Committee for Northern Ireland has worked closely with us in the preparation of this report and is in full accord with its contents and the recommendations for law reform which we make. The Committee proposes to recommend to the Secretary of State for Northern Ireland that parallel legislation should be introduced in Northern Ireland to give effect to our recommendations in this report.

The Woolf Report

1.28 In July 1996, shortly before the publication of our consultation paper, Lord Woolf published his final report ("the Woolf Report") setting out the results of his review of the civil justice system. This was accompanied by a draft of the general rules which were to form the core of a new combined code of rules for civil procedure ("the Draft Civil Proceedings Rules"). Our proposals for case management were largely modelled on the Woolf reforms, and we envisaged that our new derivative procedure would tie in to the new procedural framework.

1.29 Since then, the statutory basis for the new procedural rules, the Civil Procedure Act 1997, has come into force and work is proceeding within the Lord Chancellor's Department on completing the drafting of the rules.[43] Under the 1997 Act, the rules must be approved by the Civil Procedure Rule Committee.[44] The Lord Chancellor has, however, invited Sir Peter Middleton to undertake a review of current plans for the reform of both the civil justice system and legal aid to see if they can be improved.[45] The Lord Chancellor has made it clear that he is anxious to maintain the positive momentum for change which has been generated, but while the review is in progress, there must inevitably be some degree of uncertainty about the future of the proposals contained in the Woolf Report. Should the review recommend, and the Lord Chancellor accept, that the proposed reforms of the civil justice system should be implemented, the planned date for the new rules to come into effect is 1 October 1998.[46]

---

[42] Section 461(6) of the Companies Act 1985. See para 2.6, n 9 below.

[43] See, for example, Lord Chancellor's Department, *Access to Justice, Judicial Case Management, the Fast Track and Multi-track, A working paper* (July 1997) ("LCD Working Paper on Judicial Case Management") and Lord Chancellor's Department, *Access to Justice, Civil Procedure Rules about Costs, Consultation Paper* (August 1997). Further working papers on other aspects of the rules are expected in October. The rules are to be renamed the Civil Procedure Rules; see s 1 of the Civil Procedure Act 1997. For the purposes of this report we continue to refer to the Draft Civil Proceedings Rules.

[44] The members of this Committee were announced on 16 July 1997; Lord Chancellor's Department, Press Notice No 156/97.

[45] See Lord Chancellor's Department, Press Notice No 108/97.

[46] LCD Working Paper on Judicial Case Management, para 1.4.

1.30   So far as our own proposals are concerned, we believe that the new derivative procedure could still be introduced with little adaptation, whether or not the new rules are implemented in their current form. Only three of our case management proposals are dependent on new powers contained in the new rules,[47] and as we make clear below,[48] we do not consider that it is appropriate to introduce any separate provisions to deal solely with shareholder proceedings in respect of these particular matters. Most of our other recommendations on case management involve greater use of existing powers and need not be affected by the current review.

Structure of the report

1.31   In the consultation paper we examined the proposals for a new derivative action before our other provisional recommendations for reform. However, it is clear that the derivative action is of much less importance in practical terms than the statutory remedy under section 459. This is apparent from the reported cases and was confirmed by the responses received. We therefore propose to deal first with those recommendations which have most significance for proceedings under section 459. Accordingly, in Part 2 we deal with the proposals which relate to case management of shareholder proceedings; in Part 3 we reconsider the proposals for a new unfair prejudice remedy for smaller companies and set out our alternative recommendation for presumptions that, in certain circumstances, there has been unfairly prejudicial conduct and that, where a purchase order is made, the shares should be valued on a pro rata basis; and in Part 4 we deal with the other changes proposed in the consultation paper in respect of section 459 proceedings.

1.32   In Part 5 we set out our revised views on the proposals for new draft regulations to be inserted in Table A. In Part 6 we deal with the proposals for a new derivative action. In Part 7 we set out our recommendations on the other reform options canvassed in the consultation paper. Finally, in Part 8, we summarise our final recommendations for reform.

Acknowledgements

1.33   We are grateful to all those who responded to our consultation paper and those who have subsequently provided comments or assistance on our proposals. They are listed in Appendix K. We are also grateful to the officials of the Companies Court who assisted us in our updated statistical survey referred to in Appendix J. We would like to express our particular thanks to Professor D D Prentice of the University of Oxford, and Ms Brenda Hannigan of the University of Southampton, who have acted as our consultants throughout this project.

---

[47]   Power to dismiss a claim or part of a claim or defence which has no realistic prospect of success (recommendation 8.2(2)); exclusion of issues from determination (recommendation 8.2(5); and costs sanctions (recommendation 8.2(6)).

[48]   See para 2.34.

PART 2
CASE MANAGEMENT OF SHAREHOLDER PROCEEDINGS

Introduction

2.1 In the consultation paper, we highlighted the major problems of the length and cost of proceedings brought under section 459.[1] The wording of section 459 is extremely wide and this allows conduct going back over many years to be raised by the parties. This results in complex, often historical, factual investigations and, therefore, costly and cumbersome litigation. Prolific or weak allegations are often made by the parties to lend ballast to what are essentially their main grievances. We quoted the observation of Harman J in *Re Unisoft Group Ltd (No 3)*[2] that "[p]etitions under section 459 have become notorious to the judges of this court - and I think also to the Bar - for their length, their unpredictability of management, and the enormous and appalling costs which are incurred upon them ...".

2.2 The essence of the remedy under section 459 is that it gives the court a wide discretion to remedy conduct which may fall short of actual illegality.[3] Our provisional view, which was supported by respondents,[4] was that the very general wording of the section should remain as it now stands. However, the conduct of such proceedings should be carefully controlled. The best way to do this was by effective case management by the courts. This approach to section 459 proceedings received widespread support on consultation.[5] Accordingly, **we consider that the problems of the excessive length and cost of many proceedings brought under section 459 should be dealt with primarily by active case management by the courts.**

2.3 Although the effective use of case management techniques is particularly relevant to proceedings under section 459, our proposals in this respect are equally applicable to all shareholder proceedings, and in particular to the new derivative action which we consider in Part 6 below. There are several powers, however, which we referred to in the consultation paper, which are *only* relevant to derivative proceedings. These are considered along with the other details of the provisions for a new derivative action (in Part 6).

---

[1] See Consultation Paper No 142, paras 11.1-11.3, 11.10-11.11, and 14.5. See also para 1.6 above.

[2] [1994] 1 BCLC 609.

[3] See Report of the Company Law Committee (1962) Cmnd 1749, para 203. See also Consultation Paper No 142, paras 7.8 and 20.17.

[4] See paras 4.9-4.13 below.

[5] For an alternative view on the effectiveness of case management in general, however, see Professor Michael Zander, "Consistency in the exercise of discretionary power" (1996) 146 NLJ 1590.

2.4 We considered the issue of case management in the context of the wider review of civil procedure conducted by Lord Woolf. In his final report published in July 1996 (the Woolf Report), Lord Woolf made a number of proposals for the management of proceedings which we considered would assist in dealing with the difficulties of length, cost and factual complexity arising in proceedings under section 459.[6] Our proposals for case management were therefore modelled on the Woolf reforms, although we also proposed the greater use of some existing powers which the courts already have. This approach to more active case management of proceedings is also in line with recent decisions of the courts which emphasise the obligations of the parties and their legal advisers to co-operate in limiting the time and scope of evidence and argument.[7]

2.5 The case management powers considered in this part are discussed under the following heads: preliminary issues; security for costs; power to dismiss claim or part of claim or defence which has no realistic prospect of success; adjournment to facilitate ADR; determination of how facts are to be proved; exclusion of issues from determination; costs sanctions; and implementation of recommendations for case management. We also discuss briefly pre-action protocols.

2.6 So far as section 459 proceedings are concerned, specific procedural rules are contained in the Companies (Unfair Prejudice Applications) Proceedings Rules 1986 ("the 1986 Rules").[8] These are made in England and Wales by the Lord Chancellor with the concurrence of the Secretary of State, following consultation with the Insolvency Rules Committee.[9] Rule 2(2) provides that the rules of the High Court and County Court (as appropriate) apply where they are not inconsistent with express provisions in the Rules. We assume that if the draft Civil

---

[6] The courts in Scotland have undertaken their own review of civil procedure. Scottish courts are able to adopt procedures to improve the handling of shareholder proceedings by case management or otherwise. See Consultation Paper No 142, para 11.4, n 15.

[7] See, in particular, the case of *Ashmore v Lloyds* [1992] 1 WLR 446, 453 where Lord Templeman explained: "The parties and particularly their legal advisers in any litigation are under a duty to co-operate with the court by chronological, brief and consistent pleadings which define the issues and leave the judge to draw his own conclusions about the merits when he hears the case. It is the duty of counsel to assist the judge by simplification and concentration and not to advance a multitude of ingenious arguments in the hope that out of 10 bad points the judge will be capable of fashioning a winner. In nearly all cases the correct procedure works perfectly well. But there has been a tendency in some cases for legal advisers, pressed by their clients, to make every point conceivable and inconceivable without judgment or discrimination. In *Banque Keyser Ullmann SA v Skandia (UK) Insurance Co Ltd* [1991] 2 AC 249, 280, I warned against proceedings in which all or some of the litigants indulge in over-elaboration causing difficulties to judges at all levels in the achievement of a just result. I also said that the appellate court should be reluctant to entertain complaints about a judge who controls the conduct of proceedings and limits the time and scope of evidence and argument." See also Practice Direction (Civil Litigation: Case Management) [1995] 1 WLR 262 and Practice Direction (Chancery Division: Procedure and Case Management) [1995] 1 WLR 785, introducing the Chancery Guide.

[8] SI 1986 No 2000.

[9] Section 461(6) of the Companies Act 1985 applies the rule-making powers of s 411 of the Insolvency Act 1986 to petitions under s 459. These are made, in relation to England and Wales, by the Lord Chancellor with the concurrence of the Secretary of State. By virtue of s 413 of the Insolvency Act 1986, the Insolvency Rules Committee must also be consulted before rules are made under s 411.

Proceedings Rules are adopted, Rule 2(2) will be updated to refer to those rules instead of the existing High Court and County Court Rules.[10] In those circumstances any of the changes discussed in this Part applying to High Court and County Court actions generally are likely to apply to the unfair prejudice proceedings automatically.

Preliminary issues

2.7   Under the current law, the court may direct that preliminary issues be heard or that some issues be tried before others.[11] The Draft Civil Proceedings Rules draw particular attention to these powers as a means by which the courts should actively manage cases.[12]

2.8   We gave examples of when this power could be used to manage cases under section 459.[13] We pointed out that in some cases the real issue between the parties is not whether unfairly prejudicial conduct occurred, but the value at which shares should be sold or purchased. We suggested that it may save time and costs if the value of the shares is determined first, on the basis of stated assumptions agreed between the parties and accepted for that purpose by the court, that certain unfairly prejudicial conduct had occurred. The effect of deciding valuation issues at an early stage may be to demonstrate to the parties whether or not it is worth pursuing litigation at all and thus dispose of the case before they incur large legal costs.[14]

2.9   It may be that in most cases it is in fact more appropriate for issues relating to valuation to be determined *after* those relating to the conduct have been decided. Several respondents commented on the fact that costs are often wasted by parties in preparing valuations at too early a stage in the proceedings. This is for two reasons: first, parties often have to prepare several valuations on alternative assumed bases because they do not know the terms on which any purchase order will be made;[15] secondly, if it transpires that the conduct has not been unfairly prejudicial, or that the court is unwilling for other reasons to make a purchase order, the costs of any valuation will have been unnecessary.[16] The correct

---

[10]   The Lord Chancellor has power under s 4(1) of the Civil Procedure Act 1997 to amend any enactment to the extent he considers it necessary or desirable in consequence of the Civil Procedure Rules.

[11]   RSC, O 33, r 3.

[12]   Draft Civil Proceedings Rules, r 1.3(a), (b), and (e).

[13]   See Consultation Paper No 142, paras 17.11-17.12.

[14]   But see *Re Bird Precision Bellows Ltd* [1986] Ch 658 where the parties sought, in a consent order, to focus solely on the valuation of the shares. Oliver LJ said that "[u]nless unfair prejudice was proved, the court was simply being asked to undertake a sort of arbitration in vacuo, which it had no jurisdiction to do"; *ibid*, at p 672.

[15]   In particular the basis of valuation, the date on which the valuation is to be made, and any adjustment which may be ordered to take account of misappropriation of assets or mismanagement; see Consultation Paper No 142, paras 10.13-10.22.

[16]   See *Quinlan v Essex Hinge Co Ltd* [1996] 2 BCLC 417 where the court directed the issues should be determined in the following order: (1) whether or not there has been unfair prejudice; (2) what remedy is to be ordered; (3) if the remedy is purchase of shares, (i) the

approach for the court to take will of course depend on the circumstances of the particular case.

2.10 Our provisional view that greater use should be made of this power was supported by the vast majority of respondents. A few respondents urged caution, pointing out that directing the trial of a preliminary issue may not shorten proceedings, and might in fact have the reverse effect. There will clearly be cases where it will not be appropriate for court to direct the trial of a preliminary issue, or to direct that some issues be tried before others. As now, great care will be needed to ensure that trial of preliminary issues will shorten the proceedings.[17] But we do not consider that this detracts from the general proposition that the courts should, in appropriate cases (for example where there is a self-contained issue as to whether some impropriety occurred), make greater use of their powers in this regard. **We therefore recommend that greater use should be made of the power to direct that preliminary issues be heard, or that some issues be tried before others.**

Security for costs

2.11 We raised the question of whether the jurisdiction to order security for costs should be extended so that the court could make an order whenever it thinks fit. Currently the grounds for making such an order are limited to the following situations: the plaintiff is ordinarily resident outside the jurisdiction;[18] the plaintiff sues for the benefit of another and there is reason to believe he will be unable to pay the costs of the defendant; the plaintiff's address is not given or is given incorrectly in the originating process; or that he has changed his address in the course of litigation with a view to evading the consequences of it.[19] The purpose of this extension would be to discourage nuisance litigation.

2.12 Our provisional view was that such an additional power would be unfounded in principle and might discourage meritorious litigation. The vast majority of respondents agreed with this view and we therefore consider that there should be no change to the court's existing power to order security for costs.

---

basis of valuation, (ii) the date of valuation, and (iii) any adjustments to be made in valuation.

[17] At least if they are decided in one way; see *Carl Zeiss Stiftung v Herbert Smith & Co* [1969] 1 Ch 93.

[18] On the question of plaintiffs resident in another state of the European Union, see *Fitzgerald v Williams* [1996] 2 All ER 171 and *Chequepoint SARL v McClelland* [1997] QB 51. See also *Supreme Court Practice* (1997) vol 1, paras 23/1-3/3A.

[19] RSC O 23, r 1. Where the plaintiff is a limited company, the provisions of s 726 of the Companies Act 1985 also come into play (ie it appears by credible testimony that there is reason to believe that the company will be unable to pay the defendant's costs if successful in his defence). Neither the Woolf Report nor the Draft Civil Proceedings Rules directly addressed the issue of security for costs. The Lord Chancellor's Department is currently reviewing the position in the context of its continuing work in implementing the Woolf proposals.

Power to dismiss claim or part of claim or defence which has no realistic prospect of success

2.13 We recommended provisionally that the court should have the power to dismiss any claim or any part of the claim or any defence thereto which, in the opinion of the court, has no realistic prospect of success. This is a key feature of the proposals put forward in the Woolf Report[20] and we considered that it was central to the effective streamlining of shareholder litigation. The proposed new power is set out in Part 14 of the Draft Civil Proceedings Rules.[21] This new power would take the place of the provisions for summary judgment and striking out.[22]

2.14 As we have indicated above,[23] we drew attention in the consultation paper to the fact that the tendency of parties to make prolific or weak allegations is a particular problem in section 459 cases. We also noted that a large number of the reported cases are applications by the respondents to strike out the petition under RSC O 18, r 19(1) and/or under the inherent jurisdiction of the court.[24] But strike out applications are not ideally suited to deal with this problem. They are made on the basis that the factual allegations made by the petitioner are presumed to be true. The court cannot make any findings of fact, and the proceedings cannot be struck out merely because the case is weak.[25] Although the courts will, in appropriate cases in proceedings under section 459, consider the evidence to see whether the facts alleged, if proved, would constitute unfairly prejudicial conduct.[26]

2.15 The new power will give the courts a much greater ability to refine claims under the section so as to remove those parts based on trivial or otherwise weak allegations and so shorten and reduce the length and cost of such claims. For example, if the applicant alleges that a company was formed on the basis that there is a relationship of mutual trust and confidence between the shareholders (so as to give rise to a claim that the court should give effect to legitimate expectations not found in the company's articles),[27] the court will be able to examine the evidential basis for the allegations and see whether the allegations stand any real chance of being proved. For this purpose, it may permit oral evidence to be called. This would be an improvement in the present situation because in some cases, allegations of this nature are made on the basis of minimal evidence, but they cannot be struck out before trial because it is only then that the evidence can be tested by witnesses giving evidence and being cross-examined. The allegations may be fact-intensive and

---

[20] Woolf Report, ch 12, paras 31-36 and Recommendations 132-133. Woolf Interim Report, ch 6, paras 17-21.

[21] See Appendix I. In making our recommendation at para 2.18 below, we assume that the new power will be introduced for all proceedings.

[22] Currently under RSC, O 14 and O 18, r 19 respectively.

[23] Para 2.1.

[24] Consultation Paper No 142, paras 11.23-11.25.

[25] See *AG of Duchy of Lancaster v L & N W Railway* [1892] 3 Ch 278 and *Wenlock v Moloney* [1965] 1 WLR 1238. See also *Supreme Court Practice* (1997) vol 1, para 18/19/6.

[26] See *Re Saul D Harrison & Sons plc* [1995] 1 BCLC 14; and see Consultation Paper No 142, para 11.24.

[27] See paras 3.5-3.7 below.

require a complex and expensive investigation of events occurring many years previously.

2.16 The new power may also assist applicants with a good case in obtaining relief more quickly. In such cases, it may be possible for the applicant to show that the defence (or the relevant part of it) has no realistic prospect of success and invite the court to grant relief without the need for a full trial.[28]

2.17 In the context of the new derivative action, this power is relevant to the question of the imposition of a threshold test in relation to the merits of the action at the leave stage.[29]

2.18 The vast majority of respondents agreed with the provisional view that in shareholder proceedings the court should have this new power. Accordingly **we recommend that in shareholder proceedings the court should have the power to dismiss any claim or part of a claim or defence thereto which, in the opinion of the court, has no realistic prospect of success at full trial.**[30]

Adjournment to facilitate ADR

2.19 There already exists a power to adjourn proceedings at any stage to enable the parties to make use of mechanisms for alternative dispute resolution ("ADR") for disposing of the case or any issue in it. RSC, O 35, r 3 gives the High Court a general power of adjournment.[31] In addition, a number of practice directions in various divisions of the High Court have addressed more specifically the question of ADR.[32] We suggested in the consultation paper that an express reference to the power to adjourn to enable parties to make use of ADR in the rules relating to shareholder remedies would serve to encourage parties to consider other means for resolving disputes and issues between them. The vast majority of respondents agreed that this would be helpful.[33] We agree. There are often grievances between the parties which go beyond the pleaded allegations and for which ADR is suitable.

---

[28] This may be particularly relevant if the presumptions recommended in Part 3 are introduced. Note that at present it is not possible to obtain summary judgment in proceedings under s 459 as RSC, O 14 is only available in actions begun by writ.

[29] See paras 6.71-6.72 below.

[30] Assuming this power will be introduced for all proceedings.

[31] For the equivalent rule for the County Court, see CCR, O 14, r 3.

[32] See Practice Statement (Commercial Cases: Alternative Dispute Resolution) [1994] 1 WLR 14 and Practice Statement (Commercial Cases: Alternative Dispute Resolution) (No 2) [1996] 1 WLR 1024; and see also Practice Direction (Civil Litigation: Case Management) [1995] 1 WLR 262 and Practice Direction (Chancery Division: Procedure and Case Management) [1995] 1 WLR 785.

[33] For instance, the Chancery Bar Association said in their response: "Many unfair prejudice petitions are in our view good candidates for ADR".

2.20   The 1996 Commercial Court Practice Statement[34] makes more detailed provision, inter alia, as follows:

> If it should appear to the judge that the action before him or any of the issues arising in it are particularly appropriate for an attempt at settlement by ADR techniques but that the parties have not previously attempted settlement by such means, he may invite the parties to take positive steps to set in motion ADR procedures. The judge may, if he considers it appropriate, adjourn the proceedings then before him for a specified period of time to encourage and enable the parties to take such steps. He may for this purpose extend the time for compliance by the parties or either of them with any requirement under the Rules of the Supreme Court or previous interlocutory orders in the proceedings.
>
> ...
>
> Should the parties be unable to resolve their differences by ADR or otherwise within the period of any such adjournment as may be ordered, they may restore the summons for directions or other summons for the purpose of reporting back to the judge what progress has been made by way of ADR (such report to cover only the process adopted and its outcome, not the substantive contact between the parties and their advisers) and whether further time is required for the purposes of ADR and, where efforts towards settlement by means of ADR have proved fruitless, for the purpose of obtaining further interlocutory directions in the proceedings.

2.21   The 1996 Commercial Court Practice Statement also encourages the use of early neutral evaluation either by a judge or another independent person. A similar practice could also be considered for inclusion in the rules for unfair prejudice proceedings.[35]

2.22   The Draft Civil Proceedings Rules make reference in general terms to the court's duty to encourage parties to use ADR procedure if the court considers that appropriate and to facilitate the use of such procedure.[36] ADR is not widely used at present, and if we are right in our view that many shareholder disputes are apt for resolution in this way, we consider it would be advantageous, at least while ADR remains comparatively unknown, to have an express reference to it in the 1986 Rules. Furthermore, if this course is taken, we consider that detailed

---

[34]   Practice Statement (Commercial Cases: Alternative Dispute Resolution) (No 2) [1996] 1 WLR 1024.

[35]   We have been informed by Mr Justice Colman, Judge in Charge of the Commercial List, that as at June 1997 orders for early neutral evaluation had been made in two cases. We think that it is thus to early for us to form a view as to whether early neutral evaluation would be beneficial in shareholder disputes.

[36]   Draft Civil Proceedings Rules, Rule 1.3(c). In addition, the LCD Working Paper on Judicial Case Management proposes an automatic stay for mediation in certain cases prior to allocation of the case to a track; *ibid*, at paras 2.96-2.98. There are of course advantages in promoting ADR at later stages in the proceedings.

provisions along the lines of the 1996 Commercial Court Practice Statement quoted in paragraph 2.20 above (which include provisions for reporting back to the court as to the outcome), are more likely to yield results. Accordingly, **we recommend that the Lord Chancellor consider changes to the 1986 Rules (governing unfair prejudice proceedings) so as to include an express reference to the power to adjourn at any stage to enable the parties to make use of mechanisms for ADR for disposing of the case or any issue in it, together with provisions for reporting back to the court as to the outcome along the lines of the 1996 Commercial Court Practice Statement.**

2.23   As for other proceedings (including derivative proceedings) we consider that the court should have the same power in relation to ADR in as it has in other litigation. We do not therefore recommend any specific rule for this purpose. The question of early neutral evaluation[37] should be kept under review.[38]

Determination of how facts are to be proved

2.24   The court already has flexible powers under the current rules as to the nature of the evidence to be put before it.[39] However, the Civil Procedure Act 1997 specifically provides that the new rules of court may modify the rules of evidence.[40] The Draft Civil Proceedings Rules give the court additional powers relating to, for example, the use of video evidence[41] and witness statements.[42] Rule 28.1 imposes a duty on the court to control the evidence by deciding (a) the issues on which it requires evidence, (b) the nature of the evidence which it requires, and (c) the way in which any matter is to be proved. Our provisional view was that there could be substantial savings in time and costs if, on each occasion the case is reviewed, the court considered making directions as to how facts should be proved.[43] For example, the court may dispense with a witness being called if he has given a witness statement to one of the parties on which the other parties do not wish to cross-examine him. By way of further example, the court might in an appropriate case direct that expert evidence be given by means of a written report. In both these ways, costly time in court would be saved. This view received widespread support on consultation and accordingly, **we recommend that the court's power to determine how facts are to be proved should be used pro-actively by the court.**

---

[37]   See para 2.21 above.

[38]   See n 35 above.

[39]   See, for example, for powers relating to the use of affidavit evidence, RSC, O 38, r 2; CCR, O 20, r 6; as to witness statements, RSC, O 38, r 2A; CCR, O 20, r 12A; and as to evidence of particular facts and how they may be proved, RSC, O 38, r 3; CCR, O 20, r 8.

[40]   Civil Procedure Act, sched 1, para 4.

[41]   Rule 28.3.

[42]   Rule 28.4.

[43]   We stressed that the proposal was not intended to change the procedural rules relating to hearsay evidence in civil proceedings; see Consultation Paper No 142, para 17.18.

Exclusion of issues from determination

2.25 Currently the court cannot exclude evidence, provided it is legally relevant and admissible, and the rules of court applicable to its admissibility have been complied with.[44] However, Rule 5.1 provides that the court may "... exclude an issue from determination if it can do substantive justice between the parties on the other issues and determining it would therefore serve no worthwhile purpose".

2.26 We have already mentioned on several occasions the excessively large number of allegations frequently raised in section 459 proceedings on which the parties seek to adduce evidence. We canvassed in argument in the consultation paper the possibility of a power which would enable the court to exclude evidence where it was satisfied that it would not have a bearing on the issues that needed to be decided.[45] However, we concluded, provisionally, that the proposed power to exclude issues contained in Rule 5.1 of the Draft Civil Proceedings Rules would be sufficient for these purposes.

2.27 The vast majority of respondents agreed with the provisional view and accordingly we consider that the power to exclude issues as proposed in the Draft Civil Procedure Rules is sufficient for the purposes of enabling the court to exclude issues in appropriate circumstances in shareholder proceedings. This power would enable the court to avoid the necessity of evidence being called on an issue which the court is satisfied would not on any basis be determinative of the case before it. This might arise, for instance, if the applicant alleged that a respondent shareholder/director had acted in breach of duty, and there was other unchallenged evidence which would result in the court relieving him of his breach of duty under section 727 of the Companies Act 1985.[46] **We recommend that in shareholder proceedings the court should have the power to exclude an issue from determination if it can do substantive justice between the parties on the other issues and determining it would therefore serve no worthwhile purpose.[47]**

Costs sanctions

2.28 This is not an issue on which we made any specific recommendation in the consultation paper. However, the power of the court to penalise parties in costs is clearly an important weapon in the court's armoury in seeking to manage cases effectively.

---

[44] *Hollington v Hewthorn* [1943] 2 All ER 35, 39 *per* Goddard LJ; and see *Cross & Tapper on Evidence* (1996) p 56, and Adrian Keane, *The Modern Law of Evidence* (4th ed 1996) p 18. But note the comments of Hoffmann LJ in *Vernon v Bosley, The Times* 8 April 1994 that although a trial judge had no discretion to exclude admissible evidence, his ruling on admissibility could involve a balancing of the degree of relevance of the evidence against other considerations that was in practice indistinguishable from the exercise of discretion.

[45] Consultation Paper No 142, para 17.19.

[46] The text of s 727 is set out in para 1.9, n 23 above.

[47] Assuming this power will be introduced for all proceedings.

2.29   A number of respondents drew attention to the decision of the Court of Appeal in *Re Elgindata (No 2)*[48] in which they considered the court had made some unhelpful comments on the flexibility of the court's discretion in this regard. They considered that this decision restricted the courts' ability to use costs sanctions to encourage parties to focus their claims in proceedings under section 459 and to leave out irrelevant or weak allegations. There are two aspects to this.

2.30   First, the Court of Appeal held that the court could not order a successful party to pay the costs of an unsuccessful party in respect of an issue which had failed, unless that issue had been unreasonably or improperly raised by the successful party. The only sanction was to disallow part of the successful party's costs. This ruling was based on RSC, O 62, r 10.[49] We agree with the suggestion put forward by several respondents that it would help to deter parties from litigating issues which are likely to fail if the court could also order costs *against* the successful party in respect of issues on which he had failed, without the need to show that those issues had been raised unreasonably or improperly. We consider that *Re Elgindata (No 2)* should be reversed in this respect.

2.31   Secondly, the Court of Appeal disapproved of the approach of the trial judge in treating different categories of complaints of unfairly prejudicial conduct as separate issues for the purposes of awarding costs, and in disallowing costs in respect of those which he regarded as "thin".[50] As we have indicated, the proliferation of weak or insubstantial allegations relating to the conduct of parties is a particular problem in section 459 cases. In future, many of these should be weeded out by active case management during the course of proceedings. But this is not always possible, and we consider that the costs orders available to the trial judge should be as flexible as possible to deal with this.

---

[48]   [1993] BCLC 119. See also the case of *Rostron v Elliot* 7 June 1996 (unreported, Court of Appeal).

[49]   This provides as follows: "(1) Where it appears to the Court in any proceedings that anything has been done, or that any omission has been made, unreasonably or improperly by or on behalf of any party, the Court may order that the costs of that party in respect of the act or omission, as the case may be, shall not be allowed and that any costs occasioned by it to any other party shall be paid by him to that other party." The Court of Appeal considered that it was implicit in the principles derived from this rule that a successful party who neither improperly nor unreasonably raises issues or makes allegations on which he fails ought not to be ordered to pay any part of the unsuccessful party's costs; [1993] BCLC 119, 125.

[50]   Nourse LJ commented: "[Counsel for the respondents] sought to treat the four categories of complaints of unfairly prejudicial conduct as separate issues and even to go further and subdivide them into the individual allegations made in the petition. I wholly reject that approach"; [1993] BCLC 119, 126. Beldam LJ also stated: "In my view it is only if it is possible so to isolate an issue in the case that it can properly be said that it is unnecessarily pursued as having no bearing on the real questions in the suit that it would be proper to deprive the successful party of all costs of that issue. Otherwise a more general assessment should be made." He went on to give the following example: "The complaint of lack of consultation, though thin, was neither immaterial nor could it be said to be irrelevant. It may have been exaggerated, but that in itself is no ground for depriving the party making the allegation of all the costs"; *ibid*, at p 129.

2.32   Both these criticisms of the decision in *Re Elgindata (No 2)* appear to be consistent with the approach taken by Lord Woolf[51] in respect of costs and new draft rules recently circulated by the Lord Chancellor's Department for consultation appear to address these concerns.[52] Accordingly, **we recommend that, in proceedings under section 459, the court should have greater flexibility than at present to make costs orders to reflect the manner in which the successful party has conducted the proceedings and the outcome of individual issues.**

Implementation of recommendations for case management

2.33   The recommendations made at paragraphs 2.10 (preliminary issues) and 2.24 (in part) (determination of how facts are to be proved) involve the use of existing powers and we do not propose that there should be any new provisions to implement them. Rather, these recommendations go to the approach which we consider courts should take in future to shareholder proceedings.

2.34   The recommendations made at paragraphs 2.18 (power to dismiss claim or part of claim or defence which has no realistic prospect of success), 2.24 (in so far as use can be made of increased powers in relation to evidence in the Civil Procedure Act 1997), 2.27 (exclusion of issues from determination) and 2.32 (costs sanctions) will require the introduction of new rules of court. However, these matters are being addressed in the context of the implementation of the Woolf Report and we do not consider that it is necessary or appropriate to introduce any separate provisions to deal solely with shareholder proceedings. Accordingly, no draft provisions in respect of these matters are contained in this report.

2.35   As regards ADR, we recommend so far as section 459 proceedings are concerned, that the inclusion of an express provision in the 1986 Rules should be considered. With respect to other proceedings, we consider that the implementation of the Woolf proposals will give sufficient impetus to this approach and that no additional provision should be made in the new rule for derivative actions.

---

[51] See, in particular, Woolf Interim Report, ch 25, para 24 and Recommendation 121; Woolf Report, ch 7, paras 8 and 24, and Recommendations 61 and 62. Lord Woolf recommends that: "Courts, in making orders for costs, should pay greater regard than they do at present to the manner in which the successful party has conducted the proceedings and the outcome of individual issues"; Woolf Report, Recommendation 61. He also comments that: "Orders for costs should reflect not only whether the general outcome of the proceedings is favourable to the party seeking an order in his favour but also how the proceedings have been conducted on his behalf. ... Judges must therefore be prepared to make more detailed orders than they are accustomed to do now. The general order in favour of one party or another will less frequently be appropriate"; Woolf Report, ch 7, para 24.

[52] See Lord Chancellor's Department, *Access to Justice, Civil Procedure Rules about Costs, Consultation Paper* (August 1997), Draft Rule C 1.7. Unlike the current rules, it contains a detailed list of matters which might be relevant when the court is deciding whether to depart from the general rule that it must order the unsuccessful party to pay the costs of the successful party. This is intended to encourage the court to be more ready to depart from the general rule in any particular case. The conduct of the parties will be relevant, including pre-commencement conduct. The proposed rule also enables the court to have regard to whether a party has succeeded on a particular issue, and whether it was reasonable for a party to pursue a particular issue. This is intended to widen the limits on the court's powers arising from *Re Elgindata (No 2)*. *Ibid*, Part C1, para 14.

Pre-action protocols

2.36 The Woolf Report recommended the development of pre-action protocols to encourage well informed settlements and, if pre-action settlement is not achievable, to lay the ground for expeditious conduct of proceedings.[53] The Lord Chancellor's Department has recently set out in its working paper on Judicial Case Management[54] its proposals for the manner in which the courts will utilise them in practice. The consultation document sets out the items which should be contained in any pre-action protocol. These include: a clear statement of the area of litigation and litigants which the protocol aims to cover; standard form communications (eg letters before action and letters instructing experts); timetable for communications; reference to other methods of pursuing complaints; arrangements regarding experts reports; and arrangements regarding pre-action disclosure. It is envisaged that pre-action protocols may be embodied in practice directions and may influence the exercise of the courts' discretion after proceedings have begun on matters such as costs and requests for extensions of time.[55]

2.37 We believe that consideration should be given to the introduction of pre-action protocols in relation to proceedings under section 459. We set out below one particular area in which we consider that the development of a pre-action protocol would be desirable (namely the service of a "buy out" notice where a party is proposing to rely on the presumption we are recommending in relation to share purchase orders).[56]

Conclusion

2.38 To summarise, we consider that the most effective way to deal with the problems of the excessive length and cost of many proceedings under section 459 is by active case management by the courts. We consider that the new powers contained in the Draft Civil Proceedings Rules relating to the dismissal of claims which have no realistic prospect of success (rule 14.2) and the exclusion of issues from determination (rule 5.1) will in future give the courts much greater ability to manage claims under the section, but that the courts can and should use their existing powers to manage cases more actively where possible.

---

[53] Woolf Report, ch 10.

[54] LCD Working Paper on Judicial Case Management, Annex C.

[55] *Ibid*, at para C20.

[56] See paras 3.63-3.64 below.

PART 3
A NEW ADDITIONAL UNFAIR PREJUDICE REMEDY FOR SMALLER COMPANIES

Introduction

3.1 In the consultation paper we put forward for discussion proposals for a new unfair prejudice remedy for smaller companies.[1] The aim of such a remedy would be to provide a more streamlined procedure for dealing with some of the most common disputes which are currently brought under section 459, thereby reducing the time and costs spent on such disputes. In this part we consider the proposed new remedy and set out our reasons for rejecting it. We then explain our recommendation for presumptions that in certain circumstances (a) conduct will be presumed to be unfairly prejudicial, and (b) where the court grants a purchase order in favour of the petitioner his shares should be valued on a pro rata basis.[2] Finally, we discuss briefly the issue raised in the consultation paper of whether there should be a remedy in certain situations in which there is no fault.

The scheme proposed in the consultation paper

3.2 The suggested wording for the new remedy was as follows:

(1) Where the conditions in sub-section (2) are satisfied a member of a private company may apply to court for an order under this section on the grounds of his exclusion from participation in management of the company/removal of a director (in either case) save for gross misconduct.

(2) Such an application may only be made if there are a minimum of two and a maximum of five members in the company and if:

(a) the company is an association formed or continued on the basis of a personal relationship, involving mutual confidence;

(b) before the applicant's exclusion from management, there was an agreement or understanding between all the shareholders that he or she should participate in the conduct of the business.

(3) Under this section the court is empowered only to make an order that the shares of any members of the company are to be purchased by other members or by the company itself and, in the case of a purchase by the company itself, the reduction of the company's capital accordingly, but such purchase will be at fair value without a discount for the fact that the applicant's shares represent a minority shareholding.

---

[1] Consultation Paper No 142, Part 18.

[2] See para 3.8 below for a brief explanation of the difference between a "discounted" and "pro rata" basis of valuation.

24

Statistical survey

3.3   The elements of the proposed scheme were based on our statistical survey of petitions brought under section 459 in 1994 and 1995.[3] Essentially, three features were identified in that survey:

> (i)   the vast majority of companies involved in proceedings brought under section 459 were private companies with five or fewer shareholders;

> (ii)   by far the most commonly pleaded allegation was exclusion from management;

> (iii)   the remedy most commonly sought was the purchase of the petitioners' shares by the respondent.

3.4   The new remedy was therefore directed at disputes involving these elements. But in addition, the proposal expressly set out two other aspects which arose from the case law on disputes of this kind.

Ebrahimi considerations

3.5   As we explained in the consultation paper,[4] the Court of Appeal in *Re Saul D Harrison & Sons plc* ("*Saul D Harrison*")[5] laid down "guidelines" as to when conduct might be regarded as "unfairly prejudicial". The starting point was to ask whether the conduct was in accordance with the articles of association. But the court could also consider whether the applicant had a "legitimate expectation" over and above the legal rights conferred by the company's constitution and arising out of a relationship between the shareholders which fell within the categories or analogous situations set out in the case of *Ebrahimi v Westbourne Galleries Ltd* ("*Ebrahimi*").[6] These were:

> (i)   an association formed or continued on the basis of a personal relationship, involving mutual confidence - this element will often be found where a pre-existing partnership has been converted into a limited company;

> (ii)   an agreement, or understanding, that all, or some (for there may be "sleeping members"), of the shareholders shall participate in the conduct of the business;

---

[3]   See Consultation Paper No 142, Appendix E. An updated version of this survey is set out in Appendix J.

[4]   *Ibid*, at paras 9.21-9.26 and 20.17.

[5]   [1995] 1 BCLC 14.

[6]   [1973] AC 360. In this case, the House of Lords was considering the circumstances in which it might be "just and equitable" to order a company to be wound up under s 222(f) of the Companies Act 1948 (now s 122(1)(g) of the Insolvency Act 1986).

(iii) restriction upon the transfer of the members' interest in the company - so that if confidence is lost, or one member is removed from management, he cannot take out his stake and go elsewhere.[7]

3.6 In companies of this kind,[8] the letter of the articles may not fully reflect the understandings upon which the shareholders are associated. Wider equitable considerations might arise which may entitle a shareholder to say it would be unfair in certain circumstances for those who control the company to exercise a power conferred by the articles upon the board or the company in general meeting.[9]

3.7 Accordingly, in order for a petitioner to show, in proceedings under section 459, that his exclusion from management of the company was unfairly prejudicial, he will generally have to show that the relationship between the members of the company involved elements of the kind highlighted in the *Ebrahimi* case, and that he had a "legitimate expectation" of being able to continue to participate in the management.[10] In the proposal for a new remedy, we included express reference to the first two *Ebrahimi* elements as requirements which must be satisfied before an application could be made.[11]

Basis of valuation

3.8 We also drew attention to the difficulties involved in valuing shares for the purposes of a purchase order. One of the matters often in dispute is the basis of valuation of the shareholding.[12] This frequently turns on whether the shares should be valued on a "discounted" basis or "pro rata". We explained that a minority shareholding in a company is generally regarded as having a lower value per share than a majority shareholding. This reflects the fact that a minority shareholder may have limited voting power, and therefore limited control over the management and day to day running of the affairs of the company. Where the valuation is reduced to reflect this the shares are said to be valued on a "discounted" basis. Where, on the other hand, the shares are valued as a proportion of the value of the company as a whole, they are often said to be valued "pro rata".

---

[7] *Ibid*, at p 379.

[8] Often called "quasi-partnerships" in the cases; see Consultation Paper No 142, para 8.10.

[9] See *Re Saul D Harrison & Sons plc* [1995] 1 BCLC 14, 19.

[10] Even so, the petitioner's exclusion will not necessarily be unfair. The court will look at the conduct leading up to the exclusion to see if it was justified and, more importantly, at the terms on which the exclusion was effected to see if they were fair; see Consultation Paper No 142, para 9.34.

[11] The third element was not included because the courts have tended to focus on the other two elements, and because in practice private companies invariably have a restriction on transfer in their articles, so that the third element is almost invariably present in any event.

[12] See Consultation Paper No 142, para 10.12. Another is the date on which it is to be valued.

3.9   In fixing a value for the purposes of a purchase order in proceedings under section 459, the overriding requirement is "fairness".[13] Nevertheless, as we explained in the consultation paper,[14] the cases show that a pro rata basis of valuation is generally ordered where *Ebrahimi* type considerations are present. We therefore suggested that this should be reflected in the new remedy, and that in order to reduce the number of contested issues the remedy should provide that there should be no discount for a minority shareholding.

Suggested wording

3.10   Accordingly it was proposed, for discussion, that the new remedy would be available to a shareholder in a private company with a minimum of two and a maximum of five shareholders, between whom there was a relationship such as that set out in *Ebrahimi* if the shareholder could show that he had been excluded from management without good reason.[15] The only order which the court could make would be an order for the purchase of the applicant's shares on a "non-discounted" basis.[16]

Our provisional view

3.11   We set out wording for consideration, but did not make any provisional recommendation in advance of consultation. We accepted that any new remedy along the lines proposed was likely to be somewhat "rough and ready". However, we considered that such a remedy could be useful if it meant that fewer issues of fact would need to be proved, thereby leading to shorter, cheaper litigation than a full blown section 459 case.

3.12   We highlighted a number of specific concerns which we considered could give rise to problems.[17] These included the specified number of shareholders; the meaning of the wording taken from the judgment of Lord Wilberforce in *Ebrahimi*; the grounds of the claim; and the risk of increasing litigation. However, we noted that litigation under the new remedy was likely to be more focused than much of the current litigation under section 459, and that active case management could assist in dealing with any problems of increased litigation.

Update of statistical survey

3.13   We have conducted an identical survey of petitions filed at the High Court in London during 1996. We have incorporated the new statistics into the survey and the revised statistics for the period from January 1994 to December 1996 appear at Appendix J. These show very little change to the previous figures on the most

---

[13]   *Re Bird Precision Bellows Ltd* [1984] Ch 419; see Consultation Paper No 142, para 10.11.

[14]   See Consultation Paper No 142, Para 10.15-10.17.

[15]   The suggested wording referred to "gross misconduct"; see para 3.2 above.

[16]   The suggested wording is set out in full in para 3.2 above.

[17]   Consultation Paper No 142, paras 18.7-18.11.

commonly pleaded allegation, and the most commonly sought remedy.[18] Also, the vast majority of companies involved still have five or fewer members.[19]

Respondents' views

3.14 Views on whether there should be a new unfair prejudice remedy for smaller companies along the lines proposed were almost evenly split, with just a small majority in favour.

3.15 The main reason given by respondents who were not in favour of the new remedy was that it appeared to add little to the current section 459, but might in fact complicate proceedings. The new remedy would cover much of the same ground as the existing provision, but with the obvious limitation that the matters enabling the court to grant relief would be narrower. If the two remedies were to be cumulative,[20] shareholders were likely to invoke simultaneously the new jurisdiction and section 459, leading to further complications in already complex proceedings; if, on the other hand, the jurisdictions were to be mutually exclusive, shareholders' advisers would have a potentially difficult choice in deciding whether to seek to invoke the new jurisdiction or to rely upon the existing provision.

3.16 Another aspect which concerned a number of respondents was the lack of flexibility of the new remedy. This point was made in particular about the relief which the court could grant. Several respondents indicated that they were not in favour of the new remedy because they considered that it would be wrong for the court to order the purchase of the applicant's shares on a non-discounted basis *in every case*. In fact, it appeared that a majority of respondents who commented on the wording of the new remedy considered that it should be possible for the court to make a different order in appropriate circumstances.

3.17 A similar point about lack of flexibility was made in respect of the grounds for the application under the new remedy. Some respondents pointed out that the applicant's exclusion from management may not have been unfair, for example, because the applicant may continue to receive substantial benefits from the company, and/or because his exclusion could be justified in the interests of the company even without gross misconduct.

3.18 A further point which appeared to concern a large number of respondents was the fact that the new remedy was proposed to be limited to companies with five or fewer shareholders. Several respondents simply suggested that the limit was too low. Some of these considered that 10 may be a more appropriate number, although others did not give a specific figure. A number of other respondents did not consider that there should be any limit at all. The point was made that if the remedy was limited to companies which were formed on the basis of mutual trust and confidence there was no need for a restriction on the number of members.

---

[18] The most commonly pleaded allegation remains exclusion from management (64%), and the most common remedy sought remains the purchase of the petitioner's shares (69%).

[19] 82%.

[20] Which is what we provisionally suggested; see Consultation Paper No 142, para 18.11.

Concern was also expressed that it would be possible for a member to divide his holding amongst a number of nominees to get round the remedy.

Our final view

3.19 We identified in our statistical survey that petitions brought by minority shareholders in small private companies[21] seeking to have their shares purchased on the grounds of exclusion from management made up the majority of petitions brought under section 459. We still consider that it would be desirable to provide a disaffected minority shareholder, who has been excluded from participation in the management of the company, with a speedy and economical exit route in appropriate cases at a fair (and, so far as possible, readily ascertainable) price. Not only is this desirable from the point of view of the minority shareholder who will wish to remove his stake in the company in order to pursue other interests, but also from the point of view of the majority shareholders (and the company) who will wish to be able to dispose of any dispute quickly so that they can concentrate on the continued running of the business.

3.20 Our proposals for an exit article were widely supported on consultation.[22] Clearly it would be preferable for the parties to make provision in the articles for what will happen if their relationship breaks down. Our proposed exit article will assist in encouraging the parties to do this. But it can only go so far, and there will continue to be many disputed cases brought under section 459 on the grounds of exclusion from management.

3.21 The proposed new remedy could have provided a quicker and cheaper alternative to section 459 for resolving many of these cases. But we accept that it is likely that parties would invoke simultaneously the new jurisdiction and section 459 (if permitted) and that this could complicate the proceedings. Even though we consider that active case management could, to a large extent, deal with any problems which might arise,[23] the approach to shareholder proceedings which we are recommending already relies heavily on effective case management and we do not wish to add unnecessarily to this task by encouraging the proliferation of remedies.

3.22 Even with effective case management, there may be circumstances in which the introduction of a new remedy along the lines proposed would simply extend the length of proceedings and add to the costs. For example, if a minority shareholder relied on both the existing provision and the new remedy, the court might, in an appropriate case, determine that the issues raised by the application based on the new remedy should be heard first, and that, in the meantime, there should be an order staying the remaining issues. If the minority shareholder is successful under the new remedy, then that should be the end of the matter and the proceedings should have been more focused, and therefore quicker and cheaper. But if the

---

[21] Most of these were moreover alleged to be companies where *Ebrahimi* type considerations applied. Obviously we cannot tell from our survey whether those allegations would have succeeded.

[22] See para 5.6 below.

[23] See Consultation Paper No 142, para 18.11.

minority shareholder fails under the new remedy, he may well seek to resurrect the remaining issues relevant to the claim under the existing provision. He may have to proceed to trial on those issues, and, with the delay involved in trying the earlier issues relevant to the new remedy, the time taken to dispose of the proceedings as a whole (and the overall costs of doing so) may in fact have increased.

3.23 We are not so convinced by the concerns expressed by respondents about the lack of flexibility of the new remedy. To a certain extent this issue is an echo of the much wider debate surrounding the more general proposals put forward in the Woolf Report. The ideal may well be to have an open textured discretion as in section 459. But if a shareholder cannot afford to pursue litigation under section 459, or if the costs involved in doing so outweigh any benefit that either party will eventually obtain from the proceedings, then, however good the remedy in theory, it is of little benefit to the parties in practice. There is clearly an argument for a more "rough and ready" remedy which, although not perfect, can do substantial justice between the parties.

3.24 A remedy along the lines proposed in the consultation paper would be of much less benefit if the court retained a discretion as to the basis on which the shares are to be valued. The parties are likely to introduce many of the arguments and allegations which would otherwise have been excluded from the new remedy in seeking to persuade the court to apply a particular basis of valuation. The new remedy would therefore add little to the existing provisions of sections 459-461. A similar point can be made in response to the suggestion that the court should continue to be able to consider whether the applicant's exclusion from management was "fair" (irrespective of the issue of gross misconduct).

3.25 In short, we are concerned that the introduction of a new remedy along the lines proposed in the consultation paper may lead to duplication and complication of shareholder proceedings. Also, if the remedy were to be made more flexible, as appears to be desired by many respondents, it would largely defeat its purpose and would add little to the existing provisions. For these reasons we do not favour the introduction of a new unfair prejudice remedy for smaller companies along the lines proposed for discussion in paragraph 18.4 of the consultation paper.

An alternative approach

3.26 However, there is an alternative approach which we consider goes a long way towards achieving the policy aim set out in paragraph 3.19, but which would not involve duplication of remedies, and which would retain some flexibility. It is based on a proposal put forward by two respondents.[24]

3.27 Under this alternative approach, sections 459-461 would be amended to raise presumptions that, in certain circumstances: (a) unless the contrary is shown, the affairs of the company have been conducted in a manner which is unfairly prejudicial to the petitioner; and (b) where the court orders his shares to be bought out, the appropriate order (unless the court otherwise orders) is that the shares should be valued on a pro rata basis. The details of the circumstances

---

[24] Michael Crystal QC and Simon Mortimore QC, with whom Richard Adkins QC agreed.

giving rise to the presumptions are discussed below,[25] but the main feature of the presumptions is that the petitioner has been excluded from the management of the company.

3.28   This approach has the advantages of providing some degree of certainty for the parties on the position which the court is likely to take, and in this respect it would have much the same effect as the new remedy proposed in the consultation paper. It should also mean that cases can be dealt with more quickly when proceedings are in fact issued. For example, assuming the relevant circumstances are made out, the respondent will have to show good reason why the presumptions should not apply, and this will limit the factual allegations which the court will have to consider. Alternatively, if the respondent has made (or makes during the course of the proceedings) a fair offer for the purchase of the petitioner's shares without a discount, then save in exceptional circumstances (and subject to the question of costs), the petition should be dismissed.[26]

3.29   On the other hand, this proposal will allow the court the flexibility, in an appropriate case, to find, for example, that the petitioner's exclusion from management was not in fact unfair,[27] or that the appropriate basis on which the petitioner's shares should be valued for a purchase order is on a discounted or some other basis. Also, this approach will not involve the introduction of a new remedy, and so will not give rise to the problem of duplication highlighted above.[28]

3.30   Accordingly, **we recommend that there should be legislative provision for presumptions in proceedings under sections 459-461 that, in certain circumstances, (a) where a shareholder has been excluded from participation in the management of the company, the conduct will be presumed to be unfairly prejudicial by reason of the exclusion; and (b), if the presumption is not rebutted and the court is satisfied that it ought to order a buy out of the petitioner's shares, it should do so on a pro rata basis.**

3.31   We now consider the details of this proposal. We begin by considering the general approach which should be taken to the conditions for the application of the presumptions. Next we examine the details of the proposed conditions under the following heads: private company limited by shares; exclusion from management; make-up of the company. We then go on to explain the content of the first and second presumptions. Finally we set out an additional pre-action procedure which we consider could usefully be included in a pre-action protocol governing unfair prejudice applications, namely a buy out notice.

---

[25]   See paras 3.32-3.53 below.

[26]   This is in line with the current case law. See *Re a Company (No 003096 of 1987)* [1988] BCC 80, and see Consultation Paper No 142, paras 8.15-8.17, and para 9.51, n 136.

[27]   See paras 3.37 and 3.54 below.

[28]   See paras 3.15 and 3.21 above.

General approach to conditions for presumptions

3.32 The circumstances giving rise to the presumptions need to be as easily ascertainable as possible. Otherwise the presumptions would not assist the parties in predicting the outcome of proceedings and would not, therefore, have the intended effect of encouraging settlements. Also, it could generate additional argument during the course of proceedings (on whether the presumptions in fact applied), rather than reducing the issues which would need to be litigated if agreement could not be reached. On the other hand, the presumptions should not, so far as possible, rely on arbitrary factors; rather they should be based on clear principles.

3.33 The new remedy which we proposed in the consultation paper included express reference to the first two factors set out by Lord Wilberforce in *Ebrahimi*.[29] A similar approach could be taken in respect of the presumptions. However, a number of objections could be made to this.

3.34 First, it could be said that the meaning of the wording taken from the judgment of Lord Wilberforce in *Ebrahimi* is not clear.[30] However, this may be less of a problem than might at first be imagined. There is now a good deal of authority on the wording, and it has become very familiar to courts and practitioners alike. The views of respondents on whether this might be a problem in the context of a new remedy for smaller companies were fairly evenly split.

3.35 Secondly, there is the potential for complex factual disputes of a historical nature. The point was made by the two respondents who put forward the proposal for a presumption, that conditions based on the *Ebrahimi* relationship focus on the past, rather than on the immediate circumstances occasioning the need for relief. It is rare for the nature of the relationship between the shareholders to be subject to a clear agreement. Generally, the court will have to infer an understanding from the events which have happened. Accordingly, the petitioner will be encouraged to delve into the past to try to justify the case coming within the concepts of "personal relationship", "mutual confidence", and "understanding ... that he or she should participate in the conduct of the business", and the respondents will be encouraged to deny those allegations. This may prevent a speedy and economic resolution to the dispute. It was suggested that it would be preferable to identify conditions which can be ascertained by reference to objective and less disputable circumstances.

3.36 Thirdly, if the presumptions simply referred to the *Ebrahimi* factors, this would add little to the current position since it is fairly clear from the case law what the likely result will be where those factors are present.[31] The creation of the presumption will not exclude argument as to whether a relationship of the kind

---

[29] Consultation Paper No 142, paras 18.4-18.5. See also para 3.5 above.

[30] The point was also made in the consultation paper that it could be said to be undesirable to embody words from judgments in statute as this could hamper the development of the law; see Consultation Paper No 142, para 18.7, n 9.

[31] See Consultation Paper No 142, para 10.14.

envisaged in *Ebrahimi* exists, but will shift the onus to the party which is likely to be the stronger of the two to argue that it does not.

3.37   We are persuaded by these last two points in particular. We consider that the presumptions should be based on "structural" factors (for example the percentage holding of the petitioner and the fact that he was a director) rather than the expectations of the parties. Clearly, these matters are less open to factual disputes than conditions derived from *Ebrahimi*. They have the advantage of being readily ascertainable by reference to the current (or recent) state of affairs. It is true that they may be regarded as somewhat arbitrary. However, unlike the new remedy which was proposed in the consultation paper, this proposal only sets out a presumption. If a case does not satisfy the conditions for the presumption to arise, the application of section 459, as it stands without the presumption, is not affected. Moreover, even if the presumption applied, it would still be open to the court to find that the petitioner's exclusion from management was not unfair, either because the petitioner's conduct justified his removal, or because it was not a situation where the petitioner had a legitimate expectation as a shareholder of continuing as a director, or that his shares should be purchased on a discounted basis. The respondents would be able to call evidence to rebut the presumption. We now turn to the details of our proposed conditions.

Details of proposed conditions

Private company limited by shares

3.38   We consider that the presumptions should only apply to private companies. It is extremely unlikely that the courts would find that a shareholder in a public company (particularly a listed company) could have a legitimate expectation of being able to continue to participate in the management of the company founded on some informal agreement or arrangement.[32]

3.39   In addition, we consider that the presumptions should only apply to companies limited by shares. There are very few reported cases involving members of other types of companies[33] bringing proceedings under section 459, and none that we are aware of where the facts would fall within the terms of our presumptions. The presumptions are directed at commercial companies where an owner-manager is excluded from participation in the management of the business and seeks a purchase order in respect of his shares. Such companies are extremely unlikely to be constituted as companies limited by guarantee or unlimited companies.[34] Our intention is for the presumptions to be as simple as possible and cover the straightforward cases.[35] We do not, therefore, consider that it is necessary or appropriate to extend the presumptions to companies other than those limited by

---

[32]   *Ibid*, at paras 18.4 and 18.7. Note also s 319 of the Companies Act 1985.

[33]   Ie companies limited by guarantee or unlimited companies.

[34]   See s 1(2) of the Companies Act 1985.

[35]   We note, also, that s 461(2) of the Companies Act 1985 refers expressly to the purchase of a members *shares* in the company, but does not include express reference to the purchase of a member's interest in a company limited by guarantee with no share capital.

shares. **We recommend that the presumptions should only apply where the company is a private company limited by shares.**[36]

Exclusion from management

3.40 The presumptions should apply where the petitioner has been excluded from participating in the management of the company. By this we mean that he has been removed as a director, or has been prevented from carrying on all or substantially all his functions as a director.

3.41 In many of the reported cases, the alleged exclusion from management has consisted of removing the shareholder from his position as a director.[37] The case of *R A Noble & Sons (Clothing) Ltd*,[38] however, gives an example of the sort of situation where a shareholder could be excluded from participating in the management without any need to be formally removed as director. In that case, the respondent failed to consult with the petitioner on major decisions (such as the purchase of company cars) and failed to invite him to board meetings or supply any other information. We consider that conduct such as this would constitute exclusion from management of the company for the purposes of the presumptions. (In fact, the exclusion in *R A Noble & Sons (Clothing) Ltd* was considered fair in the circumstances because of the petitioner's own disinterest in the affairs of the company).

3.42 We did consider whether the presumptions should cover situations where the person who is removed as a director (or otherwise excluded from participation in the management) is a spouse of or person nominated by the shareholder (rather than the shareholder himself). A shareholder could arrange for a spouse or nominated person to be a director and have a legitimate expectation, as a member, that the spouse or nominated person would remain as a director. However, our presumptions are directed at the relatively simple and straightforward cases. We consider that in more complicated factual situations it is appropriate that the onus should be on the petitioner to show that the exclusion (in this case of the spouse or nominated person) was unfairly prejudicial to his interests as a member.[39]

3.43 Accordingly, **we recommend that the presumptions should apply where the petitioner has been removed as a director or has been prevented from carrying out all or substantially all of his functions as a director.**

Make-up of the company

3.44 What we are concerned with essentially are owner-managed companies. There are two elements by which we propose to describe the make up of such companies.

---

[36] As defined in s 1(3) of the Companies Act 1985.

[37] See, for example, *Re Ghyll Beck Driving Range Ltd* [1993] BCLC 1126; *Re Haden Bill Electrical Ltd* [1995] 2 BCLC 280; *Quinlan v Essex Hinge Co Ltd* [1996] 2 BCLC 417.

[38] [1983] BCLC 273.

[39] For situations in which the owner-manager may declare a trust of his shares or vest them in a nominee or company which he controls, see para 3.50 below.

3.45   The first is that the petitioner should hold not less than 10% of the voting rights. We consider that if his holding was less than 10%, it is improbable that the necessary personal relationships, agreements and understanding would be present.[40]

3.46   This requirement must be qualified, however. There may be different classes of shares, some with weighted voting rights and/or the right only to vote on certain issues. What we are concerned with is the right to vote on the company's affairs overall. We therefore propose that the provision should require the petitioner to hold 10% of the voting rights capable of being exercised at general meetings of the company on all, or substantially all, matters.[41]

3.47   In addition, we consider that, for the purposes of this 10% threshold, the shares carrying the voting rights should be held by the member in his own name. This requirement prevents a shareholder from meeting the requirement by agreeing with another shareholder that they will hold their shares jointly. It also means that a member cannot take into account shares which are vested in a nominee. We consider that in owner-managed companies a member is likely to retain a holding in his own name, and that it is a reasonable requirement for the operation of the presumption that he hold a minimum 10% stake in the company in his sole name.[42] On the other hand, we do not consider that the member should have to show that he is the beneficial owner of the shares for the purposes of this threshold. We deal with the situation of trusts below.

3.48   The second element by which we propose to describe the make up of companies to which the presumptions will apply, is that all, or substantially all, of the members are directors. As indicated above, we are trying to target owner-managed companies. In some cases, there may well be one or two shareholders who are not

---

[40]   This percentage is also consistent with other minimum share holding requirements under the Companies Acts, such as s 368(2) (power to requisition an extraordinary general meeting); s 370(3) (power to call a meeting); s 373(1)(b)(ii) (right to demand a poll), but these requirements can be met by members acting together. There are other minimum thresholds in provisions of the Companies Act, but they are also generally aggregated percentages; see, eg, ss 5, 54, 127, 376.

[41]   See sched 10A to the Companies Act 1985, which deals with parent and subsidiary undertakings. The draft Bill contains provisions such as are found in that schedule to cover the case where, eg, voting rights are temporarily incapable of being exercised. This might occur where a shareholder had died and a transfer to his personal representatives had not been registered.

[42]   We have reviewed all the cases reported in Butterworth's Company Law Cases in the last ten years (1988-1997) where *Ebrahimi* was cited (these are not *necessarily* cases where the petitioner was claiming exclusion from management or had a legitimate expectation of continued participation). Out of 31 cases listed, there were only four where the petitioner had less than 10% of the voting rights. These were *Re BSB Holdings (No 2)* [1996] 1 BCLC 155 (where it was not alleged that the *Ebrahimi* considerations were present), *Re Saul D Harrison & Sons plc* [1995] 1 BCLC 14, *Re J E Cade & Son Ltd* [1992] BCLC 213, and *Re Ringtower Holdings plc* [1989] BCLC 427. In all these cases the petition failed or was struck out and in only one of them (*Re J E Cade & Son Ltd*) was the allegation that the *Ebrahimi* considerations applied regarded as sustainable. (In addition, there were four cases where the voting rights were not apparent from the judgment).

actually directors but the company is still in essence "owner-managed". It is for this reason that we refer to all *or substantially all* of the members being directors.

3.49   There is, however, a qualification in respect of this second element in respect of joint holders. Some shares may be held in joint names (for reasons unconnected with the section).[43] For instance, a shareholder may have declared a trust over some of his shares, nominating two trustees. For the purposes of determining whether all or substantially all the shareholders are directors only one of the joint holders should count. The joint holder to be counted is the first-named joint holder or, if one of the joint-holders is a director, the first-named joint holder who is also a director.

3.50   Members of private companies may place some or all or their shares on trust for their children or others. We have considered whether voting rights attached to shares in respect of which a member has declared a trust, for family members, or which he has vested in a nominee,[44] or a company which he controls, should be aggregated with voting rights attached to other shares registered in his name for the purpose of calculating the percentage of voting rights which a member has for the purposes of the first element and of calculating whether the second element is satisfied. Our view is that this would result in complexity. Provisions of that nature might be appropriate in an anti avoidance provision, but all we are proposing is a presumption. The absence of an aggregation provision will not prevent the court from granting the same relief where the presumption does not apply. Moreover, if the shares are not held in the member's own name, this would tend to throw doubt on whether the company is in fact owner-managed. A shareholder who wants to have the benefit of the presumption will not be prevented from creating a trust of his shares, but if he does so he must remain sole holder at least of shares carrying 10% of the voting rights.[45] As respects other shares over which he creates a trust, it will be sufficient if he ensures that he is a trustee and becomes the first-named joint holder.

3.51   In each case, we propose that these elements should be present immediately before the exclusion from participation in management. So, for example, if the petitioner ceased to hold 10% of the shares, and then a year later was dismissed as a director, we do not consider that the presumption should apply. Indeed, we consider that even if he was dismissed a few days after he ceased to hold the necessary 10%, the presumption should not apply. The elements should be present effectively at the time of the dismissal. The reason we refer to "immediately before" is that the very removal from office of the petitioner might have the effect of removing one of the qualifying criteria (ie it may mean that not all or substantially all of the shareholders are directors). So one has to look at the situation immediately before the removal.

---

[43]   We have already indicated that for the purposes of the first element, the member should have a minimum shareholding *in his own name*; see para 3.47 above.

[44]   Compare para 7 of sched 10A to the Companies Act 1985; and s 346 of that Act. It is probably less common for shares to be vested in the name of a nominee in a private company.

[45]   See n 42 above which indicates that this requirement is likely to be easily met in practice.

3.52 We did consider the possibility of imposing a limit on the number of shareholders. However, we take the view that this is unnecessary. This is because the requirement that all, or substantially all, of the members are directors will inevitably place a limit on the size of companies which come within the terms of the presumptions. We consider that any additional restriction is unnecessary and could lead to arbitrary results.

3.53 **We recommend that the presumptions should apply where, immediately before the exclusion from participation in the management, (a) the petitioner held shares in his sole name giving him not less than 10% of the rights to vote at general meetings of the company on all or substantially all matters, and (b) all, or substantially all of the members of the company were directors. (For the purposes of (b), only one joint holder should be counted as a member).**

The first presumption

3.54 We propose that where these conditions are present, the affairs of the company will be presumed to have been conducted in a manner which is unfairly prejudicial to the petitioner for the purposes of section 459(1), unless the contrary is shown. In other words, the onus will be on the respondent to show that the affairs of the company have not been conducted in a manner which is unfairly prejudicial to the petitioner. It is therefore open to the respondent to show, for example, that the petitioner had no legitimate expectation of being able to continue to participate in the management of the company; or that the removal was justified by the petitioner's conduct.

3.55 It is not proposed that the presumption should affect any situations which do not fall within it. In particular, it should still be possible for a petitioner to show that exclusion from management was unfairly prejudicial under the current case law, even if the facts do not satisfy the conditions set out in the presumption. It is not intended that there should be any counter-presumption, that just because a situation does not fall within the conditions, exclusion from management is not unfair.

3.56 **We recommend that the first presumption should provide that, where these conditions are present, the affairs of the company will be presumed to have been conducted in a manner which is unfairly prejudicial to the petitioner, unless the contrary is shown.**

The second presumption

3.57 We propose that where the first presumption has not been rebutted and the court is satisfied that it ought to make an order that one or more of the respondents should purchase the petitioner's shares, the shares should be valued on a pro rata basis unless the court otherwise orders. This is confirmatory of the position established by the case law under the section applicable to these circumstances.[46]

---

[46] See paras 3.9 and 3.36 above.

3.58   We do not consider that the legislation should go on to set out by whom the shares should be purchased. This will be a matter for the court. Purchase orders can be very complex where there are a number of respondents and we do not consider that it is possible or appropriate to bind the court's discretion in this regard.

3.59   We have referred above to the question of whether shares should be valued on a discounted basis or pro rata.[47] By providing that the valuation should be on a pro rata basis, what we are proposing is that the company as a whole should be valued, and then that value should be apportioned rateably to the individual shareholdings. In other words, a 30% shareholding would be valued at 30% of a 100% shareholding. In order to meet the point that in private companies there is often no market for a shareholding we have provided that the market value should be ascertained on the basis that the whole of the share capital is being sold, and in addition that the buyer and seller are to be presumed to be willing. We believe that this will reduce the scope for unnecessary argument and produce a fair result as the situation will be one in which the court is satisfied that unfair prejudice has occurred for which the respondent is responsible. The reference to market value enables the court to take account of a special purchaser for the company if one is known to exist.

3.60   On the other hand the court may provide for the presumption to be displaced if the only shares to be purchased are for example preference shares with limited rights to receive dividends and capital. The court may consider that some simpler method of valuation would be appropriate. We think it unlikely that there will be many cases under the new section where there will be shares other than ordinary shares. Likewise if the company has a claim against the respondent who is being ordered to purchase the shares which cannot be adequately reflected in the market value of the shares the court may order some other purchase price.

3.61   The court has very wide power under section 461(1) to give ancillary directions, and the addition of the presumption will not affect this. Thus the court could as now determine the date as at which the shares to be purchased should be valued in accordance with the presumption. If the presumption contained a date for valuation there might be less room for argument as to what that date should be but we consider that the new section cannot satisfactorily specify a single date which should be presumed to be the appropriate date for this purpose.[48] The appropriate date depends on what is fair in the particular case.

3.62   **We recommend that the second presumption should provide that where the first presumption has not been rebutted and the court is satisfied that it ought to make an order that one or more of the respondents should purchase the petitioner's shares, the shares should be valued on a pro rata basis unless the court otherwise orders.**

---

[47] See para 3.8 above.

[48] See Consultation Paper No 142, paras 10.18-10.20.

Buy out notice

3.63   There is a further requirement which we consider could usefully be introduced into the procedure for unfair prejudice claims. We suggest that the petitioner should be required to serve a notice on the other members of the company and the company requiring them to purchase his shares valued on a pro rata basis if, at the time of starting the proceedings, he intends to rely on the second presumption. The purpose of the notice mechanism would be to encourage parties to settle disputes, or at least set out their respective positions on the question of a buy out, before proceedings are commenced. We do not consider that the application of the presumptions should be dependent on a notice along these lines. Instead, we would propose that the court should have the power to sanction failure to comply with the notice requirement in making appropriate costs orders.

3.64   We have already drawn attention to the proposals in the Woolf Report on pre-action protocols.[49] We consider that a notice procedure of the kind proposed above would be ideally suited to a pre-action protocol of this kind set out in a practice direction.[50] **We therefore recommend that, if our recommendations for the presumptions are implemented, the Vice Chancellor should be invited to consider whether there should be a practice direction requiring the petitioner to serve a notice on the other members of the company and the company requiring them to purchase his shares valued on a pro rata basis before he starts his proceedings if he then intends to rely on the second presumption.**

A possible remedy for "no-fault" situations

3.65   One of the issues raised in the consultation paper was whether there should be a statutory remedy in situations where there is no fault.[51] Several consultees commented on this issue in the course of their responses. Some suggested that it should be open to shareholders in "quasi-partnership" type companies to exit at will (as if the company was in fact a true partnership). Others suggested that there should be provision for owner-managers of small companies to leave the company in certain circumstances (eg on retirement as a director) or for their beneficiaries to sell the shares they receive on the death of the owner-manager.

3.66   In our view there are strong economic arguments against allowing shareholders to exit at will. Also, as a matter of principle, such a right would fundamentally contravene the sanctity of the contract binding the members and the company which we considered should guide our approach to shareholder remedies.[52] This guiding principle was strongly supported by a large majority of respondents. The presumptions we have proposed above are consistent with this approach.

---

[49]   See para 2.36 above.

[50]   In some cases, of course, injunctive relief may be required, and it may not be possible to comply with a pre-action notice requirement.

[51]   See Consultation Paper No 142, para 18.10.

[52]   *Ibid*, at para 14.11.

3.67 It may be that there are particular situations where it would be useful for a shareholder to be able to dispose of his shares in circumstances where there has been no fault. We mentioned two such situations in the consultation paper:[53] those where all the parties are agreed that certain members should leave the company but it is not possible to reach agreement as to the terms of departure; and those where there is no question of fault by any officers or members, but some members have acquired their shares by transmission or operation of law and want to dispose of them.[54]

3.68 However, our view is that such situations are best dealt with in the articles of association. In Part 5 we deal with proposals for an exit provision in the articles of association.

Conclusion

3.69 To summarise, we are not in favour of a separate remedy dealing solely with exclusion from management in smaller companies. We do, however, recommend the introduction of presumptions into proceedings under sections 459-461 that in certain circumstances, (a) where a shareholder has been excluded from participating in the management of the company, the conduct will be presumed to be unfairly prejudicial by reason of the exclusion; and (b) if the presumption is not rebutted and the court is satisfied that it ought to order a buy out of the petitioner's shares, the shares should be valued on a pro rata basis unless the court otherwise orders.[55]

3.70 We consider that the best way to deal with situations where there has been no fault on the part of the members, but one of them (or the successor of a member who has died) wishes to dispose of his shares, is by provision in the articles of association.

---

[53] *Ibid,* at para 18.10.

[54] In New Zealand the appraisal remedy provides a statutory form of buy out that allows a dissenting minority shareholder to withdraw his investment by making the company repurchase his shares at a judicially assessed fair value, upon the occurrence of certain corporate acts. There is no need to show that the action complained of was unfair or unreasonable or not in the best interests of the company. For a discussion of the relevant provisions in the New Zealand Companies Act 1993, see G Shapira, "Problems with the Minority Buy out Rights" (1994) 1 BCSLB 3.

[55] See clauses 3 and 4 of the draft Bill at Appendix A.

PART 4
OTHER REFORMS RELATING TO PROCEEDINGS UNDER SECTIONS 459-461

4.1 In the consultation paper, we canvassed a number of other reforms relating to proceedings under sections 459-461.[1] These ranged from fairly major changes to the wording of the sections to relatively minor procedural matters. Although all of these may be regarded as seeking to rationalise proceedings under the sections, some were more obviously directed at limiting the difficulties caused by the wide ranging nature of the remedy, while others addressed potential or perceived lacunae in the remedy.

4.2 We set out in this part our views on these options in the light of the responses received. First we consider amendments to the wording of section 459, and clarification of its scope by other means; then we consider the imposition of a limitation period; next we consider adding winding up to the relief available under section 461; we then look at two procedural aspects of proceedings - the power to determine relief as between respondents, and the advertisement of petitions; finally we consider whether former members should be able to bring claims under the sections.

Amendments to wording of section 459

4.3 In the consultation paper, we put forward two alternatives for amending the wording of section 459. Each had a rather different purpose.

4.4 The first, which we provisionally recommended, was to make clear that it is specific conduct, rather than the affairs of the company overall, that has to be shown to be unfairly prejudicial.[2] We suggested that the relevant part of the section could read:

> A member of a company may apply to the court by petition for an order under this Part on the ground that *conduct within the affairs of the company is or has been* unfairly prejudicial to the interests of the members generally or some part of its members (including at least himself) ...

4.5 The intention of the amendment was not to limit the conduct on which a party could rely, but to focus attention on specific conduct. We noted in the consultation paper that irrelevant or weak allegations are often made by parties to "lend ballast" to what are essentially their main grievances.[3] We considered that the proposed new wording would demonstrate that it was not every aspect of the company's affairs in the relevant period that is in issue, and so assist in reducing the number of tactical allegations made.

---

[1] See Consultation Paper No 142, paras 20.5-20.31 and 20.35-20.38.

[2] *Ibid*, at paras 20.15-20.16.

[3] *Ibid*, at paras 9.35, 11.1-11.3, 17.16. See also para 2.1 above.

4.6   This proposal received a mixed reception from respondents, only half agreeing with the provisional view. Three main reasons were put forward by those who disagreed with the provisional view. First, that the amendment was, or may be, confusing. The current wording had been in existence for some time and was reasonably well understood. There would need to be a very good reason to change it. Secondly, the amendment was unnecessary; in so far as proceedings needed to be focused, this was a matter for effective case management. Thirdly, the amendment could be counter-productive and prevent the court being able to consider conduct in the round in appropriate cases.

4.7   We accept that there are a few cases where it is the cumulative effect of a number of matters arising in the running of the company which may be regarded as unfairly prejudicial to the petitioner, rather than isolated acts. Clearly, we would not want to amend the section in such a way that the court could not look at all the circumstances in an appropriate case. Nevertheless, it is apparent that in many cases there are several main grievances on which the proceedings turn, and the tendency of petitioners to include numerous peripheral allegations is detrimental to the efficient resolution of these cases.[4] However, we agree that the best way to deal with this problem is by effective case management, and we have set out above our recommendations on this point.[5] We are reluctant to recommend a change to the wording which could give rise to unforeseen problems when it has not received the whole-hearted support of those responding to the consultation paper.

4.8   Accordingly, we do not now consider that the wording of section 459 should be amended to make it clear that it is specific conduct, rather than the affairs of the company overall, that has to be shown to be unfairly prejudicial.

4.9   The second alternative for amending the wording which we considered, but provisionally rejected, was to define the words "unfairly prejudicial" in section 459.[6] The reasoning behind this suggestion was not so much to make it easier for parties to predict whether or not a claim is likely to succeed;[7] rather, it was to ensure that the section would continue to be construed broadly.

4.10   We have drawn attention above to the decision of the Court of Appeal in *Saul D Harrison*[8] which laid down "guidelines" for the application of the section. These may appear to limit the availability of the remedy, in cases where there is no invasion of legal rights, to situations where the shareholder has a "legitimate expectation" over and above the legal rights conferred by the company's

---

[4]   See the recent case of *Re Arvin & Sons Ltd* [1997] 1 BCLC 479, where Sir Richard Scott V-C commented: "Judges should, to my mind, be astute to prevent section 459 petitions degenerating into an unnecessary raking over old grievances or settling of old scores"; *ibid*, at p 494.

[5]   See Part 2 above.

[6]   See Consultation Paper No 142, paras 20.17-20.23.

[7]   The Commission considered separately the question of clarification by authoritative guidance; see para 4.14 below.

[8]   [1995] 1 BCLC 14; see para 3.5 above.

constitution and arising out of the relationship between the shareholders which satisfies the criteria set out in *Ebrahimi*.[9]

4.11   In the consultation paper, we noted that it appeared to be the original intention of the Jenkins Committee[10] that conduct could be unfairly prejudicial without there being a breach of the rights belonging to the shareholder or to the company. We suggested that if such conduct could be unfairly prejudicial for the purposes of section 459 only where there was a legitimate expectation of the kind set out in *Saul D Harrison*, conduct which would appear to be deserving of a remedy may be left unremedied, contrary to the expectation (as we saw it) of the Jenkins Committee.[11]

4.12   However, our provisional view was that the courts will find that new situations not mentioned in *Saul D Harrison* are, in appropriate cases, capable of constituting unfairly prejudicial conduct. We were reluctant to suggest that section 459 should be amended to make this clear as any amendment would run the risk of introducing some other limitation into the section. We provisionally concluded, therefore, that it was preferable to keep the very general wording of the section as it now stands.

4.13   An overwhelming majority of respondents agreed with the provisional conclusion and accordingly we remain of the view that the words "unfairly prejudicial" should not be defined in section 459.

Clarification of its scope by other means

4.14   In addition, we canvassed the possibility of authoritative guidance on the application of section 459 by means other than legislation. We noted that those who are not experts in company law may have difficulty in predicting whether or not a claim under the section is likely to succeed, and put forward (without making any provisional recommendation) suggestions for ways in which guidance could be given.[12]

4.15   A majority of respondents were not in favour of authoritative guidance of this kind. Several reasons were given. One, to which we had drawn attention in the consultation paper,[13] was that guidance can become out of date and misleading. Another was that it would be impractical to give authoritative guidance on section 459 cases as they were largely fact driven. Another respondent suggested that the width of the discretion under section 459 made it undesirable to provide authoritative guidance as it would be unduly restrictive. We are persuaded that these arguments outweigh the potential benefit which could be derived from the

---

[9]   See Consultation Paper No 142, paras 8.5-8.12.

[10]   Report of the Company Law Committee (1962) Cmnd 1749. The Committee's recommendations formed the basis for the current wording of section 459; see Consultation Paper No 142, paras 7.8-7.12.

[11]   Consultation Paper No 142, para 2.18.

[12]   Eg leaflets drawn up by or on behalf of the DTI setting out examples from case law.

[13]   Consultation Paper No 142, para 20.8.

publication of such guidance and accordingly we recommend against the provision of authoritative guidance on the application of section 459 by means other than legislation.

Imposition of limitation period on claims under the section

4.16 There is currently no limitation period for bringing claims under section 459.[14] We have already referred on several occasions to the large number of allegations made in section 459 proceedings.[15] We pointed out in the consultation paper that these frequently involve conduct going back over a number of years[16] and that the historical nature of the investigations in such cases adds to the unwelcome length and cost of the cases.

4.17 More rigorous case management should assist in dealing with this problem.[17] However, we also considered, provisionally, that there should be a limitation period on claims under section 459. This was desirable not only because it would limit the matters on which claims could be based, and therefore help to reduce the length and cost of proceedings, but also because it would produce greater certainty for businesses.

4.18 We did not make any provisional recommendation on the length of limitation period,[18] but we did express a provisional view on two other matters. First, we considered that the limitation period should run from the date when the petitioner ought reasonably to have known the relevant facts; and secondly, we considered that the court should not have discretion to permit proceedings brought outside the limitation period to continue.

4.19 We distinguished conduct which forms the basis of the claim for unfairly prejudicial conduct (to which we considered a time limit should be applied) from other "background" matters which parties may wish to refer to in order to support or refute the claim. There was an argument for prohibiting parties from adducing any matters in evidence which occurred before a certain date (eg seven years before the proceedings). This would have the advantage of reducing the age of the factual allegations in dispute and the consequential poor quality of evidence. However, we noted that this could cause injustice if a party needed to rely on older conduct to justify his more recent behaviour. It would also cause severe injustice if it prevented a party adducing evidence that the company was formed on the basis of a relationship of the kind described in *Ebrahimi*.[19]

---

[14] Although it seems that delay in presentation of the petition may render it inequitable to grant relief under the section; see Peter Gibson J in *Re D R Chemicals Ltd* [1989] BCLC 383, 397-398. See also Consultation Paper No 142, para 9.3, n 11.

[15] See paras 2.26, 3.24 and 4.7 above.

[16] Consultation Paper No 142, para 20.9.

[17] And in particular the powers recommended at paras 2.18 and 2.27 above.

[18] Although where the alleged conduct amounts to an invasion of legal rights, or some duty owed to the petitioner or the company, we provisionally recommended that the period ought to be no less than that (if any) which applies to the wrong.

[19] See para 3.5 above.

Accordingly we provisionally recommended that there should be no limit on the age of the allegations upon which parties can rely in section 459 proceedings.

4.20 A majority of respondents who considered the point agreed with the provisional view that there should be a limitation period on claims under section 459. Two particular points were made by those who disagreed. Firstly, several respondents expressed concern that it was difficult to define a moment in time when the relevant cause of action accrued; the earliest act or omission may not on its own be sufficient to justify a remedy, whereas a whole series would. Secondly, a number of respondents drew attention to the difficulties which would arise in respect of concealed wrongdoing.

4.21 So far as the second of these points is concerned, we do not consider that this problem is any different from that which may arise in any other situation where a potential claimant does not become aware of matters relevant to his claim until some time later. Dealing with the first point, we accept (as we did in the consultation paper)[20] that it is in the nature of the phrase "unfairly prejudicial" to include a conglomeration of allegations producing a particular consequence. However, we do not consider that this would give the court any particular difficulty in applying the limitation period; time would be taken to run from the first of such allegations on which the applicant relies. The petitioner must of course have a reasonable opportunity to recognise and consider whether the circumstances give rise to a claim (and whether to pursue it), but that is also the case with any other type of claim and we do not consider that any special considerations apply to proceedings under section 459.

4.22 Indeed, it may be said that in the interests of commercial certainty there is an argument that stricter rules should apply in the case of shareholder proceedings than some other types of civil claims. However, we are of the view that the general rules relating to the length of the limitation period and the date from which the period should run should apply.[21] Responses received on these points did not highlight any special factors applying to claims under section 459. The Law Commission is carrying out a separate project on limitation,[22] and we consider that there is no reason why the general rules which are to be recommended in due course should not apply to proceedings under section 459.[23] **We therefore recommend that there should be a time limit for bringing claims under section 459, but that the length of the limitation period and the other relevant details (such as the date from which the limitation period should**

---

[20] Consultation Paper No 142, para 20.10.

[21] As should those relating to whether the court should have discretion to permit proceedings brought outside the limitation period to continue; see para 4.18 above in respect of our provisional view.

[22] A consultation paper (entitled "Limitation Periods") is in the process of being drafted and is hoped to be published before the end of the year. In Scotland, the question of time limits would need to be addressed in a reform of the law of prescription.

[23] Account may need to be taken of the fact that the alleged conduct could also amount to a wrong in respect of which a limitation period already applies; see n 18 above.

run) should be considered in the context of the Law Commission's current project on limitation.

4.23   The vast majority of respondents who addressed this point also agreed that there should no limit on the age of allegations of background facts (eg as to whether the company was formed as a "quasi-partnership") on which the parties can rely. We have already referred to the injustice which might arise if a party was prevented from relying on older conduct to justify his more recent behaviour, or if he was prevented from adducing evidence that the company was formed on the basis of a relationship of the kind described in *Ebrahimi*.[24] Accordingly, we confirm our provisional view that that there should not be a limit on the age of the allegations upon which the parties can rely in section 459 proceedings.

Adding winding up to the remedies available under section 461

4.24   Another reform option which we canvassed (although no provisional recommendation was made) was adding winding up to the remedies available under section 461.[25] Although the powers given to the court to make orders for giving relief in respect of the matters complained of in section 459 proceedings are very wide,[26] they do not include the power to order the company to be wound up. A shareholder seeking a winding up order must pursue a claim under section 122(1)(g) of the Insolvency Act 1986. Although this may be done in the same petition[27] as a claim in respect of unfairly prejudicial conduct under section 459, there are differences between the two jurisdictions which can complicate matters.[28]

4.25   We suggested that it may assist in streamlining shareholder remedies if the court was permitted to grant a winding up order on the grounds of unfairly prejudicial conduct. This would increase the range of remedies under section 461 and thus the flexibility of the court's powers to deal with shareholders' problems. We also

---

[24]   See para 4.19 above.

[25]   Consultation Paper No 142, paras 20.24-20.28.

[26]   These include regulating the conduct of the company's affairs; requiring the company to do, or refrain from doing certain acts; authorising civil proceedings to be brought in the name and on behalf of the company; and ordering the purchase of shares; section 461(2). These specific powers are without prejudice to the terms of section 461(1) which gives the court a discretion "to make such order as it thinks fit for giving relief in respect of the matters complained of".

[27]   Note, however, the Practice Direction (Ch D) (Companies Court: Contributory's Petition) [1990] 1 WLR 490 which discourages the practice of pleading the two petitions in the alternative; see para 4.29 below.

[28]   In particular, facts which satisfy the test under s 459 may not necessarily satisfy the test under s 122(1)(g) and vice versa. Contrast the cases of *R A Noble & Sons (Clothing) Ltd* [1983] BCLC 273 and *Re a Company (No 00314 of 1989), ex parte Estate Acquisition and Development Ltd* [1991] BCLC 154; see Consultation Paper No 142, para 8.18, n 52. Also, the court should not make a winding up order if it is of the opinion that the petitioner has another available remedy and is unreasonably failing to pursue it; s 122(2) of the Insolvency Act 1986 and see Consultation Paper No 142, paras 8.13-8.15. No such statutory restriction applies in relation to s 459 proceedings, although similar consideration may enter into the exercise of the court's discretion to grant relief; see Consultation Paper No 142, para 8.16. Another difference relates to who may bring a petition under the two sections; see Consultation Paper No 142, paras 8.3-8.4 and 11.12-11.14.

pointed out that in a number of foreign jurisdictions with similar statutory "oppression" provisions,[29] winding up is one of the remedies that can be granted.[30]

4.26   We drew attention to a number of potential objections that might be raised in respect of such an amendment.[31] First, there was the very different nature of the remedies available under section 461 from winding up; the former may be regarded as remedying difficulties arising during the course of the continuing life of the company, while the latter seeks to bring the company's very existence to an end.[32] However, we noted that this did not necessarily give the whole picture. As a result of a purchase order under section 461, some shareholders may leave the company, having sold their shares to others who continue to run the business. Exactly the same result may follow from a winding up, if some shareholders buy the business from the liquidator and continue to run it.

4.27   Secondly, the amendment might be seen as encouraging shareholders to seek winding up in proceedings under section 459. We had already drawn attention to the difficulties which could be caused to a company's business by pleading section 122(1)(g) in the alternative to section 459. Under section 127 of the Insolvency Act 1986, any disposition of the company's property made after the commencement of the winding up is void unless the court otherwise orders. The winding up is deemed to have commenced at the time of the presentation of the petition. The effect of this section is that any payments out of the company's bank account (or into an overdrawn account) after the presentation of the petition can be set aside and reclaimed by the liquidator once the company has been wound up.[33] In practice this means that as soon as a bank receives notice of a winding up petition it will freeze the company's bank accounts.[34]

4.28   It is of course open to the company, either before or after the event, to apply to the court to validate a transaction or series of transactions. Where the company is solvent, the court will generally validate a transaction which falls within the powers of the directors where there is evidence that it is necessary or expedient in the opinion of the directors in the interests of the company and the reasons given for it are ones which an intelligent and honest man could reasonably hold.[35] However, because of the potential uncertainty and disruption which could be caused to a company's business, the tactic of pleading winding up as an alternative to section 459, even where this was not an appropriate remedy, allowed the

[29]   Notably, Australia, New Zealand and Canada.

[30]   See Consultation Paper No 142, para 20.24 and Appendices F and G.

[31]   *Ibid*, at paras 20.25-20.27.

[32]   See the comments of Mummery J in *Re a Company (No 00314 of 1989), ex parte Estate Acquisition and Development Ltd* [1991] BCLC 154, 161.

[33]   *Re Gray's Inn Construction Co Ltd* [1980] 1 WLR 711.

[34]   See the comments of Warner J in *Re a Company (No 001363 of 1988), ex parte S-P* [1989] BCLC 579, 586 and Hoffmann J in *Re XYZ Ltd* [1987] 1 WLR 102, 110. See also *Re Doreen Boards Ltd* [1996] 1 BCLC 501.

[35]   See the comments of Slade J in *Re Burton & Deakin Ltd* [1977] 1 WLR 390, 396.

petitioner to put maximum pressure on respondents to settle the case as soon as possible.

4.29 It was to alleviate these difficulties that a practice direction was introduced in 1990 ("the 1990 Practice Direction").[36] This has two main features. First, it seeks to discourage the practice of pleading the two sections in the alternative and states that a claim for winding up should be included "only if that is the relief which the petitioner prefers or if it is considered that it may be the only relief to which he is entitled".

4.30 Secondly, the practice direction introduced a standard form validation order in respect of payments and transactions in the ordinary course of the company's business and requires the petitioner to state in the petition whether he consents to an order in those terms. If he does, the registrar will make an order without further enquiry; if the petitioner objects, the company can make an application to the judge for an order (ex parte if urgent).

4.31 Our concern was that the policy behind this practice direction may be undermined if the proposed amendment was seen as encouraging petitioners to seek winding up under section 459. However, we pointed out that the mere availability of the remedy under section 461 need not have this effect, and suggested that it may be possible for a revised practice direction to make this clear. We also suggested that, as an additional protection, the court's leave could be required for a petitioner to apply for winding up in proceedings under section 459. This is considered further below.[37]

4.32 The third potential objection to which we drew attention was the fact that the presence of a winding up remedy in section 461 would not deter petitioners from pleading section 122(1)(g) in the alternative since there are cases that satisfy the latter test which will not satisfy the test of unfairly prejudicial conduct.[38] Thus, it would not necessarily have the effect of reducing the allegations in issue. However, we suggested that active case management was the best answer to situations where section 122(1)(g) was pleaded unnecessarily or improperly. We also suggested that a leave requirement could be considered. This is dealt with below.[39]

4.33 Although most respondents who commented did not consider that the absence of winding up from section 461 caused particular problems in practice, a majority of respondents who addressed this question considered that winding up should be added to the remedies available under section 461. Where reasons were given, they were similar to those which we gave in the consultation paper (namely the desirability of streamlining shareholder proceedings and giving the courts

---

[36] Practice Direction (Ch D) (Companies Court: Contributory's Petition) [1990] 1 WLR 590. For recent consideration of this practice direction, see the cases of *Re Arvin & Sons Ltd* [1997] 1 BCLC 479 and *Re Copeland & Craddock Ltd* [1997] BCC 294. In the former, a prayer for winding up under section 122(1)(g) was struck out; in the latter an application to strike out was refused.

[37] See para 4.40 below.

[38] See n 28 above.

[39] See para 4.42 below.

maximum flexibility). One respondent in particular pointed out that in the course of proceedings under section 459 facts and matters emerge, or events unwind, which make other forms of relief impractical. A petitioner may set out with no intention to seek a winding up order, but find that no-one else can buy his shares, and the only way of realising their value is on a winding up.[40]

4.34   The main reason given by several respondents for opposing the inclusion of winding up in the remedies available under section 461 was the fact that once winding up becomes a possibility, the position of creditors has to be considered. This makes the proceedings more complex and cumbersome, and means that it becomes less easy to grant adjournments to facilitate settlements.[41]

4.35   We accept that safeguards are necessary both to protect creditors and to ensure that the company's business is not disrupted unnecessarily or excessively. However, we do not consider that this gives rise to any greater difficulties than currently arise from the availability of proceedings under section 122(1)(g), and we consider that it is desirable to have a single remedy which gives the court the maximum flexibility to deal with the matters before it. Accordingly, **we recommend that winding up should be added to the remedies available to a petitioner in proceedings under section 459**. We now consider the details of the proposal.

Who may seek winding up under the new provision

4.36   We have drawn attention above to the differences between the jurisdictions under section 459 and section 122(1)(g).[42] One of these relates to who may present a petition. There are restrictions on members seeking winding up under section 122(1)(g) of the Insolvency Act 1986 which do not apply to proceedings under section 459. For example, a member must have been registered for 6 months before presenting a petition under section 122(1)(g). There could be a risk that a new member would get round this restriction by seeking a winding up order under the amended section 461, instead of section 122(1)(g).

4.37   However, we do not consider that there is any need to make special provision for the member to have held shares for a qualifying period in the new provision. The tests for the two sections are different (one is that there has been unfairly prejudicial conduct, the other that it is just and equitable to wind the company up) and there is no reason why the persons who can petition under each should necessarily be the same.[43] Also we consider that it would complicate the drafting of the new provision, since the definition of the person entitled to present a petition

---

[40]   The court may also decide that no relief is capable of being devised which would meet the justice of the case and which would be more advantageous than winding up; see *Linos Antoniades v Landy Chet Kin (Re Full Cup International Trading Ltd)* 5 March 1997 (unreported, Court of Appeal).

[41]   Since in considering the question of adjournments, the court must look beyond the interests of the parties to those of others (in particular creditors) who may be affected.

[42]   See para 4.24 above.

[43]   Although there may well be considerable overlap with respect to the conduct caught by both sections.

under section 459 would depend on the nature of the relief sought. Moreover, as indicated below,[44] we are proposing a requirement for leave to seek winding up under the amended section 461 so that the court would have power to refuse to allow a "new" shareholder to petition for winding up in inappropriate cases.

4.38 Accordingly, we propose that any person who is able to present a petition under section 459 (ie a "member of the company"; section 459(1)) should, prima facie, be entitled to seek a winding up order under the new provision.

The requirement for leave

4.39 As we have explained,[45] under the current law it is not uncommon for a petitioner to seek a winding up order as a means of putting pressure on the other side when it is not the relief which he prefers or is most likely to obtain. There is a real risk that a company will suffer reputational damage and loss of confidence among its suppliers and customers if an application for winding up is made unjustifiably. This risk may be increased by a new provision permitting petitioners to seek winding up under the new provision.

4.40 The 1990 Practice Direction has sought to discourage the practice of claiming winding up under section 122(1)(g) "as a matter of course" in proceedings under section 459. It could be extended so that similar discouragement was given to the practice of including a claim for winding up under the new provision. However, the practice direction does not appear to have been entirely successful,[46] and we do not consider that it would be a sufficient deterrent against claiming winding up in inappropriate cases, particularly as the new power may be seen as encouraging claims for winding up. Accordingly **we recommend that a petitioner should require the court's leave to apply for winding up under sections 459-461**.

4.41 We envisage that on the leave application the court would consider, for example, whether the petitioner was seeking to exert unjustified pressure on the respondents by claiming winding up, or was acting unreasonably in seeking a winding up.[47] We would stress that winding up should remain a remedy of last

---

[44] See paras 4.39-4.40 below.

[45] See paras 4.27-4.30 above.

[46] See para 4.42 below.

[47] Compare in the case of a petition under s 122(1)(g), s 125(2) of the Insolvency Act 1986, which provides:

> If the petition is presented by members of the company as contributories on the ground that it is just and equitable that the company should be wound up, the court, if it is of opinion—
>
> > (a) that the petitioners are entitled to relief either by winding up the company or by some other means, and
> >
> > (b) that in the absence of any other remedy it would be just and equitable that the company should be wound up,
>
> shall make a winding-up order; but this does not apply if the court is also of the opinion both that some other remedy is available to the petitioners and that they are acting unreasonably in seeking to have the company wound up instead of pursuing that other remedy.

resort. The court would also consider whether it may be better to defer the application to a later stage when it would be clearer what the allegations were and whether winding up was a real possibility. The court could also take into account any other relevant factor. The effect of our Bill is that the court could not make a winding up order unless leave had been obtained.[48]

4.42   There is a risk that applicants will circumvent the leave requirement by seeking a winding up order under section 122(1)(g) (instead of under the new provision) in conjunction with section 459 proceedings. The current practice direction may not be effective in preventing this. Several practitioners expressed concern that petitioners were continuing to plead section 122(1)(g) in the alternative to section 459 in inappropriate cases, despite the introduction of the practice direction. We therefore consider that the proposed leave requirement should also apply to petitioners seeking winding up under section 122(1)(g) in conjunction with proceedings under section 459. This will necessitate legislation and cannot be achieved simply by changes to the Insolvency Rules. It will also render part of the 1990 Practice Direction unnecessary. **We therefore recommend that a petitioner should also require the leave of the court to apply for a winding up order under section 122(1)(g) of the Insolvency Act 1986 in conjunction with an application under section 459.**

Effect of presentation of petition (sections 127-129 of Insolvency Act 1986)

4.43   As indicated, we accept that where winding up is in issue, the protection of creditors and other persons dealing with a company becomes an issue. Even if the company is solvent at the start of proceedings, there is a risk that it will become insolvent on winding up due to loss of good will and going concern values attached to assets.

4.44   We propose that the safeguards set out in Part IV of the Insolvency Act 1986 in relation to the period between the commencement of the winding up and the winding up order which apply to a contributory's petition, should equally apply where winding up is sought under an amended section 461. The most important of these is section 127 which avoids dispositions of company property made after the commencement of the winding up. Other safeguards are contained in sections 126 (power for the company or a creditor or a contributory to apply to stay or restrain proceedings against the company) and 128 (avoidance of attachments).[49]

This provision would not apply to a claim for winding up under s 461, but we consider that the imposition of the leave requirement is likely to have the same effect.

[48]   See clause 5(1) and 5(3). Clause 5(1) provides that a petitioner can only include a claim for winding up in the petition if the court gives leave. We consider that if a petitioner, without first obtaining leave, included in his petition a claim for winding up under s 461 of the Companies Act 1985 or (see para 4.42 below) s 122(1)(g) of the Insolvency Act 1986, the court could either strike out that part of his claim or grant leave retrospectively; see *Re Saunders* [1997] 3 All ER 992, in which Lindsay J declined to follow the earlier decisions at first instance in *Wilson v Banner Scaffolding Ltd, The Times* 22 June 1982, and *Re National Employers Mutual General Insurance Association Ltd (in liquidation)* [1995] 1 BCLC 232.

[49]   For Scotland, the equivalent to s 128 of the Insolvency Act 1986 is s 185 of that Act which incorporates the provisions of the Bankruptcy (Scotland) Act 1985.

4.45   However, there is one important qualification which we consider needs to be made in respect of section 129. This section provides that winding up is deemed to commence at the time of the presentation of the petition for winding up. Where winding up is sought at the outset, this does not present any particular problem. But where a petition is amended, the amendment takes effect from the date of the original petition it amends, not from the date of the amendment.[50] Thus, where a petition is amended to include a claim for winding up, the "time of the presentation of the petition for winding up" is the original date on which the petition is presented, not the date on which the amendment is made. The combined effect of sections 127 and 129 is therefore that dispositions may be avoided in respect of the period before any claim for winding up is included in the petition. We do not consider that this is appropriate.

4.46   At present, this situation can already arise where a claim for winding up under section 122(1)(g) is added to a petition under section 459 during the course of the proceedings. To get round this problem, the courts can require a new petition to be presented. We consider that this is wasteful in terms of time and costs, and may be overlooked. We propose, therefore, that where a section 459 petition is amended, after it has been presented, to include a claim for winding up either under the new section 461 or under section 122(1)(g), the winding up should be deemed to commence at the time of the amendment, and not the time of the original presentation of the petition. No disposition will be avoided, therefore, in respect of the period before a winding up order is sought. Consistently with this, executions which occur after the petition is presented but before it is amended will not be avoided under section 128, as they would have been but for our recommendation. **We therefore recommend that where a petition under section 459 is amended to include a claim for winding up (whether under section 122(1)(g) or under the new provision) the winding up should be deemed to commence from the date of the amendment**.

4.47   So far as the validation of transactions after the date on which a claim for winding up is included in the petition is concerned, we consider that this is best dealt with by way of practice direction. The court will have occasion to consider that matter on the application for leave. We propose that there should be provision in a new practice direction for a standard form validation order along the lines of the one currently contained in the 1990 Practice Direction. Accordingly, **we recommend that the Vice Chancellor should be invited to consider whether there should be an amended practice direction setting out a standard form validation order where winding up is sought under the new provision**.

Court's decision on whether to make the order

4.48   We propose that the court should have jurisdiction to make a winding up order on a petition under section 459 on the same basis that it can make other orders; that is to say that once a claim for unfairly prejudicial conduct has been made out, the

---

[50]   See the notes to Order 20, r 8 (20/5-8/1) of the *Supreme Court Practice* (1997) vol 1, which deals with the amendment of documents generally.

court will have a discretion as to what order (if any) to make.[51] In exercising its discretion the court is likely to consider whether any other order under section 461 or other remedy available to the petitioner is more appropriate, but we do not consider that there is any need to make express provision in this respect in the legislation.[52]

Other relevant provisions and rules

4.49 So far as the other provisions of the Insolvency Act are concerned, we recommend that, except where they are inconsistent, those provisions which apply to winding up by a contributory under section 122(1)(g) should apply to winding up under the new provision.[53] Rules can be made under section 461(6) of the Companies Act 1985 which either draw on or incorporate the relevant parts of the Insolvency Rules.

The power to determine relief as between respondents

4.50 We pointed out in the consultation paper that third party claims and contribution claims between defendants did not appear to be available in proceedings brought under section 459.[54] Although the court may be able to get around this difficulty in practice,[55] we considered provisionally that it would be desirable for the court to be given the same procedural powers as it has in a writ action to order joinder and contributions and indemnities between respondents or respondents and non-parties.[56] All but one of the respondents who considered this issue agreed with the provisional view. This anomaly may be removed when new rules of court are adopted pursuant to the Civil Procedure Act 1997.[57] Otherwise an amendment to the 1986 Rules would be needed.[58]

4.51 However, these procedural changes would still leave a gap in the substantive law. No right of contribution exists under the Civil Liability (Contribution) Act 1978 where a person is ordered to make redress (whether by purchasing the claimant's

---

[51] On the width of the court's discretion in respect of orders under s 461, see the recent case of *Linos Antoniades v Landy Chet Kin (Re Full Cup International Trading Ltd)* 5 March 1997 (unreported, Court of Appeal).

[52] See para 4.41, n 47 above.

[53] In the draft Bill we recommend that the following sections should not apply: s 122, s 124 and s 125.

[54] Under RSC, O 16.

[55] By joining parties under r 2(2) of the 1986 Rules (and/or under RSC, O 15) and using its discretion to grant relief in such a way as to apportion the burden between the relevant parties. But it can only do this where the applicant makes a claim against all the respondents; cf *Re Little Olympian Each-Ways Ltd (No 3)* 7 October 1994 (unreported, Evans-Lombe J) where the applicant's claim against the party from whom contribution was sought had been settled.

[56] Or similar powers. Alternatively the parties could be given similar rights to issue third party or contribution notices to those they would have had in a writ action under RSC, Ord 16.

[57] And are incorporated into the 1996 Rules; see para 2.6 above.

[58] For Scotland, the court has a limited power to fix contributions under s 3 of the Law Reform (Miscellaneous Provisions) (Scotland) Act 1940, but this power does not appear to be as broad as that available under the Civil Liability (Contributions) Act 1978.

shares or otherwise) and his liability arises simply by virtue of section 459. The 1978 Act only applies where parties are liable in respect of the same damage.[59] For this purpose, the person who suffered the damage must be "entitled to recover compensation from him in respect of that damage (whatever the legal basis of his liability, whether tort, breach of contract, breach of trust or otherwise)".[60] This would not be satisfied where relief under section 461 had been ordered solely against the person claiming contribution. Even if that difficulty did not exist, there might well be no entitlement to compensation.

4.52   However, we do not make any recommendation for the amendment of the 1978 Act for three reasons. First, it was not raised as a question for consultees. Second, the court can grant relief in such a way that those who are parties only bear their fair share of the burden of the relief in any event.[61] Thus in most cases[62] a right of contribution is unnecessary. Third, where the unfairly prejudicial conduct consists of a wrong for some other reason, for example where the respondent against whom an order to pay compensation is made and the person from whom he seeks contribution are both liable for a breach of trust which is held to constitute unfairly prejudicial conduct, rights of contribution exist under the general law.

4.53   **We recommend that the Lord Chancellor consider changes to the 1986 Rules (governing unfair prejudice proceedings) so as to give the court the procedural powers to allow contribution and indemnity claims in proceedings under section 459 if this matter is not dealt with in the general rules introduced under the Civil Procedure Act 1997.**

Advertisement of section 459 petitions

4.54   In the consultation paper we pointed out how damaging to a company the dissemination of the information that a petition has been filed under section 459 can be. Strictly, unlike in the case of petitions seeking winding up under section 122(1)(g),[63] the presentation of a petition under section 459 has no legal effect on the conduct of the company's business. However, even where a petition seeks relief under section 459 alone, the company's customers and creditors are likely to be wary of doing business with the company, both because of the risk that the petition might be amended and a winding up order sought, and the disruption which is likely to be caused to the company as a result of the proceedings.

---

[59]   Sections 1 and 3.

[60]   Section 6(1).

[61]   See *Little Olympian Each-Ways Ltd (No 3)* 7 October 1994 (unreported, Evans-Lombe J) at p 15.

[62]   There is a possibility that the justice of the position as between respondents or as between respondents and non-parties may differ from that as between the claimant and the respondent. *Ibid*, at p 15.

[63]   Under s 127 of the Insolvency Act 1986, any disposition of the company's property made after the commencement of the winding up is void unless the court otherwise orders. The winding up is deemed to have commenced at the time of the presentation of the petition. See para 4.27 above, and see Consultation Paper No 142, paras 8.19-8.21.

4.55 When a petition is issued under section 459 the court fixes a return date at which a number of matters, including advertisement of the petition, can be considered.[64] It is inherent in the rules that no advertisement should take place unless the court directs that it should.[65] It is also now clear from the case law, that advertisement for these purposes does not simply mean advertisement in the Gazette, but any notification to an outsider of the existence of the petition.[66] There should, therefore, be no notification of the existence of a petition under section 459 to outsiders until the court has had an opportunity to consider the question of advertisement on the return day; nor indeed should there be any advertisement thereafter, except in accordance with an order of the court. In practice, it is by no means clear that this restriction is observed and we considered that it would be helpful to include an express provision to the effect that no advertisement of section 459 petitions should be allowed prior to the return date. In fact, on further consideration, we consider that the provision should be to the effect that there should be no advertisement at all except in accordance with an order of the court. This is in accordance with the current case law, and covers the situation where the court does not consider the question of advertisement on the return date.[67]

4.56 Nearly all of the respondents who addressed this point agreed with our provisional view. It was suggested by one respondent that it should also be made clear in the rules that the prohibition extends to all forms of advertisement, not just to formal advertisement. We agree that it would be useful to make the position as clear as possible. Accordingly, **we recommend that the Lord Chancellor consider changes to the 1986 Rules (governing unfair prejudice proceedings) so as to include an express provision stating that no advertisement of section 459 petitions should take place except in accordance with an order of the court, and so as to confirm the meaning given by the courts to "advertisement" in this context by an appropriate definition.**

Permitting former members to bring proceedings under section 459

4.57 At present an application can only be made under section 459 by a current member of the company.[68] We considered in the consultation paper whether the

---

[64] Companies (Unfair Prejudice Applications) Proceedings Rules 1986, Rule 5.

[65] See the comments of Roger Kaye QC, sitting as a deputy High Court Judge in *Re a Company (No 002015 of 1996)* [1997] 2 BCLC 1. See also *Re Doreen Boards Ltd* [1996] 1 BCLC 501 (which concerned a contributory's winding up petition).

[66] See *Re a Company (No 002015 of 1996)* [1997] 2 BCLC 1. See also *Re a Company (No 00687 of 1991)* [1992] BCLC 133; *Re Bill Hennessey Associates Ltd* [1992] BCC 386; and *Re Doreen Boards Ltd* [1996] 1 BCLC 501 (which concerned contributory's petitions to wind up the company).

[67] See *Re a Company (No 002015 of 1996)* [1997] 2 BCLC 1.

[68] Section 459(1) provides simply that "a member of a company" may apply. It omits any reference to former members. However, s 459(2) deals with an earlier problem regarding personal representatives by extending the section to "... a person who is not a member of a company but to whom shares in the company have been transferred or transmitted by operation of law".

remedy ought also to be available to former members, but did not form a provisional view on this point.

4.58 Although we were unable to cite any examples of particular problems which had arisen in practice as a result of this limitation, we did set out a factual situation where it may be appropriate for a former member to bring a claim. This is where directors have made personal profits at the expense of the company and then induce a minority shareholder to leave, giving him a price for his shares which represents an under value because of their wrongdoing.[69] However, we pointed out that the former shareholder may be able to obtain a remedy by other means: for example, by proving an actionable misrepresentation; or by establishing that the directors owe him personally a duty of disclosure.[70] We also pointed out that the shareholder should be able to protect himself in most situations by obtaining appropriate covenants and warranties in any agreement to sell his shares.

4.59 We also drew attention to the risk of increased litigation if former shareholders were permitted to sue. This was particularly relevant in the context of takeover situations, where an increase in litigation might make it difficult to effect and implement a rationalisation of the acquired company's business.[71] This would be undesirable.

4.60 A majority of respondents who addressed this question considered that former members should not be permitted to bring claims under section 459. Where reasons were given, they were similar to those set out above. No respondent gave any concrete examples of where undue hardship had been caused in practice by the lack of availability of the remedy to former members.[72] We consider that any potential problems which may arise under the current law are outweighed by the disadvantages of the extension which have been highlighted above. Accordingly we recommend against permitting former members to bring claims under section 459.

Conclusion

4.61 To summarise, we remain of the view that the words "unfairly prejudicial" should not be defined in section 459, and we recommend against the provision of

---

[69] Ie the price reflects the reduced value of the company, and that value has only been reduced because of the directors' wrongdoing. We also gave two other examples of situations where a former member may wish to bring proceedings; see Consultation Paper No 142, paras 20.35 and 20.37. See also the example set out by Marsden in "Prejudicial Relief?" (1994) 15 Co Law 178.

[70] *Re Chez Nico (Restaurants) Ltd* [1992] BCLC 192, 208, *per* Sir Nicholas Browne-Wilkinson V-C.

[71] Former shareholders are, however, given an express right to claim payments to a director on a takeover which have not been properly disclosed; see s 315 of the Companies Act 1985.

[72] On the separate question of whether a beneficial owner of shares held by nominees can present a s 459 petition, see *Ennis v Murphy and another* 20 June 1996 (unreported, Court of Appeal). As we pointed out in the consultation paper, we have not addressed in this project the problems which arise through shares being held by nominees; Consultation Paper No 142, para 1.10. As to the ability of a beneficial owner to compel a registered member to bring an action, see para 6.50, n 74 below.

authoritative guidance on the application of section 459 by means other than legislation.

4.62 We consider that there should be a time limit for bringing claims under the section but see no reason why the general provisions relating to the limitation of actions should not apply. As these are currently under review in a separate Law Commission project, we make no specific recommendation in this report on the details of the limitation provisions which should apply to section 459 proceedings.

4.63 We recommend that winding up should be added to the remedies available under section 461, but should be subject to a leave requirement.[73] We also recommend that a petitioner should be required to obtain leave of the court where he seeks winding up on just and equitable grounds in conjunction with proceedings under section 459.[74]

4.64 Where a petition under section 459 is amended to include a claim for winding up (whether under the amended section 461 or section 122(1)(g)) we consider that the winding up should be deemed to commence from the date of the amendment, rather than the date of the original presentation of the petition.[75] We also recommend that consideration should be given to the introduction of an amended practice direction setting out a standard form validation order where winding up is sought under the new provision.

4.65 We consider that the courts should have in relation to proceedings under section 459 the same or similar procedural powers to allow indemnity and contribution claims as they have in relation to writ actions.

4.66 We consider that the rules on the advertisement of petitions under section 459 should be clarified so as to confirm that no advertisement of a section 459 petition is allowed without the court's leave, and so as to confirm the meaning of advertisement in this context.

4.67 Finally, we do not recommend that section 459 is amended so as to permit former members to bring proceedings under that section.

---

[73] See clauses 5 and 6 of the draft Bill at Appendix A.

[74] See clause 7 of the draft Bill at Appendix A.

[75] See clause 6 of the draft Bill at Appendix A.

PART 5
ARTICLES OF ASSOCIATION

Introduction

5.1 In the consultation paper we provisionally recommended that it was desirable to include additional regulations in Table A. These would therefore form part of any new company's articles of association unless specifically excluded. The aim of the regulations was to encourage shareholders to provide in advance for what would happen if there was a dispute. We hoped that this would help to avoid litigation in many cases, or at least substantially reduce the issues in dispute. We also pointed out that recent cases had emphasised the need for better protection in the articles.[1] This approach is consistent with our fourth guiding principle (sanctity of contract) set out in paragraph 1.9 above.

5.2 Our approach received widespread support on consultation. A few respondents disagreed with the approach. Two reasons given by those who disagreed were that the articles would only apply to new companies (and so would not apply to the large number of existing companies); and of those new companies, many would routinely exclude any novel provisions. However, we remain of the view (which was supported by the vast majority of respondents) that Table A could serve a useful educational purpose in encouraging parties to address potential areas of dispute at the outset. **We therefore recommend that appropriate provisions should be included in Table A to encourage parties to sort out areas of potential dispute at the outset.**

5.3 In the consultation paper, we put forward three specific draft regulations which we suggested should be included in Table A.[2] These were: a shareholders' exit article for smaller private companies; an arbitration article; and a valuation procedure article. Changes to Table A can be made by statutory instrument under section 8 of the Companies Act 1985. We consider each of the proposed new regulations in turn.

Shareholders' exit article for smaller private companies

5.4 This regulation was intended to encourage shareholders in smaller private companies to make arrangements to deal with the situation where a disaffected shareholder wants to leave the company. In the consultation paper we noted that it was often the case that shareholders in such companies resorted to proceedings under section 459 in order to try to have their shares bought out, and that this often resulted in costly and cumbersome litigation.

5.5 Under the regulation appended to the consultation paper:

---

[1] In particular, the case of *Re Saul D Harrison & Sons plc* [1995] 1 BCLC 14. See Consultation Paper No 142, para 19.2.

[2] Consultation Paper No 142, Part 19.

- exit rights could be attached to particular shares by passing an ordinary resolution;

- the exit rights would be exercised by service of a notice requiring those on whom it was served to purchase the shares of the outgoing shareholder;

- no particular circumstances which would trigger the exit rights were set out, leaving it to the company to set these out (if required) in the resolution;

- if there was a disagreement the shares were to be valued on a basis which required the valuer to disregard the fact that the shares formed part of a minority shareholding;

- the outgoing shareholder could force the company to be wound up if the purchase of his shares did not go through within the timescale laid down in the regulation;

- the company had to be a private company with fewer than ten members.

5.6 There was widespread support from respondents for an exit article along the lines proposed. A few respondents expressed reservations. Three particular points were made. First, some of these were concerned that the proposed regulation was not of sufficiently general application to be included in Table A. One respondent drew a comparison with pre-emption provisions which had never been included in Table A even when there was a separate part for exempt private companies, and although such provisions were often expressly included in the articles of such companies.[3] There was never any common form suitable for Table A. The point was made that an exit provision would either be deleted, or adopted without sufficient thought, leading to difficulties.

5.7 Secondly, another respondent was concerned that providing exit routes too readily may be economically damaging, leading to the break up of small businesses at the first sign of disagreement. Thirdly, several other respondents were concerned that serving an exit notice might enable shareholders to exert pressure improperly, knowing that the other party could not afford to pay for his shares.

5.8 Dealing with the last two points, we have already indicated that we consider that there are strong economic arguments against exit rights at will for shareholders.[4] But the proposed regulation does not go that far. It requires the shareholders to take a positive decision by passing a resolution that exit rights will attach to particular shares. This is reinforced in the revised draft by a requirement that every shareholder subject to it should have expressly agreed to the resolution. We do not consider that the article will have the effect of causing businesses to break up any more frequently than at present. Indeed, it is hoped that by encouraging

---

[3] Table A does not contain a standard form pre-emption article, that is an article giving members a right of first refusal if a member wishes to dispose of his shares. If a company wishes to adopt a pre-emption article and an exit article it would have to make suitable amendments to avoid a conflict between the two provisions.

[4] See para 3.66 above.

the parties to make provision for a future breakdown in their relations, the regulation will have the opposite effect and allow parties to manage the break down in such a way as to cause the minimum disruption to the business itself. There can of course be no guarantee that a party does not seek to take advantage of any rights he has in the event of a dispute, but we do not consider that the regulation as proposed will give rise to any particular difficulties in this respect.

5.9 So far as the first point is concerned, the regulation in the consultation paper leaves it to companies to decide when the exit rights will apply (either by passing a resolution, or by modifying the regulation to set out the relevant circumstances). The article is therefore very versatile and does not suffer from the difficulties to which a standard form pre-emption article would give rise. As we stated above, we believe that the inclusion of the article will encourage companies to consider what circumstances might be appropriate for their company at the outset. We are also supported in this view by the fact that a large majority of respondents who considered this question were in favour of a regulation along the lines proposed.

5.10 Turning to the details of the provision, we have altered the emphasis to require the shareholders to make positive choices about, in particular, the basis of valuation and the choice of the valuer when the resolution is passed applying the regulation. If they do not do so, the regulation will not be effective. This reflects concerns expressed by a number of respondents that the article could operate unfairly. We are not in favour of an exit article which would apply automatically (ie unless excluded by incorporators) as appeared to be favoured by several respondents. We consider that this would increase enormously the risk of shareholders becoming subject to exit rights inadvertently. On the other hand, if the parties did want an "automatic" no-fault type provision, they could simply make the giving of notice at any time a specified event for the purposes of the new draft regulation.[5]

5.11 We have taken into account the responses received on the regulation and in order to meet as many as we can of the points that were made we are recommending a redrafted regulation 119 which will be found in Appendix C. The main features of the regulation are:

- exit rights must be conferred by an ordinary resolution;[6]

- every shareholder who is to have or be subject to exit rights must be named in the resolution and must consent to it;

- the resolution must set out the events in which the exit rights are to be exercisable. The exit right could be exercisable by personal representatives on the death of a named shareholder;

---

[5] See para 5.20 below.

[6] Particulars of the resolution would need to be sent to the Registrar of Companies in accordance with s 128(3) of the Companies Act 1985.

- when an exit right is exercisable the shareholder entitled to the right may require other shareholders named in the resolution to buy his shares at a "fair price";

- those shares must be shares he held when the resolution was passed or shares acquired in right of them, eg on a bonus issue. The exit right does not apply to other shares which were transferred to him later;

- the resolution must state how the "fair price" is to be calculated. Various of the possible methods are suggested for convenience;

- if the shares require to be valued, the resolution must say how the valuer is to be appointed. He must be an independent person who appears to have the requisite knowledge and experience;

- the purchase must be completed within three months;

- the resolution comes to an end when one of the named shareholders dies or disposes of his shares;

- the company cannot amend the resolution or the regulation without the consent of the named shareholders.

5.12   We have gone as far as we can to prevent shareholders from creating exit rights without being aware of their consequences. The adoption of exit rights under this regulation would be an interactive process between the various shareholders involved requiring them to make a series of positive choices. The only way of protecting those who will enter into exit rights without giving them proper thought is by not having the regulation in Table A. We think that this level of protection would be excessive since it would prevent *any* shareholder from having the benefit of the regulation in Table A. We now consider the provisions of the revised draft regulation in more detail.

Restriction to companies with less than 10 members

5.13   We no longer consider that the availability of the article should be limited to companies with less than 10 members. We accept the concerns of those who considered that the limit could be evaded by splitting shareholdings so as to increase the number of members beyond 10. We also agree that, since the company has to pass a resolution to bring the article into effect, there is already a sufficient restriction on its applicability. On further consideration we are of the view that the 10 member limit is unnecessary and could be arbitrary.

Circumstances giving rise to exit rights

5.14   The views of respondents appeared to be evenly split between those who considered that the article should set out specific circumstances in which the exit rights should be available and those who considered that it should not.

5.15   For those who considered that the article should set out specific circumstances the point was made that, as it was primarily intended for companies without ready access to expert advice, it would be more user friendly if it did have the circumstances set out. Few attempted to list what these should be, but one respondent suggested including: (a) loss of directorship without cause; (b) misappropriation of assets; (c) non-trivial breaches of statutory provisions; (d) loss of effective right to participation in management by retirement, illness or death.

5.16   Those who were against setting out circumstances in the draft regulation gave two main reasons. First, that it may lead to disputes as to the circumstances in which the right to serve an exit notice arises; secondly, the parties would not have the opportunity to address their minds to the circumstances which would be appropriate for them.

5.17   One respondent pointed out in respect of this issue that it was not entirely clear whether the article was designed to offer a no-fault quasi-partnership retirement route, or intended to be a remedy for unfairly prejudicial conduct by the majority. He saw no reason in principle why the regulation should not deal with both types of situation, provided its terms were even-handed as between seller and buyer. Other respondents went much further and suggested that the right to serve an exit notice should apply in any circumstances (without the need for a resolution to bring the rights into effect).

5.18   Our view is that it is often impossible to apportion blame between parties in many cases where there has been a break down in relations between owner-managers in small private companies.[7] What is important is resolving the position with as little cost and disruption to the parties and the company as possible. We would envisage that the regulation would be used in the sorts of circumstances where currently claims are *brought* under section 459, although it may be that in some of the cases the petition would not in fact be successful because the petitioner could not show unfair prejudice. If the regulation assists parties in avoiding bringing such proceedings we consider that it is worthwhile as it will save the parties considerable expense, loss of time and anxiety.

5.19   We agree that it would be helpful to some companies if the regulation set out the circumstances in which the exit rights would apply. In this way the rights could be made to apply without the need for a resolution. Also, even if the companies wanted to modify the regulation, it would give them a starting point as it would set out some of the more common circumstances in which it might be appropriate for the exit articles to arise. On the other hand, we accept that it may be dangerous to include a list of circumstances in the article as they may not be appropriate for a particular company, but the company may adopt the standard Table A articles without giving proper consideration to this issue.

5.20   As a way of addressing these competing concerns, we recommend that the article should include reference to the two most common situations in which shareholders are likely to want to invoke the exit rights, but that these should only

---

[7]   In the context of allegations of exclusion from management, see the comments of Hoffmann J in *Re XYZ Ltd* [1987] 1 WLR 102, 110 where he said: "Each party blames the other but often it is impossible, even after lengthy cross-examination, to say more than the petitioner says in this case, namely that there was a 'clear conflict in personalities and management style' ".

be by way of example. It should still be up to the shareholders to set out the relevant circumstances in the resolution applying the article (or by amendment to the article itself). The two situations we have mentioned in the revised draft are: (a) the removal of a shareholder who is a director from his office as a director of the company otherwise than where he is in serious breach of his duties as a director; and (b) the death of a shareholder.[8] Neither of these events would, of course, necessarily give rise to a buy out under section 459. But we are not seeking to replicate the result which could be achieved under that section; rather we are seeking to encourage the parties to make their own provision for the type of circumstances in which *they* consider a named member should be able to leave the company on agreed terms, so as to avoid (so far as possible) the risk that legal proceedings will be commenced.

Who is bound to purchase the shares of the outgoing shareholder and when does the provision become operative

5.21   Under the previous draft of the regulation which was appended to the consultation paper, it was proposed that an exit notice should be served on all the other shareholders of the company and that this should require them to purchase the exiting members shares within three months of the notice. Under our revised draft it is only those shareholders named in the resolution who must purchase the exiting member's shares. The regulation provides that unless the resolution otherwise states or the parties make some other agreement, they must do so in proportion to the number of shares they held at the date of the resolution.[9] In addition, the revised draft provides that the resolution shall not be valid unless every shareholder who is named in it gives a notice to the company (before the resolution is passed) stating that he consents to it.[10]

5.22   The reason for these changes is to ensure that it is only those shareholders who are aware of the exit rights and have consented to them who are bound by them. We wish to avoid the situation where, for example, a person acquires shares without considering fully the articles, or without knowing that a resolution has been passed, and finds later that he is obliged to purchase shares belonging to another shareholder.

When does the resolution cease to have effect

5.23   The draft regulation contained in the consultation paper did not include any provision for the resolution to cease to have effect. This could have lead to unfairness if some of the named shareholders ceased to hold shares, but the resolution continued to be effective as between the remaining named shareholders. Those shareholders would have had an obligation to purchase a greater proportion of an outgoing shareholder's shares (if an exit right became exercisable) than they might have anticipated at the date the resolution was passed. In order to deal with this problem, the revised draft provides that the

---

[8]   See Appendix C, draft regulation 119(3).

[9]   *Ibid*, draft regulation 119(11)(a).

[10]   *Ibid*, draft regulation 119(14).

resolution shall cease to have effect (unless it states otherwise) if a named shareholder ceases to hold the shares which he had when the resolution was passed or shares allotted directly or indirectly in right of such shares.[11] This is without prejudice to any exit notice which has already been served.[12] In order to prevent a transfer which would defeat the object of the exit article rights, the regulation provides that the directors must refuse to register a transfer which would cause the resolution to be ineffective, ie a transfer as a result of which a named shareholder would cease to hold any of the shares which he held when the resolution was passed or any shares allotted directly or indirectly in right of such shares, unless all the relevant persons agree.[13]

5.24　We also consider that it would not generally be appropriate for an exit right to be enforceable against the estate of a deceased member. It could delay the administration of the estate if there was a potential liability to purchase the shares of other named shareholders which remained outstanding. For this reason, the revised draft provides that the resolution shall also cease to have effect (unless it states otherwise) when a named shareholder dies.[14] However, if the death of the shareholder is the event which triggers the exercise by his successor of the exit right, then the resolution is to continue so far as that event is concerned.[15] This is also without prejudice to any exit notice which has already been served before the death.

5.25　The draft regulation also provides that the resolution may be brought to an end by the unanimous agreement of the named shareholders (or their successors in the event that the resolution survives their death).[16] Neither the resolution nor the regulation can be varied without the consent of those persons.[17]

Who is to carry out the valuation

5.26　In the consultation paper we proposed that the valuation of the exiting member's shares should be carried out by an independent accountant, and we set out provisions for the appointment of that person in default of agreement between the parties. In our revised draft we refer to an "independent person who appears to have the requisite knowledge and skill".[18] We accept the point made by several respondents that the auditor or even an accountant may not always be the best person to value the shares. The auditor may have a conflict of interest so far as his duties to the outgoing shareholder are concerned because of his ongoing

---

[11]　*Ibid*, draft regulation 119(15).

[12]　*Ibid*, draft regulation 119(16)(a).

[13]　*Ibid*, draft regulation 119(20).

[14]　*Ibid*, draft regulation 119(15).

[15]　*Ibid*, draft regulation 119(16)(b).

[16]　*Ibid*, draft regulation 119(17).

[17]　*Ibid*, draft regulation 119(21). This provides that if a resolution is passed, a variation of the regulation or of the resolution is to be treated as a variation of the rights attaching to the shares held by the named shareholders, and that those rights may only be varied with their unanimous consent.

[18]　*Ibid*, draft regulation 119(13).

relationship with the company.[19] Moreover, share valuation requires particular skills which do not necessarily form part of an accountant's training or practice; on the other hand, there may also be experienced valuers who are not accountants.[20] Our revised draft regulation also leaves it to the resolution to specify the manner in which the independent person is to be appointed.

Basis of valuation

5.27 The regulation put forward in the consultation paper provided for only one basis of valuation, namely non-discounted. In our revised draft we include a number of alternatives which shareholders can choose when passing the resolution which brings the article into effect. These are: fair value; pro rata to the aggregate market value of the whole of the ordinary share capital; net asset value; and return of capital. This is intended to give greater flexibility so that the article can be adapted more easily to the needs of the particular shareholders, and any special factors arising on valuation, such as the fact that some shares have special rights. In order to avoid potential unfairness which might arise if the shareholders did not properly consider the basis of valuation when passing the resolution, the revised draft regulation makes it clear that the resolution will be invalid unless it sets out a basis of valuation.[21]

Provision for winding up in default

5.28 The draft of the regulation put forward in the consultation paper gave the outgoing member the power to force the company into liquidation if the remaining shareholders failed to purchase his shares within the timescale set out. A number of respondents expressed concern at the "draconian" nature of the consequences of this provision, and the increased risk that it would enable a shareholder to put unjustified pressure on the other shareholders. The point was also made that it appeared to be unfair since the provision came into effect if only one shareholder out of many failed to purchase some of the outgoing shareholder's shares. We accept these points and our revised draft does not include provision for winding up. We propose that the outgoing shareholder should have to rely on his remedy of specific performance against those shareholders who do not complete the purchase of his shares in accordance with the terms of the article. This is the position also under common form pre-emption articles.

Withdrawal of notice

5.29 We had also proposed that a shareholder could withdraw an exit notice at any time. However, on further reflection, we consider that this might lead to undesirable uncertainty, and could increase the risk that the provision is used inappropriately, as a means simply of putting pressure on the other shareholders.

---

[19] Moreover, the company may be, or become, exempt from the requirement to appoint auditors under s 249A of the Companies Act 1985.

[20] There is not yet a recognised professional qualification in the United Kingdom for share valuers. The Society of Share and Business Valuers in the United Kingdom is only in its second year of existence.

[21] See Appendix C, draft regulation 119(6).

We therefore propose that a shareholder should not be able to withdraw a notice unless all the shareholders named in the resolution agree.

Payment by instalment

5.30 In the consultation paper we raised the question of whether the regulation should provide for the purchase price to be paid by instalments.[22] Responses indicated that there were mixed views on this point, with many respondents indicating that they considered that this should be left up to the shareholders to decide. We agree that it would not be possible to include a provision in the regulation which would be suitable for all situations, and we have not sought to do so. However, it would be open to parties to make modifications to the regulation if they knew in advance what instalment arrangements they would want.

Shareholders' agreement

5.31 It would still be open to shareholders to choose to regulate their affairs by having a shareholders' agreement. Indeed, the existence of regulation 119 in Table A may prompt registration agents to encourage their clients to consider such agreements, or even provide standard form drafts.

5.32 Accordingly, **we recommend that a shareholders' exit article in the terms of the draft Regulation 119 set out in Appendix C should be included in Table A.**

5.33 In addition, we would encourage Companies House to consider whether reference can be made in the explanatory material which it supplies to persons forming companies to the desirability of addressing the issue of providing an exit mechanism for a shareholder to withdraw his investment from the company. We also hope that registration agents would, as a matter of good practice, provide information to their customers on the new draft regulation.[23]

Arbitration

5.34 This draft regulation was not limited to any particular type or size of company and required disputes between shareholders and the company to be referred to arbitration. However, it provided that the arbitration would be suspended if the parties sought to resolve the dispute through an ADR procedure (for example, mediation). The object was, of course, to encourage incorporators to consider providing for means of dispute resolution other than the courts.

5.35 The regulation made it clear that it only applied to disputes in respect of which a member could maintain legal proceedings. This was so as not to extend the areas in which a shareholder can interfere with the company's management.[24] In the

---

[22] Consultation Paper No 142, para 19.11.

[23] Publicity in legal and accountancy journals would also be helpful, as well as dissemination of information by trade organisations, professional bodies, Business Links and Chambers of Commerce; see Consultation Paper No 142, para 19.18.

[24] There are restrictions on the extent to which an individual shareholder can enforce provisions in the memorandum and articles of association. See para 7.5 below, and see

event that the parties could not agree on the choice of an arbitrator, he would be nominated by the President of the Institute of Chartered Accountants in England and Wales.

5.36 Support for an arbitration article was much less enthusiastic than for the other two draft regulations. In fact only a small majority of respondents were in favour of its inclusion in Table A, and a majority of the practising lawyers who addressed this question were against its inclusion. A number of reasons were given. First, it was said that there may be argument as to whether a dispute was one in respect of which a member could maintain legal proceedings; secondly it was pointed out that ancillary proceedings and enforcement would be dealt with in the Commercial Court rather than the Chancery Division which, for matters of this kind, would be undesirable; thirdly, it was noted that the interests of other shareholders may be affected, but it was not clear how they were to be represented; fourthly, it was suggested that there was scope for abuse as a member dissatisfied with a proposed resolution might initiate arbitration proceedings, which may not be disposed of as easily as would court proceedings; finally the point was made that legal aid would not be available for the arbitration proceedings.

5.37 There was also considerable disagreement, even amongst those in favour of the regulation, over who should nominate the arbitrator. A majority of those who considered the issue appeared to be against the nomination by the President of the Institute of Chartered Accountants as proposed in the draft regulation, but no alternative appeared to be clearly favoured by respondents.

5.38 We are reluctant to recommend the inclusion of an article into Table A which does not have the whole hearted support of respondents, particularly when a majority of practising lawyers appeared to be against its inclusion. We are persuaded that the potential difficulties which have been highlighted outweigh the benefits which may accrue. It is of course open to parties to refer any disputes to arbitration and we would wish to encourage the greater use of ADR techniques generally. However, we do not consider that this is best achieved by the inclusion of the proposed article in Table A. Accordingly, we recommend against the inclusion of an arbitration and ADR regulation in Table A.

Valuation procedure

5.39 In the consultation paper, we drew attention to the situation where all the shareholders of a company are agreed that one or more of them should sell their shares to the rest, but no agreement can be reached on value. Currently there is no remedy to which shareholders can resort in this situation in the absence of unfairly prejudicial conduct.[25] This means that shareholders may try to bring a petition under section 459 when the circumstances do not in fact justify a claim of unfairly prejudicial conduct, and when all they are seeking to resolve is a dispute

Consultation Paper No 142, paras 2.15-2.39. The draft arbitration regulation was not intended to affect these restrictions in any way.

[25] Consultation Paper No 142, paras 19.16-19.17.

about the price to be paid for the shares. This is clearly a waste of time and costs for the parties and for the court.

5.40 The draft regulation proposed in the consultation paper was designed to meet this need. It provided that where shareholders are agreed (apart from price) on the sale or purchase of particular shares in the company, they shall appoint an independent accountant to determine the fair value of the shares, and in default the President of the Institute of Chartered Accountants may do so. It stated that no discount is to be made for the fact that the shares form part of a minority shareholding. But it made no provision for default by the purchaser in completing the sale, leaving the vendor to exercise his remedies at common law if this occurred.

5.41 The valuation article received considerable support on consultation, but serious concerns were expressed by a number of respondents about how such an article might work in practice. Two particular points were made.

5.42 The first was that price is an essential element of agreement to a sale. If there is no agreement on price, what exactly is meant by shareholders being "agreed ... on the sale or purchase of particular shares"? What is necessary for the regulation to bite? This point was developed in several different ways.

5.43 One respondent considered that the concept of agreement to sell but disagreement as to price was probably impossible to define in any sufficiently realistic way to make the regulation of significant use.

5.44 Another respondent suggested that for there to be an agreement, the parties would have to have agreed that they will buy and sell subject to the price being settled under the new regulation. This would effectively convert the valuation provision into a voluntary one, and so there may be little point in including it in Table A.

5.45 A third respondent was concerned that the regulation might be regarded as being operative when shareholders were simply in negotiation about a possible sale of shares. In his view the regulation should make it clear that the provision would only become operative as and when a sale contract was entered into which expressly included the regulation as a term.

5.46 The second point made by those who disagreed with the article was that it could operate unfairly. A valuation without a minority discount would not be appropriate in every case. If the parties could not agree on the basis of valuation, it might be unfair to impose a non-discounted valuation on them; if they were able to agree on the basis of valuation, then the article would probably serve little use in practice.

5.47 On further consideration, we agree with these concerns. The parties should not be bound by the valuation procedure at too early a stage in any discussions between them. This may discourage them from entering into negotiations at all, which would clearly have the opposite effect from that which we are seeking. But if the regulation is only to apply once the parties have reached an effective agreement, then they must have either agreed on the price or a method of fixing a price. In order to avoid any potential unfairness, we consider that the parties should also be given the opportunity to choose the basis of valuation. The regulation should not have the effect of imposing a pro rata valuation where, for example, the parties have simply made an agreement that the shares be sold at a fair value to be determined by an independent third party. Otherwise, the regulation might apply where the parties had positively disagreed about the basis of valuation but reached agreement that the shares would be sold on the basis of a valuation by a third party in ignorance of the effect of the article.

5.48   We consider that if the parties are able to agree on both the method and basis of valuing the shares, then there is little that a valuation article can achieve, since the parties can set these matters out in the agreement itself. Accordingly, we recommend against the inclusion of a valuation article in Table A.

Conclusion

5.49   To summarise, we recommend that a shareholders' exit article should be included in Table A, setting out a mechanism by which shareholders can require their shares to be purchased in certain agreed circumstances. Whilst the regulation should set out a framework for the exercise of these exit rights, it should require the shareholders to make positive choices (notably in relation to the events triggering the rights, the basis of valuation and the choice of the valuer) in order to bring the regulation into effect.[26]

5.50   We recommend against the inclusion of an arbitration article and a valuation article in Table A.

---

[26]   See draft regulation 119 at Appendix C.

PART 6
A NEW DERIVATIVE ACTION

Introduction

6.1 In this part we are concerned with the law relating to the ability of a shareholder to bring proceedings to enforce a cause of action vested in the company (a derivative action). We explained in the consultation paper that there were two related principles which restrict a member's ability to bring such proceedings. The first is the majority rule principle developed as a result of the court's historical reluctance to become involved in disputes over the internal management of business ventures.[1] The second is the proper plaintiff principle which has been described as "... the elementary principle that A cannot, as a general rule, bring an action against B to recover damages or secure other relief on behalf of C for an injury done by B to C".[2] As a company is a separate legal entity, it is the proper plaintiff where it has suffered injury. These principles were applied in the case of *Foss v Harbottle*[3] and are often applied by the courts as "the rule in *Foss v Harbottle*".[4]

6.2 However, these restrictions are not absolute. If they were, they would mean that where a wrong has been done to the company by or with the support of the majority shareholders, there could never be any redress. There are cases, therefore, when the rule will not apply and an individual shareholder will be able to bring an action. These were set out by the Court of Appeal in *Edwards v Halliwell*[5] and restated in *Prudential Assurance Co Ltd v Newman Industries Ltd (No 2)* ("*Prudential*")[6] in the following terms:

> (1)   The proper plaintiff in an action in respect of a wrong alleged to be done to a corporation is, prima facie, the corporation.

---

[1] The principle is based on the doctrine of separate corporate personality and on the early partnership principle that courts would not interfere between partners except to dissolve the partnership; see Wedderburn, "Shareholders' Rights and the Rule in Foss v Harbottle" [1957] CLJ 194, 196. See *Carlen v Drury* (1812) 1 V & B 154, 158; 35 ER 61, 62: "This Court is not to be required on every Occasion to take the Management of every Playhouse and Brewhouse in the Kingdom" *per* Lord Eldon LC.

[2] See *Prudential Assurance Co Ltd v Newman Industries Ltd (No 2)* [1982] Ch 204, 210. To allow a third party to bring an action in relation to wrongs done to another could lead to multiple actions being brought against a single defendant in relation to a single wrong.

[3] (1843) 2 Hare 461; 67 ER 189.

[4] See Wedderburn, "Shareholders' Rights and the Rule in Foss v Harbottle" [1957] CLJ 194, 195-198. See also *Prudential Assurance Co Ltd v Newman Industries Ltd (No 2)* [1982] Ch 204, where the Court of Appeal referred to the rule in *Foss v Harbottle* as embracing both the "elementary" proper plaintiff principle and "... a related principle, that an individual shareholder cannot bring an action in the courts to complain of an irregularity ... if the irregularity is one which can be cured by a vote of the company in general meeting". *Ibid*, at p 210. See generally Consultation Paper No 142, paras 4.1-4.6.

[5] [1950] 2 All ER 1064, 1066-1069, *per* Jenkins LJ.

[6] [1982] Ch 204.

(2)   Where the alleged wrong is a transaction which might be made binding on the corporation and on all its members by a simple majority of the members, no individual member of the corporation is allowed to maintain an action in respect of that matter because, if the majority confirms the transaction, *cadit quaestio* [the question is at an end]; or, if the majority challenges the transaction, there is no valid reason why the company should not sue.

(3)   There is no room for the operation of the rule if the alleged wrong is ultra vires the corporation, because the majority of members cannot confirm the transaction.

(4)   There is also no room for the operation of the rule if the transaction complained of could be validly done or sanctioned only by a special resolution or the like, because a simple majority cannot confirm a transaction which requires the concurrence of a greater majority.

(5)   There is an exception to the rule where what has been done amounts to fraud and the wrongdoers are themselves in control of the company.[7]

6.3   We noted that only the fifth limb of the restatement in *Prudential* was a true "exception" to the rule in *Foss v Harbottle*, in that it permitted a shareholder to bring a derivative action (ie an action to enforce the company's cause of action) inspite of the majority rule and proper plaintiff principles.[8] The third and fourth limbs were really situations where the principles had no application; actions under those limbs can be brought by a shareholder as a personal action in his own right, and need not be brought as a derivative action.[9]

6.4   Our view was that the basic approach to the right to bring a derivative action was a sound one: an individual shareholder should only be able to bring such an action in exceptional circumstances.[10] This approach is also reflected in the first, second and fifth guiding principles set out in paragraph 1.9 above (proper plaintiff, internal management, and freedom from unnecessary shareholder interference). But we considered that the rule was complicated and unwieldy. It could only be found in case law, much of it decided many years ago; the meaning of terms such as "wrongdoer control" were not clear; and there were situations

---

[7]   *Ibid*, at pp 210-211. *Edwards v Halliwell* also makes it clear that the enforcement of the personal rights of individual members does not come within the rule, although as discussed below, the rule does have implications for such personal actions; see para 7.7 below. For a recent case where, following *Edwards v Halliwell*, the rule was held to have no application, see *Wise v Union of Shop, Distributive and Allied Workers* [1996] ICR 691.

[8]   See Consultation Paper No 142, para 16.14 and para 4.5, n 13.

[9]   See Consultation Paper No 142, para 16.14, and see para 6.56 below. Although note that where a shareholder is seeking compensation for loss caused by an ultra vires or illegal transaction, the wrong is done to the company and the claim must be brought by derivative action; see *Smith v Croft (No 2)* [1988] Ch 114. Also, it appears that an action to restrain breaches of special resolution procedures and to prevent the company from acting on resolutions passed as a result of such breaches can be either in personal or derivative form; see *Quin & Axtens Ltd v Salmon* [1909] AC 442.

[10] Consultation Paper No 142, para 4.6.

which appeared to fall outside the fraud on the minority exception when it might be desirable for a member to be able to bring an action.[11] We also expressed concern at the way in which a member was required to prove standing to bring an action as a preliminary issue by evidence which shows a prima facie case on the merits, and noted that this could easily result in a mini trial which increases the length and cost of litigation.[12] We therefore put forward proposals for a new procedure for derivative actions.

6.5 The substance of our proposal was that the new derivative action would be available to any member if the case fell within the following situation:

> that, if the company were the applicant, it would be entitled to any remedy against any person as a result of any breach or threatened breach by any director of the company of any of his duties to the company.

6.6 But this would be subject to tight judicial control at all stages. In particular, an applicant would be required to seek leave from the court by close of pleadings to continue the action and in considering whether to grant leave the court would take account of all the circumstances.[13] Our view was that, for the most part, primary legislation was not required and that this reform should be achieved by rules of court.

6.7 In examining respondents' views on these proposals and setting out our final recommendations we consider in turn the following: international developments; the need for a new derivative action; should it be implemented by primary legislation or in rules of court; the position under Scots law; availability of the new derivative action; the extent to which the common law rule should be abrogated; the procedural steps; the issues relevant to the grant of leave; and other relevant provisions.

International developments

6.8 We noted in the consultation paper a number of international developments with regard to the derivative action. Eight of the ten provinces of Canada have since 1975 replaced the rule in *Foss v Harbottle* with a requirement that the shareholder obtain leave of the court.[14] In Australia and Hong Kong there are legislative

---

[11] See Consultation Paper No 142, paras 14.1-14.3. So far as the third point is concerned, we noted that an action to recover damages suffered by a company by reason of the negligence of a director could not be brought by a minority shareholder unless it is possible to prove that the negligence conferred a benefit on the controlling shareholders, or that the failure of the other directors to bring an action constitutes a fraud on the minority. This is discussed further below; see paras 6.38-6.41.

[12] *Ibid*, at para 14.4.

[13] We provisionally recommended that express reference should be made to five specific matters which the court should take into account. In our final recommendations we have added an additional specific matter to which we consider express reference should be made. See para 6.70 below.

[14] In 1975 the Canadian federal Parliament passed the Canada Business Corporations Act (CBCA) which followed the publication of the Dickerson Report (*Proposals for a New Business Corporations Law for Canada*) in 1971. Section 239 of the CBCA sets out a statutory

---

proposals for a statutory derivative action.[15] The proposals in Australia (as in Canada) would also replace the fifth limb of the rule in *Foss v Harbottle* and require the shareholder to obtain leave from the court.[16] The court would decide whether a derivative action should be commenced on the basis of statutory criteria.[17] The Companies Act 1993 of New Zealand introduced a statutory derivative action.[18] There is a statutory derivative action in South Africa by virtue of the Companies Act No 61 of 1973.[19] In 1993, Japan changed its law so as to facilitate derivative actions.[20]

6.9   Thus the introduction of a clear set of rules for the derivative action in this country would follow the lead given in other leading jurisdictions.[21] In an age of increasing globalisation of investment and growing international interest in corporate governance,[22] greater transparency in the requirements for a derivative action is in our view highly desirable.[23]

right to apply for leave to bring an action on behalf of a corporation or to intervene in an action to which it is a party. Seven out of the ten Canadian provinces (Alberta, Saskatchewan, Manitoba, New Brunswick, New Foundland, Nova Scotia and Ontario) have enacted or amended provincial statutes so as to contain measures which are very similar to the CBCA. An eighth (British Columbia) has also enacted legislation which provides for the creation of a derivative action scheme, but differs to a significant degree from the CBCA. The remaining two provinces (Prince Edward Island and Quebec) continue to rely on the common law. See Brian Cheffins, "Reforming the Derivative Action: The Canadian Experience and British Prospects" A Paper presented at the Cambridge Conference on Shareholders' Rights and Remedies (April 1997) pp 7-8. See also Consultation Paper No 142, Appendix F and G.

[15]   For details of the draft provisions published by the Attorney-General's Department in Australia, see *Proceedings on Behalf of a Company, Draft Provisions and Commentary* (1995); See also Consultation Paper No 142, Appendix F. For the proposals in the new Ordinance for Hong Kong, see *Review of the Hong Kong Companies Ordinance Consultancy Report* (March 1997), recommendation 7.08.

[16]   See draft Bill s 245B(1) published by the Attorney-General's Department in Australia, *Proceedings on Behalf of a Company, Draft Provisions and Commentary* (1995) pp 3 and 11. See also Consultation Paper No 142, Appendix G.

[17]   *Ibid*, s 245B(2) and p 5.

[18]   See sections 165-168 of the New Zealand Companies Act 1993. See also Consultation Paper No 142, Appendix F and G.

[19]   See sections 266-268 of the South African Companies Act No 61 of 1973. See also Consultation Paper No 142, Appendix F and G.

[20]   Articles 267 to 268 of the Commercial Code of Japan; see Mark D West, "The Pricing of Shareholder Derivative Actions in Japan and the United States" (1994) 88 North Western University Law Revision 1436, and Professor Hiroshi Oda, "Derivative Actions In Japan" 48 Current Legal Problems (1995) 161.

[21]   We note that there was an opposition amendment to the Companies Bill in 1979 which was designed to introduce a derivative action subject to leave of the court. The amendment was withdrawn following discussion in Committee; see *Hansard* (HC) Standing Committee A, 22 November 1979.

[22]   See for example, interim report of the Hampel Committee, *Committee on Corporate Governance, Preliminary Report* (August 1997), para 1.5.

[23]   An alternative approach to the derivative action is to be found in the EC Draft Fifth Directive for the Harmonisation of Company Law. For the 1988 text, see J Dine, *EC Company Law* (1st ed, 1991) paras A8.20-A8.93. Under this provision proceedings are to be

The need for a new derivative action

6.10 The vast majority of respondents considered that the operation of the rule in *Foss v Harbottle* was unsatisfactory, and agreed with the problems which we had identified. However, a number of these did express reservations about the need for a new derivative procedure along the lines proposed. Three particular points were made. First, it was said that the derivative action was of such little relevance in practice that there was no point in reforming it. Secondly, some respondents expressed concerns about the adverse consequences of making the derivative action more widely available. Thirdly, several others commented that the proposed new procedure was unlikely to be simpler or more efficient than the current law.

6.11 Dealing with the first point, we accept that, as a matter of practice, derivative actions are brought far less frequently than proceedings under section 459, but we do not accept that this means that no reform should be made. There are still cases where a derivative action is the only or most appropriate route to take. Whilst we noted the tendency of applicants to bring section 459 proceedings in respect of matters which could have given rise to a derivative action,[24] we do not consider that the two should be entirely assimilated. They are different in principle - one gives rise to a personal right which the shareholder can enforce, the other relates to the company's cause of action - and although they may cover some of the same ground, this will not always be the case. As was pointed out on consultation, section 459 has largely become an exit remedy, and what is needed is a remedy for those who want to stay in the company. We consider that a separate and distinct right to bring a derivative action should remain. Section 461(2)(c) provides a means of bringing a derivative action but as we observed in the consultation paper, this has not worked satisfactorily because the court cannot make this order unless it is satisfied that unfair prejudice has occurred and that an order under section 461(2)(c) is the appropriate relief.[25]

6.12 We highlighted the problems with the current procedure with which respondents agreed and these need to be addressed. We consider that the derivative procedure should be rationalised and modernised in accordance with our provisional recommendations. As we noted in the consultation paper,[26] this may also have the added advantage of encouraging some parties to bring claims as derivative actions

commenced on behalf of a public company in respect of directors' liabilities for breach of duty if "... so requested by one or more shareholders who hold shares of a nominal value or, in the absence of a nominal value, an accounting par value which the Member States may not require to be greater than 10% of the subscribed capital. ..." (art 16). No work is currently under way on the Fifth Directive and the ultimate fate of this draft procedure for a derivative action is uncertain. See Commission Consultation Paper on Company Law (March 1997), p 7.

[24] See Consultation Paper No 142, para 16.3.

[25] Some respondents suggested that the court should be given power to make this order at an interim stage, but that course would still involve two sets of proceedings.

[26] Consultation Paper No 142, para 15.5.

which they might otherwise have brought under section 459; these are likely to be more focused than the wide-ranging proceedings under section 459.[27]

6.13   So far as the second point is concerned, we do not accept that the proposals will make significant changes to the availability of the action. In some respects, the availability may be slightly wider;[28] in others it may be slightly narrower.[29] But in all cases the new procedure will be subject to tight judicial control. As indicated in the previous paragraph, it may be that some claims will be brought under the new procedure instead of under section 459, but for the reasons given[30] we consider that this is desirable. We do not anticipate that there will be a large overall increase in litigation,[31] but we consider that where litigation is brought, the new procedure will assist in making sure that it is dealt with fairly and efficiently.

6.14   We disagree with the third point. We consider that the proposals will put the derivative action on a much clearer and more rational basis. They will give courts the flexibility to allow cases to proceed in appropriate circumstances, while giving advisers and shareholders the necessary guidance on the matters which the court will take into account in deciding whether to grant leave.

6.15   Accordingly, **we recommend that there should be a new derivative procedure with more modern, flexible and accessible criteria for determining whether a shareholder can pursue the action.**

Should it be implemented by primary legislation or in rules of court

6.16   We provisionally recommended that, since the reform will in most respects involve questions of procedure, the new derivative action should be governed by rules of court.[32] We continue to believe that the details of the new derivative action should be spelt out in rules of court. However, we consider that the basis of the action should be set out in statute. This is for two main reasons.

---

[27]   We did raise on consultation the question of whether it would be appropriate to require all claims which can be brought by or on behalf of the company to be so brought (*ibid*, at para 16.1). Our provisional view was that this would not be appropriate and that a claimant should have the right to choose whether to bring a derivative action or proceedings under s 459, or cumulative claims under both. The vast majority of respondents agreed with our provisional view. A majority of respondents also agreed with our provisional view that the court should not have the power in proceedings under s 459 to make an order in favour of the company where such an order was not in fact sought by the claimant. We maintain our provisional view on these two points.

[28]   In particular in relation to negligence of directors; see paras 6.38-6.41 below.

[29]   Where, for example, the claim does not arise out of a breach of duty by a director; see para 6.24 below.

[30]   Derivative actions are likely to be more focused and therefore easier for the courts to manage.

[31]   This is supported by the experience in Canada; See B Cheffins (S J Berwin Professor of Corporate Law (elect), University of Cambridge), "Reforming the Derivative Action: The Canadian Experience and British Prospects" A Paper presented at the Cambridge Conference on Shareholders' Rights and Remedies (April 1997).

[32]   See Consultation Paper No 142, para 15.3.

6.17 First, we are informed by the Scottish Law Commission that to make changes to analogous actions in Scotland, primary legislation will be required.[33] We consider that it is important that Scottish and English law should remain consistent in the area of company law so far as possible. It is desirable, therefore, both that the provisions relating to shareholder actions in the two jurisdictions should match each other as closely as possible, and that there should be comparable provisions in the legislation on the derivative action and the analogous action under Scots law.

6.18 Second, we consider that it is desirable to include a provision for the derivative action in the Companies Act so that it can be put on a similar footing to the unfair prejudice remedy and so as to alert shareholders, directors and others to the existence of the provisions. In this way, the Companies Act will constitute a more complete code in relation to shareholder remedies.

6.19 The proposed amendments to the Companies Act to set out the basis of the derivative action (and the analogous action in Scotland) are set out in the draft Bill at Appendix A. We propose that the more detailed provisions should be set out in a rule of court, a draft of which is set out in Appendix B. Under English law this rule may be made by the Civil Procedure Rule Committee under section 1(2) of the Civil Procedure Act 1997.[34] There is therefore no need to have an express rule-making power in the primary legislation.

6.20 For the reasons discussed in Appendix D, the draft legislation includes a provision giving the Secretary of State the power, by statutory instrument, to set out in relation to Scotland the matters of which the court should take account in considering the granting of leave and the criteria to be applied in relation to the refusal of leave. We would envisage that the Secretary of State would prescribe similar criteria and matters to those included in our draft rule. A comparable difference in rule-making powers already exists in relation to insolvency. Section 411 of the Insolvency Act provides that in relation to England and Wales rules are to be made by the Lord Chancellor,[35] and in relation to Scotland they are to be made by the Secretary of State. So far as the English rules of court are concerned, the Civil Procedure Rule Committee must consult with such persons as they consider appropriate before making or amending any rules. We would envisage that the Committee would consult with the DTI on any matters which, in relation to Scotland, would come under the rule-making power of the Secretary of State. In this way, a consistency of approach can be maintained for the two jurisdictions.

6.21 The draft rule on derivative actions which is set out at Appendix B is intended to tie in to the Draft Civil Proceedings Rules as closely as possible. We have endeavoured to adopt the vocabulary and approach of the latter in framing our own rule. However, the rules are still being prepared.[36] It may be necessary,

---

[33] See para 6.22 below and Appendix D.

[34] See, however, n 89 below.

[35] In concurrence with the Secretary of State.

[36] See paras 1.28-1.30 above on the current position in respect of the Draft Civil Proceedings Rules.

therefore, for some minor adjustments to be made to the draft rule on derivative actions to incorporate it into the general body of rules in due course.

The position under Scots law

6.22   We are informed by the Scottish Law Commission that under Scots law, there is no recognised representative or derivative action. A shareholder's right to seek a remedy for the company is conferred by substantive law and not by procedural rules. Amendment of Scots law in relation to this right, therefore, involves separate considerations and will require separate legislative provision. The Scottish Law Commission's consideration of the relevant matters and their recommendations to parallel our recommendations discussed in this part of the report, are set out in Appendix D.

Availability of the new derivative action

6.23   Three specific questions were raised in the consultation paper in respect of the availability of the new derivative action: should it only be available in respect of breaches of duty by directors (including claims against third parties as a result of such breaches); should it extend to negligence of directors where they have not benefited personally; and should it be available for breaches of duty by officers or employees. In addition, a fourth question was touched upon which is also relevant to this discussion, namely who should be able to bring a derivative action.

Should it only be available in respect of breaches of duty by a director (including claims against third parties as a result of such breaches)

6.24   The formulation proposed in the consultation paper,[37] limited the availability of the derivative action to claims arising out of a breach of directors' duties. Our provisional view was that, in general, if there is no breach of duty by a director the shareholder should not be bringing the action. We pointed out, however, that the relief sought may not be against the director personally, but against a third party.[38]

6.25   A majority of respondents who addressed this issue agreed with our provisional view. However, two particular concerns were raised by those who disagreed. The first was the potential controversy over what amounts to a duty. One respondent referred to the case of *Movitex Ltd v Bulfield*.[39] Most books, he said, had traditionally referred to a director's duty to disclose a potentially conflicting interest in a company contract; but Vinelott J had held that there was no such duty: the effect of the rule was to place a director under a disability and no more. A second point expressed by the same respondent was that it was fallacious to say that directors were under a "duty" to use their powers for a proper purposes. If they are motivated by an improper purpose, their act or decision may be set aside; but it does not follow from this that they have breached any "duty". Several other

---

[37]   And set out in para 6.5 above.

[38]   Eg for knowing receipt of money or property transferred in breach of trust or for knowing assistance in a breach of trust.

[39]   [1988] BCLC 104. This case was based on an equivalent decision on trusts by Megarry V-C in *Tito v Waddell (No 2)* [1977] Ch 106, 246-250 (which concerned a limitation issue).

respondents also expressed a concern that it may lead to litigation about what is and is not a duty.

6.26   We are not convinced by the second point. If, for example, directors arranged for a company to execute a guarantee in favour of a third party for an improper purpose, and an action was brought to set aside the guarantee, we consider that the cause of action would be regarded as arising from a breach of duty for these purposes.[40] So far as the first point is concerned, we agree that *Movitex Ltd v Bulfield* does draw very difficult distinctions,[41] and the draft Bill takes account of the present state of the law.[42] Section 317 of the Companies Act 1985 imposes a duty on a director to disclose his interest in transactions with the company in certain circumstances. The better view is that breach of this duty does not affect the transaction.[43] However, many companies have articles requiring a director to make disclosure to the board or to the company if he is interested in a transaction with the company.[44] A breach of the disclosure requirements contained in the articles, where the requirements apply, would constitute a breach of duty for these purposes.

6.27   The second concern raised by respondents was that there may be some situations where it should be possible to bring a derivative action which would fall outside the new procedure. This may be because there is *no* breach of duty by directors (even on the widest possible meaning of "duty"), or it may be because the cause of action does not *arise out of* the breach of duty. We consider both these situations in turn.

6.28   The case of *Estmanco (Kilner House) Ltd v Greater London Council*[45] was given as an example of the first type of case. In *Estmanco* the wrong found to be a fraud on the minority was conduct of the majority shareholder and not that of the directors. The facts were unusual. The company was a flat management company. The majority shareholder was the Greater London Council ("the GLC"), which owned the block of flats and which had entered into an agreement in writing with the company to sell the flats. Each purchaser of a flat received one of the shares but the shares did not under their terms of issue confer any right to vote until all

[40]   See *Rolled Steel Products (Holdings) Ltd v British Steel Corp* [1984] BCLC 466.

[41]   These are driven by s 310 of the Companies Act 1985. This section prohibits, *inter alia,* provisions in the articles which exempt a director from liability in respect of any "negligence, default, breach of duty or breach of trust". Articles often provide that a director may be interested in a contract with his company provided he makes disclosure of his interest in the manner required by the articles. Such a provision was held by Vinelott J in *Movitex Ltd v Bulfield* [1988]BCLC 104 not to infringe the predecessor of s 310 since, as the restriction on "self-dealing" was a disability, the provision did not involve exempting directors from liability for "breach of duty or breach of trust". See also *Guinness plc v Saunders* [1990] 2 AC 663; *Lee Panavision Ltd v Lee Lighting Ltd* [1991] BCC 620; and *Hely-Hutchinson v Brayhead Ltd* [1968] 1 QB 549.

[42]   See para 6.48 below and see s 458A(2) inserted by clause 1(1) of the draft Bill in Appendix A.

[43]   See the cases cited in n 41 above.

[44]   Regulation 85 of Table A sets out such a requirement.

[45]   [1982] 1 WLR 2.

the flats had been sold. In breach of its agreement with the company, the GLC decided to stop selling the flats and to offer them instead to high priority applicants on its housing list. The directors of the company started proceedings against the GLC to enforce the written agreement but the GLC procured the passing of a resolution of the company in general meeting which directed the directors to withdraw the company's action. A minority shareholder applied to the court for leave to take over the action and to continue it as a derivative action. Sir Robert Megarry V-C found that the GLC's conduct amounted to a fraud on the minority since the prospective right to vote was affected.

6.29   The fraud found by the court was the majority shareholders' conduct and not that of the directors. The formulation for the derivative action put forward in the consultation paper does not cover the situation where the wrong relied on is not a breach by the directors of their duties. This does not mean that the shareholder has no remedy, but rather that he cannot pursue one under the new procedure. He would have to proceed under section 459, claiming authority to use the name of the company in proceedings against the GLC. The Court would have to hear the section 459 application rapidly to deal with the situation, but it seems to us preferable to leave the court to do this than, at least in the first instance, to open the door to derivative litigation against third parties by having a wider rule. (In a case such as *Estmanco* it might in fact be possible to show that the directors had acted in breach of duty for the purposes of the new derivative procedure on the ground that they should not have acted on the resolution passed by the majority shareholders but should have continued to pursue the proceedings).[46]

6.30   One could envisage other situations where the majority abuse their position in a manner which affects the running of the company, but there is no obvious breach of duty by the directors. In our view, what is in issue is a shareholder's personal rights against the company because of the conduct of the majority; it is not the company's rights which are being infringed. The appropriate remedy for the shareholder is a personal action under the articles of association or (more likely) a claim under section 459, rather than a derivative action on behalf of the company. We do not consider, therefore, that the derivative action should be available where there has been no breach of duty by the directors.

6.31   So far as the second situation is concerned, one respondent gave the following example. A profitable company is a victim of a tort by a third party, and the board, although otherwise committed to the well-being of the company, have ulterior motives of their own for not wishing to enforce the remedy for the tort. Although the board would in those circumstances be in breach of duty, their breach would not have given rise to the claim.

---

[46]   Under regulation 70 of Table A, the power to manage the company is vested in the directors. It is for the directors, not the company in general meeting, to decide whether proceedings should be pursued. See the case of *Breckland Group Holdings Ltd v London and Suffolk Properties Ltd* [1989] BCLC 100 where it was held that the company in general meeting could not intervene to adopt unauthorised proceedings; the only organ which could do so was the board.

6.32   We accept that in this type of situation an individual shareholder would have no
        right to bring a derivative action against the third party tortfeasor under our
        proposals. (There would of course be a potential claim for damages against the
        directors themselves, although this may give rise to difficulties of causation or
        quantification, and it is possible that the directors may not have sufficient funds to
        meet the claim). However, we do not consider that this is an issue which needs to
        be addressed for two main reasons.

6.33   First, we are not aware of any cases under the current law where a derivative
        action has been successfully brought in circumstances such as those described in
        paragraph 6.31.[47]

6.34   Secondly, (and more importantly) it is consistent with the proper plaintiff
        principle which we endorsed in the consultation paper and which received
        virtually unanimous support on consultation. The decision on whether to sue a
        third party (ie someone who is not a director and where the claim is not closely
        connected with a breach of duty by a director)[48] is clearly one for the board. If the
        directors breach their duty in deciding not to pursue the claim then (subject to the
        leave of the court) a derivative claim can be brought against them. To allow
        shareholders to have involvement in whether claims should be brought against
        third parties[49] in our view goes too far in encouraging excessive shareholder
        interference with management decisions. This is particularly important as we are
        proposing that derivative actions are to be available in respect of breaches of
        directors' duties of skill and care.[50] A line has to be drawn somewhere and we
        consider that this is both a logical and clearly identifiable place in which to draw
        the line.[51]

6.35   There may be situations where the line is not quite so easy to draw. For example, a
        company may have a claim in negligence against an auditor who fails to spot that
        the directors have misappropriated corporate assets. The factual background to
        the claim against the auditor is the breach of duty by the directors, but the auditor
        has neither participated in the fraud nor received corporate assets. Our view is that
        it is not appropriate for a derivative action to be brought against the auditor in
        these circumstances, and we do not consider that it would be possible to bring
        such an action under the terms of our draft bill. The cause of action against the

---

[47]   We also note that in Canada, where there is no such restriction, it appears that there have
        only been two cases where the subject-matter of the proposed litigation was an action against
        a third party. In both, the judge dismissed the application and in so doing expressed
        scepticism as to whether derivative litigation was appropriate for the type of proceedings
        involved; see Brian Cheffins, "Reforming the Derivative Action: The Canadian Experience
        and British Prospects" A Paper presented at the Cambridge Conference on Shareholders'
        Rights and Remedies (April 1997).

[48]   Eg for knowing receipt of money or property transferred in breach of trust or for knowing
        assistance in a breach of trust.

[49]   Other than where the claim arises out of the breach of duty.

[50]   See paras 6.38- 6.41 below.

[51]   The shareholders do, of course, have the right to remove the directors by ordinary resolution
        if they do not approve of the manner in which the directors are managing the company; see
        s 303 of the Companies Act 1985.

auditor does not arise as a result of the directors' act, but rather their act is merely the setting against which the auditor's (separate) default operates.

6.36 One final point made by a few respondents was that there appeared to be some confusion in the consultation paper between a "shadow director" and a "de facto" director in this context.[52] We consider that de facto directors should be included for these purposes, but we consider that they are capable of coming under the definition of director in section 741 of the Companies Act 1985[53] and no express reference to them is necessary.[54] We also consider that shadow directors should be included.[55] There are many statutory provisions which now impose obligations[56] on them and we consider that a derivative action should be available where the company has a claim in respect of breaches of those obligations.[57]

6.37 We therefore consider that the new procedure should only be available for claims in respect of breaches of duty by a director (including claims against third parties as a result of such breaches), and that for these purposes director should include a shadow director.

Should it extend to negligence of directors (where directors have not benefited personally)

6.38 Our provisional view was that there was a deficiency in the current law, in that section 459 cannot be used in respect of negligence as such, but only for serious mismanagement, and a derivative action based on negligence may only be brought if it can be shown that the majority have profited by the negligence.[58] We therefore provisionally recommended that the new derivative action should be available in respect of negligence.[59]

---

[52] See Consultation Paper No 142, para 16.8.

[53] Section 741(1) provides that: "In this Act, "director" includes any person occupying the position of director, by whatever name called".

[54] See *Re Lo-Line Electric Motors Ltd* [1988] BCLC 698. For a discussion of the difference between de jure, de facto and shadow directors, see *Re Hydrodam (Corby) Ltd* [1994] 2 BCLC 180, 183.

[55] Section 741(2) provides that: "In relation to a company, "shadow director" means a person in accordance with whose directions or instructions the directors of the company are accustomed to act. However, a person is not deemed a shadow director by reason only that the directors act on advice given by him in a professional capacity."

[56] Eg Companies Act 1985, sections: 309 (directors to have regard to interests of employees); 319 (directors' contract of employment for more than 5 years); 320 (substantial property transactions involving directors). See also Insolvency Act 1986, s 214 (wrongful trading).

[57] It remains an open question whether shadow directors can also be said to owe fiduciary duties to the company, although for a contrary view, see *Pennington's Company Law* (1995 7th ed) p 712. Our provision is not intended to impose obligations on shadow directors which they do not already have. It simply enables a shareholder to enforce a cause of action which the company would already have under the current law.

[58] See Consultation Paper No 142, para 16.9. See also paras 4.10-4.11 and 9.44-9.48; cf Hollington, *Minority Shareholders' Rights* (2nd ed 1994) p 15, para 2-021.

[59] We also noted that it appeared that the Jenkins Committee had intended section 461(2)(c) to be available in the case of negligence; see the Report of the Company Law Committee (1962) Cmnd 1749, paras 206-207, and see Consultation Paper No 142, paras 7.10-7.11.

6.39   The majority of respondents who addressed this issue agreed with the provisional view. For those who disagreed, the main reason given was the risk of increased litigation by disgruntled shareholders. This was not only seen as a problem for large public limited companies but also for small and medium-sized companies. The point was made by several respondents that a shareholder takes the risk that management decisions will turn out to be misguided and that mistakes will be made; this is a business risk taken when deciding to invest. Concern was also expressed by one respondent that it would discourage people from becoming non-executive directors, and another raised the question of the availability of insurance cover for negligence.

6.40   Dealing with the last two points, we do not consider that there is any reason why suitable persons would be discouraged from becoming directors. The courts have been developing the case law on directors' duties of skill and care to work out on a case by case basis the extent of the obligations owed by directors.[60] But there is no reason to suggest that the law imposes unduly onerous burdens. As one respondent commented: "Well organised and competent companies run by directors who know and follow their respective duties will have nothing to fear ...". We also understand that insurance cover is quite widely available and generally includes cover for negligence.[61]

6.41   So far as the risk of increased litigation is concerned, we consider that this is overstated.[62] As we have indicated there will be tight judicial control of cases brought under the new procedure. Whilst we accept that investors take the risk that those who manage companies may make mistakes, we do not consider that they have to accept that directors will fail to comply with their duties. There is no reason why directors should necessarily be able to shelter behind a procedural rule to escape liability. The court will consider carefully whether litigation should proceed in the light of all the circumstances (and in particular those which we discuss further below)[63] but where directors fail to comply with their duties we consider that there is no reason in principle why a derivative claim should not be brought against them. This was also clearly the view of the majority of

---

[60]   In *Re City Equitable Fire Insurance Co Ltd* [1925] Ch 407, Romer J concluded that a director need not exhibit in the performance of his duties a greater degree of skill than may reasonably be expected of a person of his knowledge and expertise. In *Dorchester Finance Co v Stebbing* [1989] BCLC 498 Foster J held that the proposition of Romer J applied only to the exercise of a director of his skill. This duty was to be distinguished from his duty of diligence, where what was required was "such care as an ordinary man might be expected to take on his own behalf". However, in *Norman v Theodore Goddard* [1991] BCLC 1027 and *Re D'Jan of London Ltd* [1994] 1 BCLC 561, Hoffmann J in drawing from the statutory test for wrongful trading in s 214 of the Insolvency Act 1986, expressed the view that both elements of the duty of care are to be assessed objectively.

[61]   See generally V Finch, "Personal Accountability and Corporate Control: The Role of Directors' and Officers' Liability Insurance" (1994) 57 MLR 880.

[62]   We also note that the experience in Canada suggests that there will not be a dramatic increase in the amount of litigation; see Brian Cheffins, "Reforming the Derivative Action: The Canadian Experience and British Prospects" A Paper presented at the Cambridge Conference on Shareholders' Rights and Remedies (April 1997).

[63]   See paras 6.73-6.92 below.

respondents. We therefore consider that the new procedure should be available for breach of directors' duties of skill and care.

Should it be available for breaches of duty by officers and employees

6.42 In the consultation paper we gave the examples of an employee accepting a bribe and committing a wrong against a company, or a branch manager of a single branch bank misappropriating company assets and passing them to the majority shareholder. In these circumstances we suggested that it should be open for a shareholder to bring a derivative action under the new procedure, but only if he could show that the claim could have been brought under the "fraud on the minority" exception to the rule in *Foss v Harbottle*.[64]

6.43 The reason for this was that we did not wish to remove the right to bring an action in circumstances which might have been permitted under the old law. However, there were competing considerations which needed to be addressed in deciding how such actions should be dealt with. On the one hand we considered that it would be desirable to bring such claims within the new procedure;[65] but on the other hand we did not want to extend their availability as this might lead to excessive shareholder interference. Our suggested solution was therefore a compromise between these two considerations, namely that an action could be brought under the new procedure, but only if it would have satisfied the fraud on the minority test. We anticipated that it would only be in very rare circumstances that advantage would need to be taken of this provision, since in most situations there would also be a breach of duty by the directors.

6.44 The responses to the consultation paper suggested that the majority of those who considered this point were in fact against extending the availability of the new derivative procedure to breaches of duty by officers or employees at all. The main reason given was that it was a matter for the directors to decide whether to take action in such cases. One respondent, however, said that his primary concern was for the position of the employees themselves who might become embroiled in litigation, even if it was ultimately found to be unmerited, and who may not have the necessary resources to defend themselves.

6.45 On further consideration, we agree with both these points. The decision on what action to take against employees is very clearly a management decision for the board of directors. Where the claim is not against a director (or arising out of a breach of duty by directors) the board should be making an unbiased decision as to the merits of suing and will probably be much better placed than an individual shareholder to evaluate the costs and benefits involved.[66] There is clearly considerable potential for interference with what are management decisions. There is also the potential for vexatious litigation by disgruntled shareholders against employees which we agree may well be unfair to the employees concerned.

---

[64] See Consultation Paper No 142, paras 16.10-16.11.

[65] So as to avoid diverging principles and procedures; see para 6.53 below.

[66] See Brian Cheffins, "Reforming the Derivative Action: The Canadian Experience and British Prospects" A Paper presented at the Cambridge Conference on Shareholders' Rights and Remedies (April 1997) at p 16.

In public companies, in particular, there is a risk that shares will be acquired for the sole purpose of bringing proceedings against managers where the person acquiring the share is unhappy with particular management decisions. Whilst these types of applicants would no doubt be refused leave to continue the proceedings, we consider that it is preferable to avoid the possibility of such nuisance claims being brought at all.

6.46 By focusing on breaches of duty by directors, the derivative action will be placed on a more logical and rational basis. We consider that it is consistent with this approach to exclude entirely claims based on breach of duty by employees and officers other than directors (unless of course they also arise out of a breach of duty by directors). We accept that there may be a few very unusual situations involving breaches of duty by employees or other officers which could have come within the common law exceptions. But unless the directors are implicated in the wrongdoing, we do not consider that a derivative action is appropriate. Where what is in issue is the conduct of the majority shareholders (as in the second example given in paragraph 6.42 above), we consider that this is more appropriately dealt with by personal proceedings, and in particular the use of section 459.[67]

Meaning of breach of duty

6.47 We have indicated above[68] that we consider that a derivative action should be available where a cause of action arises out of a breach, or threatened breach, of duty by a director, and that for these purposes, breach of duty should include negligence. We also envisage that a derivative action should be available in respect of a statutory default by a director.[69] Whilst we consider that the expression "breach of duty" is capable of covering both negligence and statutory default, we consider that it would be preferable for the legislation to make this clear. We therefore propose that the legislative provision implementing our recommendation should adopt the expression used in sections 310[70] and 727[71] of the Companies Act 1985, namely "negligence, default, breach of duty or breach of trust".

6.48 In the light of the discussion above,[72] there may be some doubt as to whether the obligation of a director not to place himself in a position where his personal interests conflict with his duties to the company would come within the terms of this expression. We do not consider that it would be appropriate to seek to resolve this issue in the limited context of our proposals on the derivative action, since it has far wider implications for company and trust law generally. However, we consider that the legislation should make it clear that a derivative action is

---

[67] See para 6.30 above.

[68] See paras 6.5, 6.37 and 6.41.

[69] For example, the failure to obtain approval for a substantial property transaction involving a director, under s 320. See *British Racing Drivers' Club Ltd v Hextall Erskine & Co (a firm)* [1997] 1 BCLC 182.

[70] Which avoids certain provisions exempting officers and auditors from liability.

[71] Which gives the court power to grant relief in certain cases.

[72] See paras 6.25-6.26 above.

available where a cause of action arises as a result of a director putting himself in a position where his personal interests conflict with his duties to the company.

6.49 Accordingly, **we recommend that the new procedure should only be available if the cause of action arises as a result of an actual or threatened act or omission involving (a) negligence, default, breach of duty or breach of trust by a director of the company, or (b) a director putting himself in a position where his personal interests conflict with his duties to the company. The cause of action may be against the director or another person (or both). We also recommend that, for these purposes, director should include a shadow director.**

Who should be able to bring a derivative action

6.50 In the consultation paper we concluded provisionally that there was no justification for permitting former members to bring derivative actions.[73] Our view was that there is bound to be a current member who (if the wrong has not been ratified) could maintain proceedings. We saw no reason why a former member should be able to bring a derivative claim if the current members were not willing to do so. The vast majority of respondents agreed with this view. For these purposes, "member" is defined by section 22 of the Companies Act 1985.[74] **We recommend that the derivative action should be available only to members of the company.**

Extent to which common law rule should be abrogated

Should it entirely replace the common law derivative action

6.51 The vast majority of respondents agreed with the provisional view expressed in the consultation question that "an action which can be brought under the new procedure should only be capable of being so brought, and not also under the exceptions to the rule in *Foss v Harbottle*".[75] The question left open the possibility that derivative actions may still be brought under the common law in

---

[73] See Consultation Paper No 142, para 20.33.

[74] Section 22 provides as follows: "(1) The subscribers of a company's memorandum are deemed to have agreed to become members of the company, and on registration shall be entered as such in its register of members. (2) Every other person who agrees to become a member of a company, and whose name is entered in its register of members, is a member of the company." For a recent decision of the Court of Appeal of the Cayman Islands on the position of beneficial owners, see *Jonasson v Svanstrom* 4 April 1997 (unreported, Cayman Islands CA). See also J Payne, "Derivative Actions by beneficial shareholders" (1997) 18 Company Lawyer 212. As to the ability of a beneficial owner to compel a registered member to bring an action, see *Mutual Life Insurance Co of New York v The Rank Organisation Ltd* [1985] BCLC 11 (in that case, a personal action was brought by a beneficial owner to enforce the articles of association). Section 459(2) extends the meaning of "member" to include a person who has acquired shares by operation of law, and thus to include the case of a personal representative who may have been refused registration (see para 4.57, n 68 above), but we do not consider that a similar extension is required or appropriate in the case of a derivative action.

[75] Consultation Paper No 142, para 16.13.

circumstances which fell outside the new procedure.[76] However, it was apparent that many respondents considered that the new procedure should entirely replace the existing common law right to bring a derivative action.

6.52   Having considered the matter further, and in the light of the responses to the consultation paper, we consider that it would be desirable for the new procedure to replace entirely the common law right to bring a derivative action. In the consultation paper we quoted the following comments on the Canadian legislation:[77]

> It would only lead to confusion to allow both common law and statutory actions. A more orderly development of the law would result from one point of access to a derivative action and would allow a body of experience and precedent to build up to guide shareholders.[78]

6.53   We noted that diverging principles might develop between the new procedure and the procedure at common law which would add to the current confusion. This would go against our stated aim of making the law simpler. We consider that the only way to avoid this problem is for the new procedure to replace the common law derivative action entirely.

6.54   As explained in the consultation paper and noted above,[79] it is not only under the fraud on the minority exception that a shareholder can bring a derivative action. He can also bring one for loss caused by an ultra vires or illegal transaction. He also appears to have the option to bring one in respect of breaches of special resolution procedures.[80] We propose that these situations should also be replaced by the new derivative procedure so that they will be subject to the new restrictions and procedures discussed in this part.[81] We consider that where a director causes a company to enter into an ultra vires or illegal transaction or one for which a special majority is required he will be regarded as having acted in breach of duty for the purposes of the new derivative procedure.

---

[76]   The issue here is the right to bring a *derivative* action; not the right to bring a personal action, for example in respect of transactions requiring approval of a special majority, as the view is taken in the consultation paper that these fall outside the rule entirely. See para 6.56 below.

[77]   See Consultation Paper No 142, para 16.13.

[78]   S Beck, "The Shareholders' Derivative Action" (1974) 52 Can Bar Rev 159. In Canada this objective is met, however, not by express abrogation of the rule but by requiring that no derivative action be brought without the leave of the court and by laying down conditions for the granting of leave. In New Zealand the legislation expressly provides that no derivative action can be brought except as provided in the section creating the statutory derivative action; and the draft Australian provision abolishes the common law right to bring a derivative action. See Consultation Paper No 142, para 16.12 and Appendices F & G.

[79]   See para 6.3, n 9.

[80]   On the right to bring a personal action in respect of breaches of special resolution procedures, see para 6.56 below.

[81]   A shareholder will of course continue to be able to bring a personal action in respect of breaches of special resolution procedures which will not be subject to these restrictions; see para 6.57 below.

6.55 As indicated above,[82] there may be a few very rare cases which could have been brought as derivative actions under the common law but will not come within the terms of the new procedure. But we consider that if we are to put the derivative action on a new, simpler and more rational basis then this is something which cannot be avoided. As we have explained, we consider that our proposals set logical and clearly identifiable limits on the availability of the action. For any exceptional cases of hardship, there is still the possibility of bringing proceedings under section 459 and, if appropriate, seeking an order that proceedings may be brought on the company's behalf under section 461(2)(c). **We therefore recommend that the new derivative procedure should replace the common law derivative action entirely.**

Personal actions

6.56 In the consultation paper, we drew particular attention to cases falling under the fourth limb of the restatement of the rule in *Prudential*, namely claims to establish the invalidity of a transaction for which a special majority is required.[83] It appears that such actions can be brought either as derivative or personal actions. To the extent that they can be brought as personal actions, these are clearly situations where the rule in *Foss v Harbottle* does not apply. Our provisional view was that as these fell outside the rule in *Foss v Harbottle*, there was no reason why any special rules should apply to them. A member should be able to continue to bring a personal action without the need to obtain the leave of the court, or to satisfy any other particular procedural requirement. The majority of respondents agreed with our provisional view and we therefore consider that no special provision should be made for actions in respect of transactions requiring a special majority.[84]

6.57 More generally, we do not intend that our proposals in respect of the derivative action should affect any existing personal actions. We have noted above that, in addition to claims in respects of transactions requiring a special majority, a personal action may be brought to restrain an ultra vires or illegal act.[85] A personal action may also be brought in respect of breaches of personal rights arising under the company's constitution.[86] Our proposals are not intended to affect the circumstances in which or the manner in which such actions may be brought.

---

[82] See paras 6.27-6.34 above.

[83] See Consultation Paper No 142, para 16.14.

[84] A shareholder does, however, currently have the option of bringing a derivative action in respect of breaches of special resolution procedures; see *Quin & Axtens Ltd v Salmon* [1909] AC 442 and Consultation Paper No 142, para 16.14. It is proposed that this should only be possible in future in so far as it comes within the new derivative procedure; see para 6.54 above.

[85] See para 6.3.

[86] See paras 7.2-7.11 below.

Procedural steps

Notice to the company

6.58   We provisionally recommended that notice to the company should be a precondition to the grant of leave to a shareholder to maintain a derivative action. The notice period should be 28 days and the notice should specify the grounds of the proposed derivative action. However, we provisionally recommended that the requirement for notice should be waived if the shareholder could show that urgent relief was required, and/or if the court dispensed with the requirement.[87]

6.59   The vast majority of respondents agreed with the provisional recommendations. Several respondents suggested that 28 days was too short as the company may have to investigate the claim and then call a meeting to decide what action to take. We accept that there may need to be some flexibility but consider that this could be achieved under the general rules.[88] **We therefore recommend that:**

    (1)   unless the court otherwise orders, a claimant should be required to give notice to the company of its intention to bring a derivative action at least 28 days before the commencement of proceedings;

    (2)   the notice should specify the grounds of the proposed derivative action.[89]

Company fails diligently to pursue proceedings

6.60   We also drew attention to the situation where, on receipt of notice, a company commences an action but fails diligently to pursue it. We considered that it should be open to a shareholder to apply to the court for leave to take over the action in these circumstances, and that the court should have to consider the same criteria for leave as those which we proposed for derivative actions generally.[90]

6.61   Having given further thought to this point, we do not consider that the possibility of a shareholder taking over an action commenced by the company should be tied specifically to the situation where the company commences proceedings *following* receipt of a notice in the manner described above. The company could pre-empt the giving of notice by commencing proceedings before receipt of the notice with

---

[87]   Consultation Paper No 142, paras 16.15-16.17.

[88]   Rule 5(1)(c) of the Draft Civil Proceedings Rules permits the court to extend or shorten the time for compliance with any rule, practice direction or order or direction of the court. However, see n 89 below. If the notice requirement were to be included in a pre-action protocol then we consider that it should be sufficiently flexible to allow the company more time to consider the claim in appropriate cases.

[89]   We have incorporated this recommendation into the draft rule in Appendix B (Rule 50.4), as it is an integral part of the procedure that we are recommending. However, it may be that this provision should properly appear in a pre-action protocol or Practice Direction as it does not concern the procedure in court. The proposed primary legislation for Scotland contains a specific provision for notice to be given by a shareholder wishing to bring a shareholder's action (analogous to the derivative action under English law) (see s 458B(3)-(5) in clause 1(1) of the draft Bill at Appendix A) but we do not consider that a similar provision is required for England and Wales.

[90]   See paras 6.70-6.92 below.

no real intention of pursuing the proceedings. The shareholder would have only limited redress in these circumstances.[91] We therefore propose a slightly different scheme for this rule.

6.62   What we recommend is that a shareholder should be able to apply to continue, as a derivative action, proceedings commenced by the company where: (a) the claim is capable of being pursued as a derivative action;[92] (b) the company has failed to prosecute the claim diligently; and (c) the manner in which the company has commenced and continued the action amounts to an abuse of the process of the court.[93]

6.63   This last requirement is proposed in order to prevent undue interference with existing litigation by shareholders. We do not want individual shareholders to apply to take over current litigation being pursued by their company just because they are not happy with the progress being made. The provision is intended to deal with those situations where the company's real intention in commencing proceedings is to *prevent* a successful claim being brought. In the recent case of *Grovit v Doctor*,[94] the court held that for a plaintiff to commence and to continue litigation which he had no intention to bring to a conclusion could amount to an abuse of process for the purposes of an application to strike out. We consider that an action commenced by a company for the purposes of preventing a shareholder bringing a derivative action and which it has no real intention of bringing to a conclusion would amount to an abuse of the process of the court for the purposes of the new rule we are proposing.

6.64   As before, we consider that in considering the application to continue the proceedings as a derivative action, the court should consider all the circumstances including the factors specifically set out in connection with the application for leave to continue a derivative action.[95] If, for example, it forms the view that it is not in the interests of the company for the action to proceed, it should dismiss the application to continue it as a derivative action.[96]

6.65   Accordingly, **we recommend that a shareholder should be able to apply to continue, as a derivative action, proceedings commenced by the company where:**

   (1)   **the claim is capable of being pursued as a derivative action;**

   (2)   **the company has failed to prosecute the claim diligently; and**

---

[91]   The shareholder might be able to bring an action against the directors for breach of duty in failing to pursue the proceedings diligently, but he would not be able to pursue proceedings in respect of the original cause of action.

[92]   In particular, it must be a cause of action arising out of a breach of duty by a director; see paras 6.24-6.37 above.

[93]   See Draft Rule 50.9, Appendix B.

[94]   [1997] 1 WLR 640.

[95]   See para 6.70 and paras 6.75-6.91 below.

[96]   See Draft Rule 50.10 and 50.11, Appendix B.

(3) **the manner in which the company has commenced and continued the action amounts to an abuse of the process of the court.**

Consideration by the court

6.66 Our provisional view was that the court should normally consider the matter of leave at close of pleadings, but should be able to do so earlier, and that the application should normally be heard by a judge rather than a master. We also provisionally recommended that all parties to the proceedings should be parties to the application, should be entitled to receive evidence filed on it, and should be present at the hearing unless the court orders otherwise.

6.67 Most respondents who commented agreed with this view. There was some concern that it should be open to a company to dispose of vexatious litigation at an early stage (some respondents thought that leave should be sought before the action was started), and that the close of pleadings may be too late. As we explained in the consultation paper, case management conferences will be a feature of many cases under the reforms proposed by Lord Woolf.[97] Our provisional view was that where there is to be a case management conference, it will normally be convenient for the issue of leave to be dealt with at this stage. We remain of this view. Indeed, on further consideration, we consider that it would be appropriate to require the court fix a case management conference for all derivative actions.[98] Normally, all parties to the proceedings will be present at the case management conference.[99] We accept that it may be appropriate for the leave hearing to be dealt with earlier in some cases and we consider that it should be within the court's powers to direct an earlier hearing. In an appropriate case it may also be possible for a respondent to apply to strike out the claim at the outset.

6.68 On the application for leave, we recommend that the court should have the power to do the following: grant leave to continue the claim for such period and on such terms as it thinks fit; refuse leave and dismiss the claim; strike out the claim; or adjourn the proceedings relating to the application and give such directions as it thinks fit.[100] If the claimant does not apply for leave at the case management conference (or at such earlier time as the court directs), we recommend that the defendant should be able to apply to strike out the claim.[101]

6.69 Accordingly, **we recommend that:**

(1) **where a derivative action is brought, the court must fix a case management conference;**

(2) **unless the court otherwise directs, the claimant must seek leave to continue the derivative action at the case management conference.**

---

[97] See LCD Working Paper on Judicial Case Management, paras 4.6-4.9.

[98] See Draft Rule 50.5, Appendix B.

[99] See LCD Working Paper on Judicial Case Management, para 4.8.

[100] See Draft Rule 50.8(1), Appendix B.

[101] See Draft Rule 50.6(3), Appendix B.

Issues relevant to grant of leave

6.70 Our provisional view was that in considering the issue of leave the court should take into account all the relevant circumstances without limit.[102] However, we also listed five specific matters which we considered the court should take into account; the applicant's good faith; the interests of the company; that the wrong has been, or may be, approved in general meeting; the views of an independent organ; and the availability of alternative remedies. We proposed that these matters should be set out expressly in rules of court. An additional matter which was not specifically mentioned in the consultation paper, but which we consider should be included in this list, is a decision by the company in general meeting not to sue.[103] We consider each of these matters in turn, but first consider a further issue which we raised, namely whether there should be a threshold test on the merits.

Threshold test

6.71 Our provisional view was that there should be no threshold test on the merits of the case.[104] Our main reason for this was that the inclusion of an express test would increase the risk of a detailed investigation into the merits of the case taking place at the leave stage, and that such a "mini-trial" would be time consuming and expensive. There would of course be some consideration of the merits, since it would clearly be wrong for the court to allow an obviously hopeless case to proceed.[105] But we considered that it would be undesirable to encourage the parties to bring evidence to show that the case met or failed to meet a particular merits test.

6.72 Most respondents who considered this issue agreed with this approach and we remain of the view that there should be no threshold test. We consider that including a specific threshold test would lead to fine distinctions being drawn as to whether the facts of individual cases fall on one or other side of a particular line drawn and we consider that this is undesirable. We consider that it is preferable for the courts to develop a principled approach which is not tied to the rigid language of a particular rule or statutory provision. Accordingly, **we recommend that there should be no threshold test on the merits.**

Court to consider all the relevant circumstances

6.73 The majority of respondents agreed with the provisional view that the court should consider all the relevant circumstances without limit. One or two expressed concern that this would mean that the reasons for deciding whether a claim should proceed were vague and that it would make it difficult to advise clients

---

[102] See Consultation Paper No 142, para 16.25.

[103] This is considered, along with the question of whether the wrong has been, or may be, approved in general meeting, under the general heading "authorisation and ratification"; see paras 6.80-6.87 below.

[104] *Ibid*, at para 16.22.

[105] Apart from the exercise of the court's discretion to grant leave under the new procedure, the court will have the power to dismiss a case or part of a case on the grounds that it has no realistic prospect of success under the proposed new Civil Procedure Rules; see para 2.13 above.

with any certainty as to what the result of an application would be. However, we consider that it is important for the court to have the flexibility to look at all the relevant circumstances. There is a danger that any definitive criteria for granting leave would be incomplete and would not fit the circumstances of individual cases. We also consider that the concerns about the difficulties in predicting the outcome of applications for leave are overstated. As indicated, we also proposed a list of specific matters which the court should take into account, and we consider that these, together with the developing case law, will assist practitioners in advising their clients. **We therefore recommend that in considering the issue of leave the court should take account of all the relevant circumstances without limit.**

6.74   We now consider the specific matters which we recommended the court should take into account in considering the issue of leave together with the additional matter which we consider should be added to this list.[106] As we explained in the consultation paper, we consider that these matters should be set out in an express statement in the rules of court.[107]

Applicant's good faith

6.75   The first matter which we considered the court should take into account was the good faith of the applicant. We noted that it was unlikely that a court would grant leave to an applicant whom it considered was acting in bad faith (so that it may not be necessary to state this factor specifically) but considered that since it is a relevant criterion it was of sufficient importance to be mentioned expressly. Although we favoured the test of "honestly and with no ulterior motive"[108] we did not make any recommendation on whether "good faith" should be defined for these purposes. Our view was also that while the applicant's good faith was relevant, it should not be a prerequisite for leave.

6.76   There was virtually unanimous support for the view that the court should take account of the applicants good faith and the majority of those commenting also agreed that it should not be a prerequisite. Most of those commenting also considered that good faith should not be defined. A number of respondents made the point that it would be extremely difficult to define, but was generally readily recognisable. We agree. The applicant may benefit commercially if he succeeds in the derivative action, and thus has an ulterior motive in bringing it. But nonetheless, the court may consider that he is an appropriate person to bring the action and that the action ought to be brought. **We therefore recommend that the good faith of the applicant should be taken into account by the court but it should not be a prerequisite and should not be defined.**

---

[106]   See para 6.70 above and para 6.87 below.

[107]   See Consultation Paper No 142, para 16.44. Our provisional view received support from a large majority of respondents. See Draft Rule 50 at Appendix B.

[108]   As applied by Lord Denning MR in *Central Estates (Belgravia) Ltd v Woolgar* [1972] 1 QB 48, 55 (construing the Leasehold Reform Act 1967, sched 3 para 4(1)) and by Plowman J in *Smith v Morrison* [1974] 1 WLR 659, 676 (construing the Land Registration (Official Searches) Rules 1969).

Interests of the company

6.77 The second matter which we considered the court should take into account was the interests of the company. In doing so, the court should have regard to the views of directors on commercial matters. Again, we suggested that this should be a relevant criterion, but the court should not be bound to refuse leave if the proceedings were not in the interests of the company.

6.78 Although a majority of respondents agreed with our provisional view, there was some concern expressed on this last point. A significant number of respondents took the view that if the proceedings were not in the interests of the company, the court should refuse leave.

6.79 We remain of the view that it would not be appropriate to require an applicant to prove that the action was in the interests of the company in order to obtain leave. If this approach were taken in respect of all the factors which we have set out, it would have the effect of laying down a number of hurdles which an applicant would have to overcome in order to obtain leave to continue the proceedings, and lead to detailed argument on whether the applicant had (or had not) satisfied each of the relevant criteria. This may have the effect of lengthening the leave stage and adding to the costs. However, we do accept that if a court is satisfied that the proceedings are not in the interests of the company there is no reason why the proceedings should continue and the court should refuse leave.[109] Accordingly, **we recommend that the court should take account of the interests of the company, and in doing so the court should have regard to the views of directors on commercial matters;[110] however, the court should refuse leave if it is satisfied that the proceedings are not in the interests of the company.**

Authorisation and ratification

6.80 Under the current law, if a wrong[111] has been effectively ratified by the company, this will be a complete bar to a derivative action. The wrong will have been cured so that there is no cause of action in respect of which the company (and therefore the shareholder through the derivative action) can bring proceedings. In addition, if a wrong is *capable* of being ratified (ie it is ratifiable), then even if there has been no formal ratification, it may not be possible for a minority shareholder to bring a derivative action.[112]

6.81 The law on ratification is by no means clear, although we sought to resolve some of the apparent inconsistencies in the case law in our discussion of this topic in the

---

[109] See Draft Rule 50.8(3), Appendix B.

[110] This does not of course mean that the court would be bound to accept the views of the directors. The existence of a conflict of interest may affect the weight to be given to them, and the court would give no weight to views which no reasonable director in that position could hold.

[111] We include, for this purpose, the situation where a director puts himself in a position where his personal interests conflict with his duties to the company; see para 6.48 above.

[112] See, for example, *MacDougall v Gardiner* (1875) 1 Ch D 13.

consultation paper.[113] As we noted in the consultation paper,[114] where a shareholder can show fraud and wrongdoer control, purported ratification of the acts in question will be a manifestation of wrongdoer control and will not prevent a minority shareholder from bringing a derivative action. The issue of ratification is therefore closely tied up with the whole question of fraud on the minority, and in order to understand when ratification may be effective it is necessary to examine many old authorities on what constitutes fraud on the minority. There is a danger that our desire to simplify the derivative action could be undermined by the complexities which arise where it is claimed that the relevant breach of duty has been (or may be) ratified.

6.82   As we noted in the consultation paper, a number of other jurisdictions have dealt with this point by providing that ratification should only be treated as an issue which the court should take into account.[115] In framing our provisional recommendations we drew on the provisions in these other jurisdictions, but we also made it clear that our view was that "if [the ratification] was effective in law to cure the breach of duty of which the applicant complained, the court would have to dismiss any claims based on that breach of duty".[116]

6.83   The issue of whether effective ratification should be a complete bar to a derivative action was not directly addressed by many respondents and so it is difficult to draw any conclusive results from the consultation on this point. However, a number of respondents did express serious objections to any change to the substantive law of ratification, not least because of the uncertainty that this would create in certain commercial situations.

6.84   Our view remains that ratification should continue to be effective in the cases where it is currently effective to bar an action by a minority shareholder,[117] but will otherwise be only a factor to which the court has regard. In other words, the fact that a wrong is *ratifiable* will not prevent a shareholder from commencing a derivative action. However, if there *has been* effective ratification, then the action cannot proceed as there will be no subsisting cause of action vested in the company which the shareholder can pursue.[118] In some cases, a minority shareholder's action has been struck out because the wrong was ratifiable without the court investigating whether ratification would take place.[119] Thus, to a small extent, our recommendation represents a change from the position under the current law. Of course, if the court is faced with a derivative action in respect of a wrong which is ratifiable but has not been ratified, it will be open to it to adjourn

---

[113]   See Consultation Paper No 142, paras 5.6-5.17.

[114]   *Ibid*, at para 5.7.

[115]   *Ibid*, at paras 16.35-16.36.

[116]   *Ibid*, at para 16.37.

[117]   As in s 322(2)(c) of the Companies Act 1985.

[118]   This point is made clear in Draft Rule 50.8(4), Appendix B.

[119]   See, eg, *MacDougall v Gardiner* (1875) LR 10 Ch App 606; cf *Bamford v Bamford* [1970] Ch 212.

the proceedings to allow a meeting to be called for the purposes of ratification.[120] Alternatively, if it is clear that the wrong will be ratified and that no purpose will be served in holding a meeting, the court can use its discretion to refuse leave for the action to proceed.[121] Given that the project is only concerned with remedies and not, for example, with directors' duties, we do not consider that it would be within our terms of reference to consider substantive changes to the law of ratification.

6.85 We also consider that there are considerable practical difficulties with an approach which would remove the binding nature of ratification which is effective under the current law. We have already drawn attention to the uncertainty that this may cause in certain transactions.[122] As one respondent put it, the current position would be "replaced by a general discretion of the court to undo transactions or to make the directors responsible for compensating the company." Although there may be a case for modernising and simplifying the law of ratification, we are of the firm view that any changes need to be considered in the context of a comprehensive review of directors' duties. It would not be appropriate to make piecemeal changes in the context of our current project on shareholder remedies which may have wider implications. We do not therefore propose any change to the substantive law on ratification.

6.86 **We therefore recommend that the court should take account of the fact that the wrong has been, or may be, approved by the company in general meeting; but that effective ratification should continue to be a complete bar to the continuation of a derivative action.**[123]

6.87 It is open to a majority of members to resolve that no action should be taken to remedy a wrong done to the company. Such a resolution, if made in good faith and what they consider to be for the benefit of the company, will bind the minority.[124] This is not the same as ratification, which has the effect of curing the wrong.[125] Nor is it the same as taking account of the views of an independent organ,[126] which involves considering the views of a particular group within the company. Although not specifically mentioned in the consultation paper, this is

---

[120] See paras 6.100-6.103 below.

[121] See *Re Savoy Hotel Ltd* [1981] Ch 351.

[122] It would also be inconsistent with our second and fifth guiding principles.

[123] There may well be other situations in which the court would have to dismiss the action, eg if there had been a binding release; see para 6.87, n 125 below.

[124] *Taylor v National Union of Mineworkers (Derbyshire Area)* [1985] BCLC 237, 255. See also *Smith v Croft (No 3)* [1987] BCLC 355.

[125] In *Taylor v National Union of Mineworkers (Derbyshire Area)* Vinelott J made it clear that such a resolution could be effective even if the wrong could not be ratified by any majority of the members; *ibid*, at p 254. Vinelott J also drew a distinction between a resolution not to sue and a binding release. The draft rule set out in Appendix B does not refer to a release but the existence of such a release is one of the matters to which the court would have regard. If it was binding, the derivative action would have to be dismissed. We have not considered the effect of s 310 of the Companies Act 1985 on such a release.

[126] See paras 6.88-6.89 below.

clearly a matter which the court should take into account in considering whether to grant leave. Accordingly, **we recommend that the court should take account of the fact that the company in general meeting has resolved not to pursue the cause of action.**

Views of independent organ

6.88 As we pointed out in the consultation paper,[127] even if there has been no approval (or purported approval) of the wrong, the court may be informed of commercial reasons why the shareholders (or a group of shareholders), or even the directors or a committee of the directors consider that the action should not proceed. The term "independent organ" was used by Knox J in the case of *Smith v Croft (No 2)*[128] to describe a group of persons within the company whose views would be taken into account for these purposes. Essentially these are persons whose votes would not be disregarded on the grounds that they had been (or would be) "cast with a view to supporting the defendants rather than securing benefit to the company, or that the situation of the person whose vote is considered is such that there is a substantial risk of that happening."[129] Our provisional view was that the views of such an independent organ should be one of the factors which the court should take into account under the new derivative procedure in deciding whether to grant leave.

6.89 Almost all of the respondents who commented agreed with our provisional view. One or two expressed concern that the meaning of "independent organ" was not clear. However, our view is that it is not appropriate to define what this means in the rules. Knox J made clear that the appropriate independent organ will vary according to the constitution of the company concerned and the identity of the defendants.[130] We consider that the courts should be allowed to continue to develop the concept of "independent organ" in line with the current authorities.

6.90 Accordingly, **we recommend that the court should take account of the views of an independent organ that for commercial reasons the action should or should not be pursued, but as the law in this area is still in a state of development and should be left to be developed by the courts, the new rule should not provide that its views should be conclusive on the issue whether or not leave should be granted.**

Availability of alternative remedies

6.91 The final matter which we considered should be included in the list of matters which the court should take into account was the availability of other remedies. The case of *Barrett v Duckett*[131] suggests that this is a matter that the courts will

---

[127] Consultation Paper No 142, para 16.38.

[128] [1988] Ch 144.

[129] *Ibid*, at p 186.

[130] *Ibid*, at p 185. See also generally Consultation Paper No 142, paras 4.27-4.29.

[131] [1995] 1 BCLC 243.

take into account under the current law.[132] There was virtually unanimous support for this from respondents, and **we therefore recommend that the court should take account of the availability of alternative remedies, but that their availability should not necessarily be conclusive on the issue of whether or not leave should be granted.**

6.92　We explained in the consultation paper that a member cannot bring a derivative action if the company is in liquidation.[133] We intend that this should still be the position under our new procedure.

Proper plaintiff principle

6.93　As we made clear in the consultation paper,[134] in the absence of circumstances justifying the grant of leave, we consider that the proper plaintiff principle should apply since, in the words of the Court of Appeal in *Prudential*[135] it "... is fundamental to any rational system of jurisprudence".[136]

Other relevant provisions

Nature of derivative action

6.94　In the consultation paper we explained that derivative actions are brought in "representative" form; that is to say, the title to the proceedings will state that the plaintiff sues on behalf of himself and all other shareholders in the company other than the defendants.[137] Since the company has not authorised the action, the company's name cannot be used. The company must also be named as a defendant. We consider that derivative actions should continue to be brought in this manner and that the rules should provide that any decision of the court is binding on the other shareholders on whose behalf the action is brought.[138] This will prevent a different shareholder seeking to bring a derivative claim in respect of the same cause of action at a later date (since he will be bound by the result of the derivative action which has already been brought).[139]

---

[132]　See Consultation Paper No 142, para 5.19.

[133]　*Ibid*, at para 5.20. See also *Watts v Midland Bank* [1986] BCLC 15.

[134]　*Ibid*, at para 16.41. All but one of the respondents agreed with our provisional view.

[135]　[1982] Ch 204.

[136]　*Ibid*, at p 210.

[137]　Consultation Paper No 142, para 6.5.

[138]　See Draft Rule 50.2, Appendix B.

[139]　If one shareholder brought a derivative action in respect of a cause of action, and another shareholder brought a second derivative action in respect of the same cause of action while the first was continuing, it is considered that the court would have the power to revoke any leave that it had given in the action which ought to be stayed, or to stay one of the actions under s 49(3) of the Supreme Court Act 1981; see generally the notes to the *Supreme Court Practice* 1997 vol 2, paras 5202 and 5237 and the cases there cited, for instance *Slough Estates Ltd v Slough Borough Council* [1968] Ch 299. In that case the court held that a plaintiff who appealed to the Minister in respect of the grant of conditional planning permission and then issued proceedings in the High Court to determine the validity of the planning permission should be put to its election as to which remedy to pursue. It was common ground that to

6.95   However, an order of the court against a member who is only a represented party (for example for costs) cannot be enforced without the court's leave.[140]

6.96   Accordingly, **we recommend that the action should be brought on behalf of all the company's members other than any who are defendants, and a decision of the court should be binding on all the members on whose behalf the action is brought. However, any decision of the court should not be enforced against a person who is not a party to the proceedings without the court's permission.**

Additional qualifying requirement

6.97   In the consultation paper we considered and provisionally rejected a requirement that the applicant should have been a shareholder for a minimum period of time.[141] The vast majority of respondents agreed with the provisional view and we remain of the view that there should be no such additional qualifying requirement.

6.98   Also, the applicant need not have been a shareholder at the time when the alleged wrong occurred. The right to bring proceedings as a shareholder in respect of the wrong is part of the bundle of rights represented by a share and can be transferred to a transferee.

Court's power to appoint an independent expert

6.99   We also recommended that the court should not have a special power to appoint an independent expert to investigate and advise on the action along the lines of proposals in the draft Australian legislation.[142] Again, this was supported by most respondents and we maintain our provisional view on this point.

Court's power to adjourn to enable the company to call a meeting

6.100   As part of the court's case management powers in relation to derivative actions, we also provisionally recommended that the rules should expressly provide that the court has power to direct the company to convene a meeting of the shareholders to consider a resolution as to whether the proceedings should be continued.[143] At the same time, we raised for consideration the question of whether the court should have additional powers to determine whether any shareholder should or should not be permitted to vote at such a meeting.

---

obtain a stay the defendants had to establish: (1) duplication between two sets of proceedings; (2) oppression, vexation or abuse of the process of the court resulting from the continuation of the proceedings sought to be stayed; and (3) the absence of any other consideration against the relief sought (ie the application for a stay). In that case the plaintiff was the party seeking both to appeal to the Minister and to pursue the High Court proceedings, but it is considered that similar considerations would apply where different parties seek to pursue the same claim on a representative basis.

[140]   As in Draft Rule 20.3(2) of the Draft Civil Proceedings Rules which deals with other kinds of representative actions.

[141]   Consultation Paper No 142, para 16.45.

[142]   *Ibid*, at para 16.47.

[143]   *Ibid*, at para 17.7.

6.101   A large majority of respondents agreed with our recommendation but a significant number expressed reservations on the second aspect which we raised for consideration. The point was made that it was a very radical step to "disenfranchise" a shareholder. It was also pointed out that it may involve pre-judging the issue before the evidence was properly heard; when the court ordered the meeting to be convened, it may not be clear which members are connected with the board and the matters complained of.

6.102   In the light of the responses received, we agree that it would not be helpful or appropriate to give the court power to determine whether a shareholder should or should not be permitted to vote. In so far as any resolution passed purports to ratify or release the relevant cause of action, it will be up to the court on normal principles to decide whether the ratification or release is effective.[144] This it can do in the light of the evidence of the circumstances of the vote and the interests of the relevant parties. We do not consider that it is necessary or helpful for the court to decide *before the meeting* who may or may not vote on the issue. Where the resolution seeks in more general terms to elicit the views of members on whether legal proceedings should be pursued or continued, then the result of the vote will also provide the court with the information it requires (in particular on the views of any "independent organ")[145] without the need for additional powers to alter voting rights.

6.103   So far as the terms of the relevant rule are concerned, we consider, on reflection, that it is the power to grant an adjournment which needs to be expressed, rather than the power to direct the company to convene a meeting.[146] Accordingly, **we recommend that the rules on derivative actions should provide that the court has power to adjourn a hearing to enable a meeting of shareholders to be convened for the purpose of considering a resolution affecting the claim.**

Costs indemnity orders

6.104   We provisionally recommended that the court's power to make costs indemnity orders in derivative actions should remain unchanged and this view received virtually unanimous support on consultation.[147]

[144]   A resolution of the company in general meeting not to pursue the cause of action may also prevent proceedings being commenced or continued; see para 6.87 above.

[145]   See paras 6.88-6.90 above.

[146]   See *Prudential Assurance Co Ltd v Newman Industries Ltd (No 2)* [1982] Ch 204, 222 and *Hogg v Cramphorn* [1967] 1 Ch 254, 270. The court does have powers under the Companies Act 1985 to direct that a meeting be convened in certain circumstances (eg s 371), but we are not proposing any changes to these powers. For a recent discussion of s 371 where the Court of Appeal held that the court had no jurisdiction to affect shareholders' voting rights, see *Ross v Telford, The Times* 4 July 1997.

[147]   The proposed primary legislation for Scotland contains a specific provision giving the courts power to make cost indemnity orders (see s 458B(8) in clause 1(1) of the Bill) but the court already has this power in England and Wales; see eg *Wallersteiner v Moir (No 2)* [1975] QB 373.

Court's power to substitute claimant

6.105   We drew attention in the consultation paper to the fact that it may be appropriate for the court to substitute a new plaintiff in the derivative action, for example if the existing plaintiff has some conflict of interest which makes him unsuitable to be a representative plaintiff.[148] We suggested that the court's existing power to add or substitute parties should be sufficient for these purposes.

6.106   The relevant provisions on the addition and substitution of parties under the Draft Civil Proceedings Rules are contained in Part 18. These are currently being reviewed by the Lord Chancellor's Department as part of the continuing work on the implementation of the new rules.

Leave of the court for discontinuance or compromise of proceedings

6.107   We also provisionally recommended that the rules governing the new derivative action should provide that the applicant should not enter into any compromise or abandon the proceedings without the leave of the court.[149] We pointed out that the absence of such a provision could give rise to serious possibilities of collusion, with the directors buying off the plaintiff in disregard of the rights of the company and its members.[150] Our provisional view was widely supported on consultation, and accordingly **we recommend that the rules should provide that no proceedings brought by a shareholder under the provisions relating to derivative actions may be discontinued or compromised without the leave of the court.**

Remedy

6.108   A further issue which we raised was whether it should be open to the court to make an order granting a personal benefit to the shareholder bringing the derivative action, such as an order that the defendant wrongdoers buy the claimant's shares.[151] We provisionally rejected this suggestion and our provisional view has been confirmed on consultation.

Multiple derivative actions

6.109   Finally, in connection with the new derivative procedure, we raised the issue of whether a shareholder in a parent company should be able to bring a derivative action on behalf of a subsidiary or associated company within the group (which

---

[148]   See Consultation Paper No 142, para 17.9.

[149]   *Ibid*, at para 17.10.

[150]   At para 2.116 of the LCD Working Paper on Judicial Case Management, it is suggested that where parties fail to take steps in an action for a certain period of time the new Civil Procedure Rules might provide for the court to issue an order that unless the parties take steps within a specified period the case would be presumed settled (a settlement order). A failure by the claimant to take those steps pursuant to an agreement with other parties is likely to be a compromise which requires the leave of the court. Clearly if the suggestion in the Working Paper is implemented, care will have to be taken so that it is not possible for a claimant in a derivative action to avoid the requirement for court leave for a compromise of the action by colluding in a situation in which the court makes a settlement order.

[151]   Consultation Paper No 142, paras 16.48-16.50.

we referred to, for simplicity, as a "multiple derivative action").[152] We expressed no provisional view but invited comments on this point.

6.110 Although a small majority of respondents who addressed this issue did consider that provision should be made for multiple derivative actions, we are not persuaded that it would be helpful or practicable to include such a provision. We consider that this situation is likely to be extremely rare and that any rule attempting to deal with it would be complicated and unlikely to be able to cover every conceivable situation. We consider that the question of multiple derivative actions is best left to the courts to resolve, if necessary using the power under section 461(2)(c) of the Companies Act 1985 to bring a derivative action. Accordingly, we do not consider that there should be any express provision dealing with multiple derivative actions.

Conclusion

6.111 To summarise, we recommend that the right to bring a derivative action at common law should be replaced by a simpler and more modern procedure. We recommend that the basis of the right to bring a derivative action should be set out in the Companies Acts,[153] but that the details of the procedure should be set out in rules of court so as to give maximum flexibility.[154]

6.112 The derivative action should be available to current members of the company where the cause of action arises as a result of an actual or proposed act or omission involving negligence, default, breach of duty or breach of trust by a director, or a director putting himself in a position where his personal interests conflict with his duties to the company (although the claim itself need not be against a director). For these purposes, director should include both shadow and de facto directors. However, derivative claims should be subject to tight judicial control at all stages.

6.113 We recommend that a claimant should be required to give notice to the company of his intention to bring a derivative action at least 28 days before proceedings are commenced. He should be required to obtain leave of the court in order to continue a derivative claim beyond the preliminary stages and in deciding whether to grant leave the court should take into account all the relevant circumstances. These should include: the good faith of the applicant; the interests of the company; the fact that the wrong has been or may be approved by the company in general meeting (but effective ratification should continue to be a complete bar to a derivative action); whether the company in general meeting has resolved not to pursue the cause of action; the views of an independent organ that for commercial reason the action should or should not be pursued; and the availability of alternative remedies. The court should have an express power to adjourn the proceedings to enable a meeting of shareholders to be convened for the purpose of considering a resolution affecting the claim.

---

[152] *Ibid*, at para 16.51. See, eg, *Beck v Value Capital* [1975] 1 WLR 6, 11 B-E.

[153] See clause 1 of the draft Bill at Appendix A.

[154] See Draft Rule 50 at Appendix B.

6.114   The action should continue to be brought on behalf of all the company's members other than any who are defendants, and a decision of the court should be binding on all the members on whose behalf the action is brought. No discontinuance or compromise of the proceedings should be permitted without leave of the court. It should also be possible to continue, as a derivative action, proceedings commenced by the company where the company has failed to prosecute the claim diligently and the manner in which the company has commenced and continued the action amounts to an abuse of the process of the court.

PART 7
OTHER REFORMS

7.1 In this part we consider the other reforms which we canvassed in the consultation paper. These are reform of section 14 of the Companies Act 1985 and pre-action discovery in shareholder proceedings.

Reform of section 14

7.2 The issue with which we are concerned here is the extent to which a shareholder has enforceable rights arising under the company's constitution. The constitutions of companies registered under the Companies Acts comprise two separate documents - the memorandum of association and the articles of association.[1] The legal effect of those documents is set out in section 14 of the Companies Act 1985 which provides that, when registered, they bind the company and its members "to the same extent as if they respectively had been signed and sealed by each member and contained covenants on the part of each member to observe all the provisions of the memorandum and of the articles". In essence, therefore, section 14 creates a contract which forms the basis of legal relations between the company and its members and between the members inter se.[2]

7.3 We drew attention to two potential problems in respect of the rights arising under section 14. The first is that section 14 does not expressly state that the company is bound by its own articles.[3] However, our view was that it is clear on the wording of the section that the company is bound; the only point is that it is not deemed to have executed the articles under seal. As the only practical consequence of this is in relation to the limitation period for actions against the company,[4] and as we

---

[1] In broad terms, the memorandum governs the relationship between the company and the outside world, whereas the articles represent the domestic regulations of the company and govern its internal management.

[2] The precise nature of this statutory contract has been the subject of much academic debate. See, for example: K W Wedderburn, "Shareholders' Rights and the Rule in Foss v Harbottle" [1957] CLJ 194; G D Goldberg, "The Enforcement of Outsider Rights under Section 20 of the Companies Act 1948" (1972) 35 MLR 362; G N Prentice, "The Enforcement of 'Outsider' Rights" (1980) 1 Co Law 179; R Gregory, "The Section 20 Contract" (1981) 44 MLR 526; G D Goldberg, "The Controversy on the Section 20 Contract Revisited" (1985) 48 MLR 158; R Drury, "The Relative Nature of a Shareholder's Right to Enforce the Company Contract" [1986] CLJ 219.

[3] The reason for this is historical. The source of the present wording is the Joint Stock Companies Act 1844 which relied on the existing common law method of forming companies by "deed of settlement", with a trustee covenanting on the part of the company. The Joint Stock Companies Act 1856 subsequently substituted the modern form constitution for the deed of settlement but in adopting wording similar to that now in force it did not take fully into account the new development of the incorporated company as a separate legal entity. See Consultation Paper No 142, paras 2.6-2.8.

[4] This is 6 years. If the articles were deemed to be sealed by the company, the limitation period for claims against it would be 12 years; see *Re Compania de Electricidad de la Provincia de Buenos Aires Ltd* [1980] Ch 146.

were not aware of any particular difficulties to which this gave rise, our provisional view was that there was no reason to amend section 14 in this respect.[5]

7.4 The vast majority of respondents agreed with our provisional view and we therefore remain of the view that there should be no amendment to section 14 to provide that the company is also deemed to have executed the memorandum and articles of association under seal.[6]

7.5 The second potential problem to which we drew attention was the difficulty in identifying enforceable personal rights conferred by the articles. As we explained in the consultation paper,[7] there are restrictions on a member's ability to bring a personal action to enforce the provisions of the articles of association. There are two aspects to this which we examined.

7.6 First, it seems to be generally accepted that the statutory contract only confers rights on a member in his capacity as member (sometimes referred to as "insider rights"), not in any "outsider" capacity such as his position as a solicitor or director of the company.[8] We took the view that examination of these "outsider" rights was beyond the terms of reference of the project,[9] but in any event we considered that there would normally be a contract between the company and the member in his other capacity so that there would be no need for him to seek to rely on the provisions of section 14.[10]

7.7 Secondly, the courts have classified breaches of certain constitutional provisions as "internal irregularities" for which no personal action will lie. This restriction stems from the majority rule and proper plaintiff principles discussed above.[11] The courts have held that if the internal affairs of the company are not being properly managed, then the company is the proper person to complain; there is no use in having litigation "the ultimate end of which is only that a meeting has to be called and then ultimately the majority gets its wishes".[12] But there are cases where shareholders have been entitled to bring claims based on irregularities in voting procedures, such as the wrongful exclusion of proxy votes which would otherwise have resulted in the defeat of a resolution.[13] Similarly, in cases involving defective notices of meetings, or inadequate notice of certain resolutions, the courts have

---

[5] Consultation Paper No 142, para 14.9.

[6] For a brief discussion of changes which have been made to the equivalent provision in Australia to address this point, see Brian R Cheffins, *Company Law: Theory, Structure and Operation* (1997) p 462.

[7] Consultation Paper No 142, paras 2.13-2.27 and 2.39.

[8] *Hickman v Kent or Romney Marsh Sheep Breeders' Association* [1915] 1 Ch 881. See Consultation Paper No 142, paras 2.15-2.20.

[9] *Ibid*, at paras 1.9 and 14.7.

[10] *Ibid*, at para 14.7 and para 2.20, n 41.

[11] See para 6.1 above.

[12] *MacDougall v Gardiner* (1875) 1 Ch D 13, 25.

[13] *Oliver v Dalgleish* [1963] 1 WLR 1274. See also Consultation Paper No 142, para 2.24, n 53.

allowed personal actions to proceed.[14] It was the potential difficulty in identifying membership rights to which the "internal irregularities" restriction did not apply to which we drew attention in the consultation paper.

7.8   Our provisional view, having had preliminary discussions with a number of interested parties, was that no hardship was being caused by any such difficulty. Moreover, we considered that there could never be a comprehensive definition of what constitutes a personal membership right under section 14, since regard has to be had to the terms of the particular articles in question and to the circumstances of the alleged breach.

7.9   We did, however, canvass the possibility of a non-exhaustive list of personal rights enforceable under section 14 to be included in the section.[15] This would set out the rights which the courts have to date allowed shareholders to enforce by personal action, but make it clear that the fact that these rights can be enforced by personal action does not mean that there are not others that can be enforced by the same means.

7.10   We provisionally considered that this would not be a useful addition to the statute for a number of reasons. First, the list could not state every breach of the articles which could give rise to a personal action, and so cases would still arise which were not expressly mentioned. Secondly, breaches of the articles vary from the trivial to the grave. Where they are trivial, we did not want to encourage litigation, and considered that setting out examples in a statute might have just this effect. The list would not reflect the exercise by the court of its discretion to refuse to give remedies for breaches of personal rights, for example, where a meeting had been improperly convened and another could be properly convened and take the same steps. We also reiterated our provisional view that there was no evidence of hardship being caused by the absence of a list, and noted that in practice actions to enforce personal rights appeared to be effectively eclipsed by proceedings under section 459, in which the remedies available are far wider.

7.11   The vast majority of respondents agreed that no hardship was being caused by any difficulty in identifying personal rights conferred by the articles.[16] A large majority also rejected the proposal that there should be a statutory non-exhaustive list of personal rights enforceable under section 14. The reasons given were similar to those set out in the previous paragraph. In the light of the responses to the consultation paper, we remain of the view that there should not be of a statutory non-exhaustive list of personal rights enforceable under section 14.

---

[14]   See, for example, *Alexander v Simpson* (1890) 43 Ch D 139; *Musselwhite v C H Musselwhite & Son* [1962] Ch 964; *Johnson v Lyttle's Iron Agency* (1877) 5 Ch D 687; *Kaye v Croydon Tramways Co* [1898] 1 Ch 358; *Tiessen v Henderson* [1899] 1 Ch 861; *MacConnell v E Prill & Co* [1916] 2 Ch 57.

[15]   See Consultation Paper No 142, paras 20.2-20.4.

[16]   This view is supported by Brian R Cheffins in *Company Law: Theory, Structure and Operation* (1997) where he concludes, at page 462: "Since Australia's experience indicates that reform will not be a straightforward exercise and since there is little direct evidence that section 14 is causing difficulty for shareholders, Parliament should let matters rest for the time being".

7.12 **Accordingly, we do not recommend any reform of section 14 of the Companies Act 1985.**

Pre-action discovery

7.13 Another issue which we raised for consideration, without making any recommendation, was whether shareholders should be given rights of pre-action discovery of relevant documents. There were two aspects to this: pre-action disclosure against persons who are likely to be parties to the proceedings; and pre-action disclosure against persons who are not likely to be parties to the proceedings.[17]

7.14 Under the current law, it is possible to obtain pre-action discovery of documents against persons who are likely to be parties to proceedings involving a claim in respect of personal injury or death,[18] but not in other cases. The Woolf Report recommends that the current rules for personal injury claims should be extended to all cases.[19] At present it is not possible to obtain pre-action disclosure from non-parties,[20] even in relation to claims in respect of personal injury or death. The Woolf Report included a recommendation that in respect of such personal injury and death claims the court's powers should be extended so that it may order a third party to disclose documents before proceedings have begun whether or not it is intended to join them as a defendant.[21] However, Lord Woolf stated: "Without experience of how the power would work in relation to the limited category of personal injury and death claims, I would not put it forward on a wider basis."

7.15 A majority of respondents considered that current discovery rights were generally adequate, although just under half were in favour of having a right of pre-action discovery similar to that available in relation to personal injury claims. The point was made by a number of respondents that there was no compelling reason why shareholder proceedings ought to be treated differently from others. We agree with this last point. Assuming the Woolf proposals on pre-action discovery against potential parties are to be implemented, we see no reason why these should not apply to shareholder proceedings. We see no need for them to be extended to include pre-action discovery against non-parties. If for any reason the Woolf proposals are not implemented, we do not consider that there are particular

---

[17] The issue of discovery against non-parties *during the course of proceedings* was not raised in the consultation paper. At present it is only allowed in personal injury actions; Supreme Court Act 1981, s 34. Rule 27.20 of the Draft Civil Proceedings Rules proposes limited rights of non-party disclosure in all cases (although there is no specific reference to this change in the law in the Woolf Report).

[18] Supreme Court Act 1981, s 33(2).

[19] See Woolf Report, ch 12, paras 48-50 and Recommendation 140; see also Rule 27.19 of the Draft Civil Proceedings Rules.

[20] Ie persons other than those who are likely to be parties to proceedings.

[21] Chapter 12, para 52 and Recommendation 142. However, this recommendation does not appear to have found its way into the Draft Civil Proceedings Rules.

factors which would require special rules[22] to be put in place for shareholder litigation.

7.16 **We do not recommend any extension to the right to disclosure of documents specifically for shareholder proceedings.**

Conclusion

7.17 To summarise, we do not recommend any amendment to section 14 of the Companies Act 1985 to provide that the company is deemed to have executed the memorandum and articles of association under seal. Nor do we recommend any reform to the section to assist in identifying enforceable personal rights conferred by the articles. Our view is that neither of these issues causes hardship in practice.

7.18 We do not see any particular need for specific rules on pre-action discovery in relation to shareholder proceedings.

---

[22] On the other hand, pre-action disclosure might usefully be considered in the context of a pre-action protocol; see para 2.36 above.

PART 8
SUMMARY OF RECOMMENDATIONS

Case management of shareholder proceedings

8.1 We consider that the problems of the excessive length and cost of many proceedings brought under section 459 should be dealt with primarily by active case management by the courts.[1] **(para 2.2)**

8.2 We make the following specific recommendations in this respect.[2]

Preliminary issues

(1) We recommend that greater use should be made of the power to direct that preliminary issues be heard, or that some issues be tried before others. **(para 2.10; no new provision proposed)**

Power to dismiss claim or part of claim or defence which has no realistic prospect of success

(2) We recommend that the court should have the power to dismiss any claim or part of a claim or defence thereto which, in the opinion of the court, has no realistic prospect of success at full trial.[3] **(para 2.18; to be implemented in context of Woolf reforms)**

Adjournment to facilitate ADR

(3) We recommend that the Lord Chancellor consider changes to the 1986 Rules (governing unfair prejudice proceedings) so as to include an express reference to the power to adjourn at any stage to enable the parties to make use of mechanisms for ADR for disposing of the case or any issue in it, together with provisions for reporting back to the court as to the outcome along the lines of the 1996 Commercial Court Practice Statement.[4] **(para 2.22; to be considered by Lord Chancellor)**

---

[1] Active case management for Scotland is a matter for rules of court to be drawn up by the appropriate authority. Where appropriate, the power of the Secretary of State under s 411 of the Insolvency Act 1986 to make rules, so far as it relates to a winding up petition, is also available in relation to a petition under s 459 (by virtue of s 461(6) of the Companies Act 1985). In so far as the matters covered by the recommendations set out in this summary might be appropriate for consideration as regards rules of court for the Scottish courts, any further consultation required in that regard will be a matter for the appropriate rule-making authority.

[2] Although primarily directed at claims brought under s 459, these recommendations apply to all shareholder proceedings unless otherwise indicated.

[3] Assuming this power will be introduced for all proceedings.

[4] Practice Statement (Commercial Cases: Alternative Dispute Resolution) (No 2) [1996] 1 WLR 1024.

Determination of how facts are to be proved

(4) We recommend that the court's power to determine how facts are to be proved should be used pro-actively by the court. **(para 2.24; no new provision proposed)**

Exclusion of issues from determination

(5) We recommend that in shareholder proceedings the court should have the power to exclude an issue from determination if it can do substantive justice between the parties on the other issues and determining it would therefore serve no worthwhile purpose.[5] **(para 2.27; to be implemented in context of Woolf reforms)**

Costs sanctions

(6) We recommend that, in proceedings under section 459, the court should have greater flexibility than at present to make costs orders to reflect the manner in which the successful party has conducted the proceedings and the outcome of individual issues. **(para 2.32; to be implemented in the context of Woolf reforms)**

Presumptions in proceedings under section 459

8.3   We recommend that there should be legislative provision for presumptions in proceedings under sections 459-461 that, in certain circumstances, (a) where a shareholder has been excluded from participation in the management of the company, the conduct will be presumed to be unfairly prejudicial by reason of the exclusion; and (b), if the presumption is not rebutted and the court is satisfied that it ought to order a buy out of the petitioner's shares, it should do so on a pro rata basis. **(para 3.30; clauses 3 & 4)**

8.4   The following conditions should be present for the presumptions to apply:

(1) the company is a private company limited by shares;[6] **(para 3.39)**

(2) the petitioner has been removed as a director or has been prevented from carrying out all or substantially all of his functions as a director; **(para 3.43)**

(3) immediately before the exclusion from participation in the management, (a) the petitioner held shares in his sole name giving him not less than 10% of the rights to vote at general meetings of the company on all or substantially all matters, and (b) all, or substantially all of the members of the company were directors. (For the purposes of (b), only one joint holder should be counted as a member). **(para 3.53)**

---

[5]   Assuming this power will be introduced for all proceedings.

[6]   As defined in s 1(3) of the Companies Act 1985.

8.5 The first presumption should provide that, where these conditions are present, the affairs of the company will be presumed to have been conducted in a manner which is unfairly prejudicial to the petitioner, unless the contrary is shown. **(para 3.56)**

8.6 The second presumption should provide that where the first presumption has not been rebutted and the court is satisfied that it ought to make an order that one or more of the respondents should purchase the petitioner's shares, the shares should be valued on a pro rata basis unless the court otherwise orders. **(para 3.62)**

8.7 We recommend that, if our recommendations for the presumptions are implemented, the Vice Chancellor should be invited to consider whether there should be a practice direction requiring the petitioner to serve a notice on the other members of the company and the company requiring them to purchase his shares valued on a pro rata basis before he starts his proceedings if he then intends to rely on the second presumption. **(para 3.64; to be considered by Vice Chancellor)**

Other reforms relating to proceedings under sections 459-461

8.8 We make the following additional recommendations in respect of proceedings under sections 459-461.

Imposition of limitation period

(1) We recommend that there should be a time limit for bringing claims under section 459, but that the length of the limitation period and the other relevant details (such as the date from which the limitation period should run) should be considered in the context of the Law Commission's current project on limitation. **(para 4.22; to be considered further by Commission in context of review of limitation periods)**

Adding winding up to the remedies available under section 461

(2) We recommend that winding up should be added to the remedies available to a petitioner in proceedings under section 459. **(para 4.35; clause 5(2))**

(3) We recommend that a petitioner should require the court's leave to apply for winding up in proceedings under sections 459-461. **(para 4.40; clause 5(1) & (3))**

(4) We recommend that a petitioner should also require the leave of the court to apply for a winding up order under section 122(1)(g) of the Insolvency Act 1986 in conjunction with an application under section 459. **(para 4.42; clause 7)**

(5) We recommend that where a petition under section 459 is amended to include a claim for winding up (whether under section 122(1)(g) or under the new provision) the winding up should be deemed to commence from the date of the amendment. **(para 4.46; clause 6)**

(6) We recommend that the Vice Chancellor should be invited to consider whether there should be an amended practice direction setting out a standard

form validation order where winding up is sought under the new provision. **(para 4.47; to be considered by Vice Chancellor)**

Power to determine relief as between respondents

(7) We recommend that the Lord Chancellor consider changes to the 1986 Rules (governing unfair prejudice proceedings) so as to give the court the procedural powers to allow contribution and indemnity claims in proceedings under section 459 if this matter is not dealt with in the general rules introduced under the Civil Procedure Act 1997. **(para 4.53; to be considered by Lord Chancellor)**

Advertisement of section 459 petitions

(8) We recommend that the Lord Chancellor consider changes to the 1986 Rules (governing unfair prejudice proceedings) so as to include an express provision stating that no advertisement of section 459 petitions should take place except in accordance with an order of the court, and so as to confirm the meaning given by the courts to "advertisement" in this context by an appropriate definition. **(para 4.56; to be considered by the Lord Chancellor)**

Articles of Association

8.9 We recommend that appropriate provisions should be included in Table A to encourage parties to sort out areas of potential dispute at the outset. **(para 5.2)** In particular we recommend that a shareholders' exit article in the terms of the draft Regulation 119 set out in Appendix C should be included in Table A **(para 5.32; Appendix C)**

A new derivative action

8.10 We recommend that there should be a new derivative procedure with more modern, flexible and accessible criteria for determining whether a shareholder can pursue the action. **(para 6.15)**

8.11 We make the following recommendations on the details of the procedure.

Availability of the new derivative action

(1) The new procedure should only be available if the cause of action arises as a result of an actual or threatened act or omission involving (a) negligence, default, breach of duty or breach of trust by a director of the company, or (b) a director putting himself in a position where his personal interests conflict with his duties to the company. The cause of action may be against the director or another person (or both) **(para 6.49; clause 1)**

(2) For these purposes, director should include a shadow director. **(para 6.49; clause 1)**

(3) The derivative action should be available only to members of the company. **(para 6.50; clause 1)**

Extent to which common law rule should be abrogated

(4) The new derivative procedure should replace the common law derivative action entirely. **(para 6.55; clause 1)**

Notice requirements

(5) (i) Unless the court otherwise orders, a claimant should be required to give notice to the company of its intention to bring a derivative action at least 28 days before the commencement of proceedings.

(ii) The notice should specify the grounds of the proposed derivative action.[7] **(para 6.59; rule 50.4)**

Company fails diligently to pursue proceedings

(6) A shareholder should be able to apply to continue, as a derivative action, proceedings commenced by the company where:

(i) the claim is capable of being pursued as a derivative action;

(ii) the company has failed to prosecute the claim diligently; and

(iii) the manner in which the company has commenced and continued the action amounts to an abuse of the process of the court. **(para 6.65; rules 50.9, 50.10 & 50.11)**

Consideration by the court

(7)(i) Where a derivative action is brought, the court must fix a case management conference.

(ii) Unless the court otherwise directs, the claimant must seek leave to continue the derivative action at the case management conference. **(para 6.69; rules 50.5 & 50.6)**

Issues relevant to the grant of leave

(8) There should be no threshold test on the merits. **(para 6.72)**

(9) In considering the issue of leave the court should take account of all the relevant circumstances without limit. **(para 6.73; rule 50.7(1))**

(10) These should include the following:

---

[7] We have incorporated this recommendation into the draft rule in Appendix B (Rule 50.4), as it is an integral part of the procedure that we are recommending. However, it may be that this provision should properly appear in a pre-action protocol or Practice Direction as it does not concern the procedure in court. The proposed primary legislation for Scotland contains a specific provision for notice to be given by a shareholder wishing to bring a shareholder's action (analogous to the derivative action under English law) (see s 458B(3)-(5) in clause 1(1) of the draft Bill at Appendix A) but we do not consider that a similar provision is required for England and Wales.

(i) the good faith of the applicant (which should not be defined); **(para 6.76; rule 50.7(2))**

(ii) the interests of the company (having regard to the views of directors on commercial matters);[8] **(para 6.79; rule 50.7(2))**

(iii) the fact that the wrong has been, or may be, approved by the company in general meeting (but effective ratification should continue to be a complete bar);[9] **(para 6.86; rules 50.7(2) & 50.8(4))**

(iv) the fact that the company in general meeting has resolved not to pursue the cause of action; **(para 6.87; rule 50.7(2))**

(v) the views of an independent organ that for commercial reasons the action should or should not be pursued; **(para 6.90; rule 50.7(2))**

(vi) the availability of alternative remedies. **(para 6.91; rule 50.7(2))**

(11) The court should not grant leave to continue the proceedings if it is satisfied that the action is not in the interests of the company; **(para 6.79; rule 50.8(3))**

Other relevant provisions

(12) The action should be brought on behalf of all the company's members other than any who are defendants, and a decision of the court should be binding on all the members on whose behalf the action is brought. However, any decision of the court should not be enforced against a person who is not a party to the proceedings without the court's permission. **(para 6.96; rule 50.2)**

(13) The court may adjourn a hearing to enable a meeting of shareholders to be convened for the purpose of considering a resolution affecting the claim. **(para 6.103; rule 50.3)**

(14) No proceedings brought by a shareholder under the provisions relating to derivative actions may be discontinued or compromised without the leave of the court. **(para 6.107; rule 50.14)**

Reform of section 14

8.12 We do not recommend any reform of section 14 of the Companies Act 1985. **(para 7.12)**

---

[8] This does not of course mean that the court would be bound to accept the views of the directors. The existence of a conflict of interest may affect the weight to be given to them, and the court would give no weight to views which no reasonable director in that position could hold.

[9] There may well be other situations in which the court would have to dismiss the action, eg if there had been a binding release; see para 6.87, n 125 above.

Pre-action discovery

8.13   We do not recommend any extension to the right to disclosure of documents specifically for shareholder proceedings. **(para 7.16)**

                              (Signed)   MARY ARDEN, *Chairman*
                                                      ANDREW BURROWS
                                                      DIANA FABER
                                                      CHARLES HARPUM
                                                      STEPHEN SILBER

MICHAEL SAYERS, *Secretary*
11 September 1997

APPENDIX A

Draft
Companies (Members' Proceedings) Bill

ARRANGEMENT OF CLAUSES

DRAFT

OF A

B I L L

INTITULED

An Act to amend the law relating to proceedings by members of companies and to make connected amendments.

A.D. 1997.

BE IT ENACTED by the Queen's most Excellent Majesty, by and with the advice and consent of the Lords Spiritual and Temporal, and Commons, in this present Parliament assembled, and by the authority of the same, as follows:—

5   *Derivative and analogous actions*

1.—(1) The following Part is inserted after Part XVI of the Companies Act 1985—

Derivative and analogous actions.

"PART XVIA

1985 c. 6.

DERIVATIVE AND ANALOGOUS ACTIONS

10 Derivative actions.

458A.—(1) A derivative action is an action by a member of a company where the cause of action is vested in the company and relief is sought on its behalf.

(2) A derivative action may be brought if and only if the cause of action arises as a result of an actual or proposed act or
15 omission involving-

    (a) negligence, default, breach of duty or breach of trust by a director of the company, or

    (b) a director putting himself in a position where his personal interests conflict with his duties to the
20   company.

(3) The cause of action may be against the director or another person (or both).

(4) Subsections (1) to (3) do not affect the court's power to make an order under section 461(2)(c) or anything done
25 under such an order.

(5) References in this section to a director include references to a shadow director.

EXPLANATORY NOTES

Clause 1 implements the Commission's recommendations in paragraphs 6.15, 6.49, 6.50 and 6.55 of the Report for the introduction of a new derivative procedure to replace entirely the right to bring a derivative action at common law and recommendations (1) to (17) of the Scottish Law Commission set out in Appendix D concerning the new statutory right of a member of a company to raise an action to protect the interests of the company and obtain a remedy on its behalf, to replace the common law right to raise such an action. It introduces two new sections into the Companies Act 1985: section 458A which deals with derivative actions in England and Wales; and section 458B which deals with analogous actions in Scotland. In relation to England and Wales, the remaining recommendations concerning the detail of the new derivative procedure are to be implemented by rules of court made under section 1 of the Civil Procedure Act 1997. In relation to Scotland, matters of title - which are relevant to the grant and refusal of leave - will be prescribed by the Secretary of State under the power conferred on him by section 458B(9)(b) and (10); only those matters which are procedural under Scots law will be dealt with by rules of court by the appropriate rule-making authority (see the discussion at paragraphs 9, 36 to 38 and 76 of Appendix D).

Section 458A(1) defines what is meant by a derivative action. There are three elements to this: the action is brought by a member of the company (as defined by section 22 of the Companies Act 1985); the cause of action is vested in the company; and relief is sought on the company's behalf.

Section 458A(2) (along with section 458A(3) and (5)) implements the recommendations in paragraphs 6.49 and 6.55 of the Report. It sets out the basis on which a derivative action may be brought and removes the right to bring a derivative action at common law. A derivative action may only be brought where there has been an actual or proposed act or omission involving (a) negligence, default, breach of duty or breach of trust by a director of the company, or (b) a director putting himself in a position where his personal interests conflict with his duties to the company. The wording in (b) is included to deal with the difficulty raised by the case of *Movitex Ltd v Bulfield* [1988] BCLC 104, highlighted in paragraphs 6.25-6.26 and paragraph 6.48 of the Report. "Director" is defined in section 741(1) of the Companies Act 1985, and for these purposes is intended to include a de facto director (see paragraph 6.36 of the Report).

Section 458A(3) makes it clear that the cause of action which the member seeks to enforce need not be against a director (provided it arises in the manner described in section 458A(2)).

Section 458A(4) makes it clear that the court's power to authorise proceedings to be brought in the name and on behalf of a company in proceedings under sections 459-461 of the Companies Act 1985 (protection of company's members against unfair prejudice) remains unaffected.

Section 458A(5) provides that acts and omissions of shadow directors are caught, and thus implements the recommendation contained in the final sentence of paragraph 6.49 of the Report. "Shadow director" is defined in section 741(2) of the Companies Act 1985.

(6) This section does not apply to Scotland.

Analogous actions in Scotland.

458B.—(1) In Scotland, to protect the interests of a company and obtain a remedy on its behalf, a member of the company is, with leave of the court and subject to subsections (3) to (5), entitled to raise under this section an action the cause of which arises as a result of an actual or proposed act or omission involving—

    (a) negligence, default, breach of duty or breach of trust by a director of the company, or

    (b) a director putting himself in a position where his personal interests conflict with his duties to the company.

(2) The action may be against the director or another person (or both).

(3) Subject to subsection (5), the member shall serve notice on the company that, unless within the period of 28 days beginning with the day of service the company raises an action as respects the actual or proposed act or omission, he intends to raise such an action under this section; and it shall not be competent for the member to raise it until that period has elapsed.

(4) The notice shall specify the cause of action and shall include a summary of the facts on which the action is based.

(5) The court may on cause shown disapply, or modify the application of, the provisions of subsections (3) and (4) in any case.

(6) Leave of the court shall be refused for the purposes of subsection (1) if any of the relevant criteria is shown to arise.

(7) Subsections (1) to (6) do not affect the court's power to make an order under section 461(2)(c) or anything done under such an order.

(8) In an action raised under this section the court may, on such terms as it thinks fit, grant an application by the member for an indemnity, out of the company's assets, in respect of expenses incurred, or to be incurred, by him in or in relation to the action.

(9) References in this section—

    (a) to a director, include a shadow director; and

    (b) to relevant criteria, are to such criteria as may be prescribed for the purposes of this section after consultation with the Lord President of the Court of Session.

(10) There may also be prescribed, after such consultation, matters to which the court shall have regard in reaching a decision—

    (a) at any stage, in an action raised under this section; or

EXPLANATORY NOTES

Section 458B(1) implements recommendations (1), (2), (4), (5) and (7) of the Scottish Law Commission. It sets out the basis on which a member of a company may raise an action under the new section to protect the interests of the company and to seek a remedy on its behalf. It replaces the equivalent common law right to raise such an action (subsection (1), read with subsection (12)). The cause of action must arise as a result of an actual or proposed act or omission involving (a) negligence, default, breach of duty or breach of trust by a director, or (b) a director putting himself in a position where his personal interests conflict with his duties to the company. The wording in (b) is intended to deal with the difficulty raised by the case of *Movitex Ltd v Bulfield* [1988] BCLC 104, discussed at paragraphs 6.25-6.26 and 6.48 of, and paragraph 21 of Appendix D to, the Report. "Member" is defined by section 22 of the Companies Act 1985. "Director" is defined in section 741(1) of that Act and for the purposes of section 458B is intended to include a de facto director (see paragraph 15 of Appendix D). Leave of the court is required to raise an action, and in addition, the applicant must have served notice on the company of his intention to raise the action (unless the court, on cause shown, modifies or dispenses with this requirement) (subsections (3) to (5)). The common law remedies which are currently available will be available in an action under section 458B.

Section 458B(2) implements recommendation (3)(a) of the Scottish Law Commission. It makes clear that an action may be raised under section 458B against a director, a third party, or both (provided the cause of it arises in the manner described in section 458B(1)).

Section 458B(3), (4) and (5) implement recommendation (6) of the Scottish Law Commission. A member intending to raise an action under section 458B is required to serve notice on the company of his intention to raise the action, 28 days before the action is raised. The notice must specify the cause of action and state that, if the company does not bring proceedings in respect of the cause of action, the applicant intends to raise the action. The court is given power, on cause shown, to disapply, or modify any aspect of this requirement. An explanation of why this requirement is included expressly in section 458B and not left to be prescribed by the Secretary of State is contained at paragraph 45 of Appendix D.

Section 458B(6) (along with section 458B(9)(b)) implements recommendation (15) of the Scottish Law Commission. It provides that the court must refuse leave to raise an action under section 458B if any of the relevant criteria is shown to arise. "Relevant criteria" is defined in subsection (9)(b) as such criteria as may be prescribed for the purposes of section 458B by the Secretary of State under that subsection. The discussion of what the Scottish Law Commission consider should be the criteria to be prescribed is contained at paragraphs 61 to 64 of Appendix D.

Section 458B(7) makes it clear that the court's power to authorise proceedings to be brought in the name and on behalf of a company in proceedings under sections 459-461 of the Companies Act 1985 (protection of company's members against unfair prejudice) remains unaffected.

Section 458B(8) implements recommendation (17) of the Scottish Law Commission. It gives the court power to grant an application by a member raising an action under section 458B for an indemnity, out of the company's assets, in respect of expenses incurred, or to be incurred by him in or in relation to the action. The court would have no such power at common law. The court's award need not be confined to judicial expenses: it may extend to all expenses in relation to the action.

Section 458B(9), paragraph (a) implements recommendation (3)(b) of the Scottish Law Commission. It provides that acts and omissions of shadow directors are caught as well as those of directors. "Shadow director" is defined in section 741(2) of the Companies Act 1985. Section 458B(9), paragraph (b) (along with section 458B(10)) implements recommendation (16) of the Scottish Law Commission. It confers on the Secretary of State power to prescribe criteria, any of which if shown to arise, will result in the court being required to refuse leave to raise an action under section 458B (see also subsection (6)). In exercising this power, the Secretary of State is required to consult with the Lord President of the Court of Session (see recommendation 16(b) and, for an explanation of this requirement, paragraphs 65 to 68 of Appendix D). The criteria which the Scottish Law Commission consider the Secretary of State should prescribe are discussed at paragraphs 61 to 64 of Appendix D. The Scottish Law Commission recommend that the court should refuse leave if satisfied that

(i) the action is not in the interests of the company; or

(ii) there has been effective ratification by the company of the director's conduct or effective waiver by the company of its claim against the director or third party, as appropriate (recommendation (16)(d)).

"Prescribed" is defined in section 744 of the Companies Act 1985 and for the purposes of this section means prescribed by statutory instrument.

(b) as to whether to grant leave for the purposes of subsection (1).

(11) A statutory instrument made by virtue of subsection (9)(b) or (10) shall be subject to annulment in pursuance of a resolution of either House of Parliament.

(12) This section is without prejudice to the right of a member of a company to raise an action to protect his own interests and to obtain a remedy on his own behalf."

(2) This section applies in relation to proceedings begun on or after the appointed day.

Unfair prejudice

2. Sections 3 to 6 amend Part XVII of the Companies Act 1985 (protection of company's members against unfair prejudice).

Introduction.
1985 c. 6.

3. After section 459 (member may petition court for an order) insert—

Presumption as to unfair prejudice.

"Presumption as to unfair prejudice.

459A.—(1) This section applies if—

(a) a member of a private company limited by shares petitions under section 459(1) for an order under this Part,

(b) it is shown that the member has been removed as a director or has been prevented from carrying out all (or substantially all) his functions as a director,

(c) immediately before the removal or prevention mentioned in paragraph (b) the member held at least 10 per cent of the voting rights in the company, and

(d) immediately before the removal or prevention mentioned in paragraph (b) all (or substantially all) the members of the company fulfilled the director condition set out in subsection (3).

(2) Unless the contrary is shown, it must be presumed that because of the removal or prevention mentioned in subsection (1)(b) the company's affairs have been conducted in a manner which is unfairly prejudicial to the interests of the petitioner.

(3) A member fulfils the director condition at the time concerned if he is then a director of the company.

(4) Nothing in this section affects the operation of section 459 apart from this section.

Interpretation of section 459A.

459B.—(1) The reference in section 459A(1)(c) to the voting rights in the company is to the rights conferred on shareholders in respect of their shares to vote at general meetings of the company on all (or substantially all) matters.

(2) For the purposes of section 459A(1)(c) rights of the member must be taken into account only if they are rights as sole holder of shares.

EXPLANATORY NOTES

Section 458B(10) (along with section 458B(9)(b)) implements recommendation (16) of the Scottish Law Commission. It confers on the Secretary of State power to prescribe matters to which the court must have regard in reaching a decision at any stage in an action under section 458B, including the stage of reaching a decision as to whether to grant leave. Again, the Secretary of State, in exercising his power, is required to consult with the Lord President of the Court of Session. The discussion of what matters the Scottish Law Commission consider the Secretary of State should prescribe is contained at paragraphs 48 to 60 of Appendix D, and the relevant recommendations are Recommendations (8) to (14) and (16)(c). In summary, the court should have regard to all relevant circumstances, including (as at present):
- whether the applicant is acting in good faith in bringing the action,
- whether the action is in the interests of the company, taking account of the views of the company's directors on commercial matters,
- whether the director's conduct as a result of which the cause of action is alleged to arise may be approved by the company and (if it may be) whether it has purportedly been so approved,
- whether the cause of action may be or has purportedly been waived by the company,
- whether the company in general meeting has resolved not to raise proceedings in respect of the director's conduct against the director or third party, as appropriate,
- the opinion (if any) of an independent organ that for commercial reasons the action should or should not be pursued, and
- whether an alternative remedy is available.

Section 458B(11) provides for the relevant statutory instrument made under section 458B(9)(b) or (10) to be made by negative resolution procedure.

Section 458B(12) makes clear that the right of a member of a company to raise an action to protect his own interests and to obtain a remedy on his own behalf is not affected by section 458B. This right of a member is discussed at paragraphs 7 and 31 of Appendix D.

Clauses 2 to 7 deal with proceedings under sections 459-461 of the Companies Act 1985. These relate to cases where unfair prejudice to members is alleged.

Clauses 3 and 4 implement the Commission's recommendation in paragraph 3.30 of the Report for the introduction of presumptions where a shareholder in an owner-managed company has been excluded from participation in the management of the company. They introduce three new sections into the Act: sections 459A and 459B which deal with the first presumption (as to unfair prejudice); and section 461A which deals with the second presumption (as to purchase price of shares).

Section 459A(1) and (3) set out the four conditions for the application of the first presumption in accordance with the recommendations in paragraphs 3.39, 3.43 and 3.53 of the Report. These are:
(a) the company is a private company limited by shares (see section 1(2)(a) and (3) of the Companies Act 1985);
(b) the member has been removed as a director or prevented from carrying out all (or substantially all) his functions as a director;
(c) immediately before the removal, the member held shares in his sole name giving him 10% of the voting rights in the company (see section 459B(2) which makes it clear that the shares must be held in his sole name);
(d) immediately before the removal, all (or substantially all) the members were directors of the company (the "director condition").

Section 459A(2) sets out the first presumption in accordance with the recommendation contained in paragraph 3.56 of the Report. It puts the onus on the respondent, where the conditions apply, to show that the removal of the petitioner as a director, or the prevention of his carrying out his functions as a director, was not unfairly prejudicial to the petitioner's interests.

Section 459A(4) makes it clear that the presumption does not have any effect outside those situations where it applies. In particular, it is not intended that the fact that a case does not fall within the terms of the presumption should make it any more or less difficult for a petitioner to show that particular conduct is unfairly prejudicial to his interests for the purposes of section 459(1) of the Act.

(3) For the purposes of section 459A(1)(c) rights which are exercisable only in certain circumstances must be taken into account only—

    (a) when the circumstances have arisen, and for so long as they continue to obtain, or   5

    (b) when the circumstances are within the control of the person who has the rights.

(4) For the purposes of section 459A(1)(c) rights which are normally exercisable but are temporarily incapable of exercise must continue to be taken into account.   10

(5) The following rules apply for the purposes of section 459A(1)(d) if at the time concerned a share is held by persons jointly—

    (a) if at least one of the holders is a director of the company, the director whose name appears first in   15 the company's register of members must be taken to be the only member by virtue of the share;

    (b) in any other case, the holder whose name appears first in the company's register of members must be taken to be the only member by virtue of the   20 share."

Presumption as to purchase price of shares.

4. After section 461 (provisions as to petitions and orders) insert—

"Presumption as to purchase price of shares.

461A.—(1) This section applies if—

    (a) by virtue of section 459A the presumption there mentioned applies and the contrary is not shown,   25 and

    (b) the court decides to make an order under this Part providing for the purchase of the petitioner's shares.

(2) It must be presumed that the order should provide for-   30

    (a) the purchase to be for a price which represents for each share of a particular class a rateable proportion of the market value of all the company's shares of that class;

    (b) that market value to be found by assuming a sale by a   35 willing seller to a willing buyer of all the company's issued share capital.

(3) The presumption mentioned in subsection (2) is displaced if the court orders it to be displaced."

Winding up.

5.—(1) In section 459 insert after subsection (1)—   40

"(1A) A petition for an order under this Part may include an application to the court to order the winding up of the company, but only if the court gives leave for it to include such an application."

(2) In section 461(2) (court's powers) insert after paragraph (d)—

"(e) provide for the company to be wound up."   45

EXPLANATORY NOTES

Section 459B supplements section 459A. In particular, it defines voting rights and provides that only one joint holder of shares is to be counted in determining whether all (or substantially all) the members are directors for the purposes of the director condition.

Section 461A(1) sets out the conditions for the application of the second presumption. These are (a) that the first presumption applies and has not been rebutted, and (b) that the court is satisfied that it ought to make an order for the purchase of the petitioner's shares.

Section 461A(2) and (3) set out the second presumption in accordance with the recommendation in paragraph 3.62 of the Report. Where the conditions apply, the share purchase order ought to be on a "pro rata" basis (see paragraph 3.8 of the Report) (ie the shares should be valued as a rateable proportion of the market value of all the shares of that class without any discount or enhancement by reference to the number of the shares). However, under section 461A(3) the court may order the presumption to be displaced.

Clause 5 implements the Commission's recommendations in paragraphs 4.35 and 4.40 of the Report. It adds winding up to the remedies available in proceedings under section 459-461, but provides that the court cannot make a winding up order unless an application for winding up is included in the petition. This in turn requires the court's leave.

(3) In section 461 insert after subsection (2)—

"(2A) However, the court may not provide for the company to be wound up unless the petition includes an application to the court to order its winding up."

5 **6.** After section 461A insert— Winding up: further provisions.

"Winding up: further provisions. 461B.—(1) The provisions of the Insolvency Act 1986 about winding up on the application of a contributory (except for sections 122, 124 and 125) apply in a case where an application for the winding up of a company is included 10 in a petition under section 459(1) by virtue of section 459(1A).

1986 c. 45.

(2) Subsection (3) has effect if a member of a company petitions under section 459(1) for an order under this Part and the petition is amended so as—

15 (a) to include an application for the winding up of the company by virtue of section 459(1A), or

(b) to include an application for the winding up of the company under section 122(1)(g) of the Insolvency Act 1986 (the just and equitable ground).

20 (3) In such a case section 129(2) of the Insolvency Act 1986 (winding up deemed to commence at time of presentation of petition) applies as if the reference to the presentation of the petition for winding up were to the making of the amendment of the petition."

25 **7.** In the Insolvency Act 1986 the following section is inserted after section 124— Amendment of insolvency legislation.

"Unfair prejudice. 124AA.—(1) Unless he has the court's leave, a member of a company may not—

(a) apply to wind it up under section 122(1)(g) when he 30 makes or while he is pursuing a section 459 application with regard to it;

(b) pursue an application to wind it up under section 122(1)(g) if, having made the application, he makes a section 459 application with regard to it.

35 (2) A section 459 application is an application under section 459 of the Companies Act 1985 (unfair prejudice)." 1985 c. 6.

8.—(1) Sections 3 to 6 apply in relation to petitions presented under section 459(1) on or after the appointed day. Commencement.

(2) Section 7 applies if any of the applications concerned is made on or 40 after the appointed day.

General

9.—(1) The appointed day is such day as the Secretary of State appoints by order made by statutory instrument. Meaning of appointed day.

EXPLANATORY NOTES

Clause 6 sets out further provisions in relation to winding up under the new power. It applies the general regime which applies to winding up on the application of a contributory under the Insolvency Act 1986. It also implements the Commission's recommendation in paragraph 4.46 of the Report. The effect is that where a petition under section 459 is amended to include a claim for winding up (whether under the new power or section 122(1)(g) of the Insolvency Act 1986) and a winding up order is made, the winding up is deemed to commence from the date of the amendment rather than the date of the original presentation of the petition.

Clause 7 implements the Commission's recommendation in paragraph 4.42 of the Report that a petitioner who wishes to pursue winding up proceedings under section 122(1)(g) of the Insolvency Act 1986 in conjunction with proceedings under section 459 of the Companies Act 1985 must seek leave from the court in order to do so.

(2) Different days may be appointed for different provisions or for different purposes.

Extent.

10. This Act does not extend to Northern Ireland.

Citation.

11. This Act may be cited as the Companies (Members' Proceedings) Act 1997.

5

APPENDIX B
Draft Rule on Derivative Claims

DRAFT CIVIL PROCEDURE RULES

DRAFT PART 50

Derivative Claims

CONTENTS OF THIS PART

Derivative claims - general

50.1   (1) This Part applies to derivative claims.

          (2) A derivative claim is a claim by a member of a company where the cause of action is vested in the company and relief is sought on its behalf.

Nature of derivative claim

50.2   (1) A derivative claim must state that it is brought by a claimant on behalf of all the company's members other than any who are defendants.

          (2) A decision of the court is binding on all the members on whose behalf the claim is brought.

          (3) But a decision of the court may not be enforced against a person who is not a party to the proceedings unless the person wishing to enforce it obtains permission from the court.

Adjournment of hearing

50.3   The court may at any time adjourn a hearing relating to a derivative claim to enable a general meeting of the company to be convened and held for the purpose of considering a resolution affecting the claim.

Commencement of claim

50.4   (1) Before a derivative claim is commenced—

          (a)   the claimant must serve on the company a notice which complies with paragraph (2), and

          (b)   a period of at least 28 days must elapse, beginning with the day on which it is served.

          (2) The notice must—

          (a)   set out the cause of action and a summary of the facts on which it is based, and

          (b)   state that, if the company does not take proceedings in respect of the cause of action, the claimant proposes to commence a derivative claim.

          (3) On an application by the claimant the court may order (whether because of urgency or otherwise)—

          (a)   that no notice under paragraph (1) is needed before a derivative claim is commenced, or

          (b)   that the period mentioned in paragraph (1)(b) is to be taken to be such shorter period as the court specifies.

(4) If a derivative claim is commenced contrary to paragraphs (1) to (3) the defendant may apply to the court for an order striking out the claim.

(5) On an application under paragraph (4) the court may—

    (a) strike out the claim,

    (b) stay the proceedings either generally or until a specified date,

    (c) waive any defect in a notice under paragraph (1) or in its purported service,

    (d) dispense with the need for such a notice, or

    (e) make such other order as it thinks fit.

Case management conference

50.5   If a derivative claim is commenced the court must fix a case management conference.

Leave to continue derivative claim

50.6   (1) The claimant must apply to the court for leave to continue the derivative claim.

(2) The application must be made—

    (a) at the case management conference, or

    (b) at such time (falling before or after the conference) as the court may order before the conference.

(3) If the claimant does not comply with paragraphs (1) and (2) a defendant may apply to the court for an order striking out the claim.

(4) On an application under paragraph (3) the court may—

    (a) strike out the claim, or

    (b) make such other order as it thinks fit.

(5) An application for leave to continue a derivative claim must be heard by a judge unless the court otherwise orders.

Leave to continue - relevant matters

50.7   (1) In considering an application for leave to continue a derivative claim the court must take all relevant matters into account.

(2) In particular the court must take the following matters into account—

(a) whether the plaintiff is acting in good faith in bringing the derivative claim;

(b) whether the derivative claim is in the interests of the company, taking account of the views of the company's directors on commercial matters;

(c) whether the director's activity as a result of which the cause of action is alleged to arise may be approved by the company in general meeting and (if it may be) whether it has been;

(d) whether the company in general meeting has resolved not to pursue the cause of action;

(e) the opinion (if any) of an independent organ that for commercial reasons the derivative claim should or (as the case may be) should not be pursued;

(f) whether a remedy is available as an alternative to the derivative claim.

Leave to continue - court's powers

50.8 (1) After considering an application for leave to continue a derivative claim the court may—

(a) grant leave to continue the claim for such period and on such terms as it thinks fit,

(b) refuse leave and dismiss the claim,

(c) strike out the claim, or

(d) adjourn the proceedings relating to the application and give such directions as it thinks fit.

(2) Subject to paragraphs (3) and (4), the court may give such weight as it thinks fit to the matters it takes into account as required by rule 50.7.

(3) The court must refuse leave and dismiss the derivative claim if it is satisfied that the claim is not in the interests of the company.

(4) The court must strike out the derivative claim if it is satisfied that the director's activity as a result of which the cause of action is alleged to arise has been ratified by the company.

Claim by company

50.9 (1) This rule applies if—

(a) a derivative claim is capable of being brought in respect of a cause of action, and

(b) the company commences a claim in respect of the cause of action.

(2) A member of the company may apply to the court for leave to continue the claim as a derivative claim on the ground that—

    (a) the manner in which the company commenced or continued the claim amounts to an abuse of the process of the court,

    (b) the company has failed to prosecute the claim diligently, and

    (c) it is appropriate for the member to continue the claim as a derivative claim.

Application under rule 50.9 - relevant matters

50.10   (1) In considering an application under rule 50.9 the court must take all relevant matters into account.

    (2) In particular the court must take the following matters into account—

    (a) whether the member is acting in good faith in seeking to continue the claim as a derivative claim;

    (b) whether the claim is in the interests of the company, taking account of the views of the company's directors on commercial matters;

    (c) whether the director's activity as a result of which the cause of action is alleged to arise may be approved by the company in general meeting and (if it may be) whether it has been;

    (d) whether the company in general meeting has resolved not to pursue the cause of action;

    (e) the opinion (if any) of an independent organ that for commercial reasons the claim should or (as the case may be) should not be pursued;

    (f) whether a remedy is available as an alternative to the claim.

Application under rule 50.9 - court's powers

50.11   (1) After considering an application under rule 50.9 the court may—

    (a) grant leave to the member to continue the claim as a derivative claim for such period and on such terms as it thinks fit,

    (b) dismiss the application, or

    (c) strike out the application.

    (2) Subject to paragraphs (3) and (4), the court may give such weight as it thinks fit to the matters it takes into account as required by rule 50.10.

    (3) The court must dismiss the application if it is satisfied that the claim is not in the interests of the company.

(4) The court must strike out the application if it is satisfied that the director's activity as a result of which the cause of action is alleged to arise has been ratified by the company.

Interim remedies

50.12   The claimant may apply for an interim remedy pending the determination of an application for leave to continue a derivative claim.

Costs

50.13   (1) The claimant may apply for an indemnity out of the company's assets in respect of costs incurred or to be incurred in a derivative claim.

(2) The court may grant such indemnity on such terms as it thinks fit.

(3) So far as reasonably practicable, an application under this rule must be made so as to be heard at the same time as the application for leave to continue the derivative claim.

Discontinuance or compromise - court's leave

50.14   A claimant may not discontinue or compromise a derivative claim without the leave of the court.

APPENDIX C
Draft Regulation 119: Exit Right

(1) The company in general meeting may at any time pass an ordinary resolution under this regulation, and in this regulation—

> (a) "specified" and "named" respectively mean specified and named in the resolution;

> (b) references to an independent person are to be construed in accordance with paragraph (13).

(2) The resolution may provide that if a specified event (or one of a number of specified events) affects a named shareholder he has an exit right which—

> (a) is exercisable by notice given to the company and named shareholders within a specified period, and

> (b) consists of the right to require those shareholders to buy the affected shareholder's shares for a fair price.

(3) A specified event may be, for example—

> (a) the removal of a shareholder who is a director from his position as a director, otherwise than where he is in serious breach of his duties as a director;

> (b) the death of a shareholder.

(4) The affected shareholder's shares are shares in the company which fulfil these conditions—

> (a) they must be held by him when the notice is given;

> (b) they must have been held by him when the resolution was passed or have been allotted directly or indirectly in right of shares so held.

(5) If a specified event is the death of the affected shareholder the person entitled to shares by reason of the death may exercise the exit right to which the affected shareholder was entitled.

(6) The resolution is invalid unless it contains provision as to the meaning of a fair price, and in particular it may provide for any of the following—

> (a) a price which represents a fair value as decided by an independent person (acting as an expert valuer and not as arbitrator or arbiter);

> (b) a price representing a rateable value (found as mentioned in paragraph (7));

(c) in the case of shares which carry a right to participate in surplus assets on a winding up, a price representing their net asset value as decided by an independent person;

(d) in the case of shares which do not carry a right to participate in surplus assets on a winding up, a price equal to the capital paid up on them;

and the resolution may contain different provision for different events.

(7) A rateable value of shares of a particular class (the shares in question) is one decided by an independent person (acting as an expert valuer and not as an arbitrator or arbiter) by taking the market value of all the shares of that class in issue and multiplying it by the fraction—

(a) whose numerator represents the capital paid up on the shares in question, and

(b) whose denominator represents the capital paid up on all the shares of that class in issue;

and the market value of all the shares of a particular class in issue is a value found by assuming a sale by a willing seller to a willing buyer of all the company's issued share capital.

(8) The resolution may provide that the net asset value of shares is to take account of or to disregard intangible assets (depending on the terms of the resolution).

(9) Unless the resolution otherwise provides, any value must be found by reference to the state of affairs obtaining at the beginning of the day when the notice exercising the exit right is given.

(10) The following rules apply if a value has to be decided by an independent person for the purposes of the resolution—

(a) as soon as is reasonably practicable after it receives the notice the company must instruct the independent person to decide the value;

(b) as soon as is reasonably practicable after it receives the decision the company must give notice of it to the named shareholders;

(c) half the costs of the independent person must be borne by the affected shareholder or, if he is dead, the person entitled to his shares by reason of his death;

(d) half the costs of the independent person must be borne by the shareholders who are required to buy;

(e) the shareholders who are required to buy must bear that half in proportion to the number of shares they are required to buy.

(11) Subject to any provision in the resolution and to any agreement by all the parties concerned—

(a) the shareholders who are required to buy must buy the shares in proportion to the number of shares registered in their names in the company's register of members at the beginning of the day on which the resolution was passed (treating joint holders as a single holder);

(b) all parties must do their best to secure that the purchase is completed before the expiry of the relevant period (defined in paragraph (12));

(c) at completion a buyer must pay a proper proportion of the price (in cash and in full) against delivery to him of a duly executed form of transfer.

(12) The relevant period is a period of three months starting with—

(a) the day when the company gives notice to the shareholders of the decision of the independent person (if paragraph (10) applies), or

(b) the day when the notice exercising the exit right was given (in any other case).

(13) References in this regulation to an independent person are to an independent person who appears to have the requisite knowledge and experience and who is appointed in such manner as is specified.

(14) A resolution is invalid unless every named shareholder gives a notice to the company (before the resolution is passed) stating that he consents to it.

(15) A resolution ceases to be effective if a named shareholder dies or an event occurs after which he holds none of the following shares—

(a) shares held by him when the resolution was passed;

(b) shares allotted directly or indirectly in right of such shares.

(16) Paragraph (15) has effect subject to the following rules—

(a) if a notice exercising the exit right has already been given paragraph (15) does not apply as regards that notice;

(b) if the death of the named shareholder is a specified event paragraph (15) does not apply as regards that event;

(c) paragraph (15) does not apply if the resolution disapplies it.

(17) A resolution ceases to be effective if there is agreement to that effect by all relevant persons; and a relevant person is any person who is—

(a) a named shareholder, or

(b) a person entitled to a named shareholder's shares by reason of his death.

(18) Regulations 111, 112 and 114 to 116 apply to a notice exercising the exit right as if it were a notice given by the company.

(19) If a notice exercising the exit right is given it cannot be withdrawn without the consent of all relevant persons (within the meaning given by paragraph (17)).

(20) If while a resolution is effective a named shareholder transfers shares, and after the registration of the transfer he would hold none of the shares mentioned in paragraph (15)(a) and (b), the directors of the company must refuse to register the transfer unless all relevant persons (within the meaning given by paragraph (17)) notify the company in writing that they consent to the transfer; and consent unreasonably withheld must be taken to be so notified.

(21) If a resolution is passed under this regulation—

> (a) a variation of this regulation or of the resolution is to be treated as a variation of the rights attached to the shares held by the named shareholders, and

> (b) those rights may be varied only with the consent of all relevant persons (within the meaning given by paragraph (17)).

APPENDIX D
The Shareholders' Action in Scotland, views and recommendations of the Scottish Law Commission

Introduction

1. This appendix contains the views and recommendations of the Scottish Law Commission on the shareholder's action in Scotland which achieves a similar practical result to the derivative action in England and Wales discussed in Part 6 of the Report.

Background

2. In the consultation paper, the proposal was made to introduce a new right of action by a shareholder on behalf of the company which was described as a derivative action. It was recognised that Scots law, however, did not have a derivative action and that Scots procedure differed from that of England and Wales.[1] In Scotland a shareholder has a right to raise an action in certain circumstances to protect the interests of his company and to seek a remedy on its behalf.[2] The shareholder's right of action is conferred by substantive law and not by procedural rules.

3. In Scots law, title to sue is a matter of substantive law and not of procedure. As several consultees pointed out in their responses to the consultation paper, this affects the way in which the proposed reforms can be implemented in Scotland. While in England and Wales the new remedy may be introduced in large measure by adopting new rules of court, that mechanism is not available in Scotland.

4. Our policy is to achieve, so far as possible and reasonable, consistency in substantive company law throughout the United Kingdom, as the United Kingdom is an integrated economy. It is also our policy that the mechanism for the proposed reforms should be capable of being adapted to take account of developments in company law. Although the proposed mechanism to implement the reform differs from that of England and Wales, the aim is to achieve the same practical result as a matter of substantive company law.

5. In this appendix we set out, first, the reasons why it is necessary to legislate to provide the proposed solution for Scotland, secondly, the scope of the proposed new statutory right and, thirdly, the mechanism by which the right may be implemented.

The need for legislation

6. Scots law recognises the right of a shareholder to raise an action to protect his own interests and also his separate right to raise an action to obtain a remedy for the company. However, the reasoning in the few reported cases which deal with these actions is neither consistent nor developed.

---

[1] Consultation Paper No 142, paras 1.6, n 8; 4.1, n 1 and 6.5, n 8.

[2] For a further discussion of this right, see paras 8 and 9 below.

7.   A shareholder in Scotland can raise an action on his own behalf to protect his personal interests. Thus the shareholder can raise an action against his company to prevent or nullify an *ultra vires* act.[3] He can enforce personal rights in the company's articles of association.[4] It is likely also that a shareholder can raise an action where there has been an irregularity in a resolution requiring a qualified majority.[5] A shareholder may also raise an action against an individual director or directors for damages for fraud or fraudulent misrepresentation.[6]

8.   A shareholder also has title as a matter of substantive law to raise proceedings in respect of a director's breach of duty to obtain a remedy for the company. In our view, his title to sue arises from his status as shareholder which gives him an interest in the company. The rights which the shareholder can enforce against a director or a third party are those of the company. The remedy is obtained for the company. The shareholder's right to raise proceedings is available where the action complained of is fraudulent or *ultra vires* the company and so cannot be validated by a majority of the members of the company. It is not available where a majority of members acting in good faith have validated or may validate the act complained of.[7]

9.   As a matter of substantive law two rules apply to both actions to protect a shareholder's personal interests and actions to protect the company's interests, namely that the directors of a company owe duties to the company and not to the shareholders and that the court will not interfere in matters of internal management which a majority of shareholders may sanction.[8] Thus, Scots law achieves results which are similar in effect to the first two limbs of the restatement of the rule in *Foss v Harbottle*.[9] In our view, this similar result in Scotland is not based on the procedural principles of *Foss v Harbottle* but is a matter of substantive law. However, in two cases the courts have adopted the principles of *Foss v Harbottle*.[10] This has given rise to significant doubts as to the basis on which a shareholder is acting when he raises proceedings alleging that the company has acted *ultra vires* or that it has purported to pass by simple majority a resolution

---

[3]   See for example *Smith v Glasgow and South Western Railway* (1897) 4 SLT 327, *Cameron v Glenmorangie Distillery Co Ltd* (1896) 23 R 1092 and *Lochaber District Committee v Invergarry and Fort Augustus Railway Co* 1913 1 SLT 361.

[4]   Section 14 of the Companies Act 1985. See Part 2 of Consultation Paper No 142.

[5]   *Cameron v Glenmorangie Distillery Co Ltd* (1896) 23 R 1092, 1095 per Lord Kyllachy.

[6]   *Leslie's Representatives v Lumsden* (1851) 14 D 213.

[7]   See *Lee v Crawford* (1890) 17 R 1094, *Hannay v Muir* (1898) 1 F 306, *Harris v A Harris Ltd* 1936 SC 183 and *Oliver's Trustees v W G Walker & Sons (Edinburgh) Ltd* 1948 SLT 140.

[8]   *Hannay v Muir* (1898) 1 F 306, *Brown v Stewart* (1898) 1 F 316. See also *Currie v Cowdenbeath Football Club Ltd* 1992 SLT 407.

[9]   See paragraph 6.2 of the Report.

[10] *Orr v Glasgow, Airdrie and Monklands Junction Railway Co* (1860) 3 Macq 799, *Brown v Stewart* (1898) 1 F 316.

which requires a special majority or where there has been fraud on the minority.[11] These doubts could hamper future development of Scots law in this field.

10. The proposed reform of shareholder remedies offers an opportunity to remove these doubts and place the shareholder's right of action to protect the interests of the company on a more secure foundation. Consultees for the Scottish interest expressed different views. Some considered that a new statutory right of action to protect the interests of the company is not necessary. The majority, however, considered that the importation of the principles of *Foss v Harbottle* into Scots law was both unsatisfactory and unnecessary. They considered that there is a need to clarify the basis and scope of the shareholder's right of action under Scots law. In our view, the paucity of case law and the reference in the minority of cases to *Foss v Harbottle* lead to actual and potential confusion. We consider it appropriate that this confusion should be laid to rest. Accordingly, as respects Scotland, we recommend: [12]

> **(1) that the right of a shareholder to raise an action to protect the interests of his company and to obtain a remedy on its behalf should be put on a clear statutory basis (clause 1: new section 458B).**

The scope of the proposed new statutory right and the mechanism by which it may be implemented

11. The Law Commission explain the guiding principles for their recommendations in relation to the reform of the law and procedure relating to shareholder remedies. Scots law has substantive rules which have the same effect as some of those guiding principles.[13]

12. The discussion which follows of the circumstances in which an action may be brought under the new statutory provision recommended for Scotland and other matters in relation to this right of action is structured to fit with the order in which the discussion in Part 6 of the Report is set out. For ease of understanding, the discussion in this appendix, where appropriate, follows the same headings as are used in that Part.

Should the right of action under the new statutory provision be available only in respect of breaches of duty by a director (including claims against third parties as a result of such breaches)

13. The recommendations of the Law Commission[14] encapsulate a number of policy issues. Much of the related discussion, though set in the context of the different

---

[11] See for example A Mackenzie "The problem of enforcement of directors' duties in Scotland" 1981 SLT (News) 257; A A Paterson, "The derivative action in Scotland" 1982 SLT (News) 205.

[12] The Law Commission's parallel recommendation is set out at paras 6.15 and 8.10 of the Report.

[13] See the discussion at paras 1.9-1.12 of the report and at para 9 above.

[14] See the recommendations set out at paras 6.49, 8.11(1) and (2), and the discussion at paras 6.24-6.48 of the Report.

background applicable for England and Wales (that of the derivative action which for England and Wales is a procedural mechanism), is equally relevant for Scotland. We agree with the policy which the Law Commission's recommendations seek to implement.

14. In summary, the relevant issues encapsulated in the Law Commission's recommendations are as follows:

- whether breach by a director of a duty which he owes to the company should be a necessary pre-condition for the right of action under the new statutory provision which we recommend for Scotland;

- what should constitute breach of duty for the purposes of this new provision; and

- should the right of action be available for breaches of duty by officers and employees who are not directors.

Whether breach by a director of a duty which he owes to the company should be a necessary pre-condition for the right of action under the new statutory provision which we recommend for Scotland

15. We agree with the Law Commission that if there is no breach of duty by a director, a shareholder should not be bringing the action.[15] An action should be able to be brought under the new statutory provision in respect of a breach or threatened breach of duty by a director, against the director and against a third party, where the company otherwise would be entitled to raise an action against the third party, and where that cause of action - the fact or combination of facts which must be proved to entitle the company to succeed - arises directly or indirectly as a result of the director's breach or threatened breach of duty.[16] It should be possible to raise an action against both a director and a third party, so with the possibility of joint and several liability. A director for this purpose should include a "shadow director"; we agree that de facto directors should be included and that they are capable of coming under the definition of director in section 741 of the Companies Act 1985.[17]

16. Some concern was expressed on consultation for the Scottish interest that the scope of the right to raise an action under the new provision against a third party should be free from doubt. The director's breach of duty itself would not be sufficient as a cause of action against the third party in most cases where the right of action should lie. An attempt to recover company funds or assets from the third party normally would require proof of facts other than the director's breach of duty, yet should be competent under the new statutory provision.

17. We agree that in such cases, the cause of action against the third party will not merely be the director's breach of duty. Rather, the action will be for eg,

[15] See para 6.24 of the Report - the overall issue being discussed at paras 6.24-6.37.

[16] See para 6.37 of the Report.

[17] See paras 6.36 and 6.49 of the Report.

vindication of the company's real right of ownership of company assets held by a third party on a void title; restitution of property held by a third party on a voidable title; repetition from a third party of company funds received by him in bad faith or gratuitously; recompense, where the third party has obtained the benefit of company funds or other assets but no longer holds or has consumed these; or a delictual claim where the third party has participated in the director's breach of duty, eg by complicity in theft by the director of company funds or other assets.

18. In all such cases, however, the breach of duty will be the underlying problem, giving rise to the third party's own bad faith or other actionable conduct. Where that is not the case, eg a delictual claim against the third party does not arise from a director's breach of duty,[18] we agree that the action against the third party should not be a matter for the new statutory provision. We do not envisage an action proceeding against a third party under the new statutory provision in all circumstances where the director's breach of duty is one of the facts to be proved to succeed in a claim against the third party. For example, the shareholder's action should not proceed against an auditor for professional negligence where an auditor fails to detect a misappropriation of funds by a director. In such a case there is not a sufficiently close connection with the director's breach of duty, the auditor having neither received, nor had the benefit of, the company's assets nor having participated in the director's breach of duty. In other words, the director's breach of duty is not the underlying problem which gives rise to the auditor's actionable conduct. The policy of the Law Commissions is consistent in this respect.[19]

19. So, too, we consider that the ordinary common law defences in relation to the cause of action against the third party should still be available. In an action of restitution, repetition or recompense, therefore, the pursuer should still have to prove the third party's knowledge of the director's breach of duty - so bad faith - or that the third party did not give value for the company's funds or other assets,[20] and in a delictual claim, he should still have to prove that the third party knowingly participated in the director's wrongful conduct.

What should constitute a breach of duty for the purposes of this new provision

20. We have explained above[21] that we agree that an action should be capable of being brought under the new statutory provision in respect of a director's breach of duty. We agree similarly that it should be made clear that breach of duty includes negligence[22] (regardless of whether or not any director has benefited personally)

---

[18] See the example given at para 6.31 of the Report.

[19] See the discussion at para 6.35 of the Report.

[20] See *Thomson and Others v Clydesdale Bank Ltd* 1893 20 R (HL) 59, the Lord Chancellor and Lord Watson at 61 and Lord Shand at 62; *Style Financial Services Ltd v Bank of Scotland* 1997 S.C.L.R. (OH) 633.

[21] Para 15.

[22] See paras 6.38-6.41 and the recommendation set out at paras 6.49 and 8.11(1) of the Report.

and statutory default,[23] and accordingly that the relevant legislation implementing the recommendation (and the parallel recommendation[24] made in this appendix for Scotland) should adopt the expression used in sections 310 and 727 of the Companies Act 1985, namely "negligence, default, breach of duty or breach of trust".[25]

21. We share the Law Commission's view that it is not appropriate, in the limited context of the shareholder remedies exercise, to seek to resolve the issue of whether the obligation of a director not to place himself in a position where his personal interests conflict with his duties to the company amounts to a duty and not merely a disability.[26] This is an issue of wider significance. We agree, however, that it is appropriate for the legislation implementing our respective recommendations to make clear that a shareholder has title to bring whatever action the company could bring in respect of such conduct.

Should the right of action be available for breaches of duty by officers and employees who are not directors

22. Consultation responses for the Scottish interest disclosed mixed views as regards whether the new statutory provision should allow actions to be brought against officers and employees (other than directors) in respect of a wrong or threatened wrong by them towards the company, and the circumstances in which such an action should be competent.

23. The Law Commission conclude[27] that the new derivative action for England and Wales should not extend to claims based on breach of duty by such employees and officers (unless, of course, they arise also out of a breach of duty by directors). Employees and officers other than directors, therefore, would be in the same position as other third parties.

24. We agree with that view and consider that, for Scotland, the right of action of a member of a company under the new statutory provision should be similarly confined in scope.

25. Accordingly, we agree with the Law Commission's recommendations[28] on the matters discussed in this part of the appendix. Given that, for Scotland, the context for the new statutory provision is different from that for England and

---

[23] See the discussion at para 6.47 and the recommendation set out at paras 6.49 and 8.11(1) of the Report.

[24] See para 25 below.

[25] See para 6.47 of the Report.

[26] See paras 6.25-6.26 and the discussion there of *Movitex Ltd v Bulfield* [1988] BCLC 104 and para 6.48 and the related recommendations set out in paras 6.49 and 8.11(2)(i) of the Report.

[27] See paras 6.42-6.46.

[28] The recommendations are set out paras 6.49 and 8.11(1) and (2) of the Report.

Wales,[29] it is appropriate to set out equivalent recommendations framed to fit the Scottish background. Accordingly, we **recommend:**

> **(2) that a shareholder should be entitled to raise an action under the new statutory provision for Scotland if the cause of it arises as a result of an actual or threatened act or omission involving**
>
> > **(a) negligence, default, breach of duty or breach of trust by a director of the company, or**
> >
> > **(b) a director putting himself in a position where his personal interests conflict with his duties to the company (clause 1: new section 458B, subsection (1)); and**
>
> **(3) that**
>
> > **(a) the action might be against the director or some other person, or both (clause 1: new section 458B, subsection (2)); and**
> >
> > **(b) for the purposes of the new statutory provision, "director" should include a shadow director (clause 1: new section 458B, subsection (9)(a)).**

Who should be able to bring a shareholder's action

26. The Law Commission recommend[30] that the new derivative action for England and Wales should be available only to members of the company, and not to those who have ceased to be members of it.

27. No qualifying period of membership is recommended.[31] A majority of the consultees for the Scottish interest considered that there should be no such requirement, with one considering that there should be. On balance, we agree that such a requirement is not appropriate. Any current member should have the right to raise an action under the new statutory provision. Accordingly, we similarly **recommend:**

> **(4) that the right of action under the new statutory provision for Scotland should be available only to members of the company (clause 1: new section 458B, subsection (1)).**

---

[29]   See the discussion at paras 2 to 9 above.

[30]   See the recommendation set out paras 6.50 and 8.11(3) and the discussion at para 6.50.

[31]   See paras 6.97-6.98 of the Report.

***Extent to which common law right of shareholder to raise action to
protect interests of company and obtain remedy on company's behalf
should be replaced***

28.   The Law Commission recommend[32] that, for England and Wales, the new
        procedure should replace entirely the common law right to bring a derivative
        action, with section 459 of the Companies Act being available for any exceptional
        cases of hardship.

29.   We agree that it is important also for Scotland that the existing common law right
        of a member to raise an action to protect the company's interests and to obtain a
        remedy on its behalf and the new statutory right to raise such an action do not co-
        exist. If they did, this would lead only to confusion. Rather, our aim is to make the
        law more accessible and simpler. If the existing shareholder's common law right of
        action were to remain, alongside the new statutory right, then abrogation for
        England and Wales of the common law derivative action as an exception to the
        rule in *Foss v Harbottle* would necessarily lead to speculation and uncertainty as to
        the effect for the future of the Scottish cases which appear to have imported that
        rule and that exception into Scots law.[33] Further, it would be reasonable to expect
        that there would be attempts made to clarify what the distinction was between the
        scope of the common law right and that of the new statutory right. We consider
        that this would lead to unsatisfactory results.

30.   As discussed above,[34] we consider that there is clear authority under Scots law that
        a shareholder has a direct right of action to protect the interests of the company
        and to seek a remedy for it in respect of a director's breach of duty. We have also
        explained our view that we consider that the case of *Foss v Harbottle* and what have
        become known as the qualifications and exceptions to the rule in that case do not
        need to be relied on to ascertain or confine the scope of that right of action. We
        consider it appropriate, therefore, that for Scotland what has become known as
        the rule in that case and the qualifications and exceptions to it are laid to rest in
        respect of such an action. Accordingly, we recommend:

> **(5) that the right of action under the new statutory provision for
> Scotland should replace the common law right of a shareholder to
> raise an action to protect the interests of the company and seek a
> remedy for the company in respect of a director's breach of duty
> (clause 1: new section 458B).**

***Actions by a shareholder of a company to protect his own interests and to
seek a remedy for himself***

31.   As discussed above, a shareholder has a separate right to raise actions to protect
        his own interests.[35] We propose no changes to the law in respect of such personal

---

[32]   See the recommendation set out paras 6.55 and 8.11(4) and the discussion at paras 6.51-
       6.55.

[33]   See the discussion at para 9 above.

[34]   Para 8.

[35]   Para 7.

actions. We recognise that dicta in *Brown v Stewart*[36] which refer to the principle of *Foss v Harbottle* have created doubts about the basis on which the shareholder raises such proceedings. We consider however that the case goes no further than to confirm two substantive rules of common law, namely that a director owes his duties of good faith etc to the company and not to individual shareholders, and that a minority shareholder who wishes to challenge a transaction, which may be made binding on the company, may be overruled by the majority of shareholders if they choose to ratify the transaction.

Additional restrictions which should apply to right to bring action under new statutory provision

32.   The existing common law right of a shareholder under Scots law to bring an action to protect the company's interests and to seek a remedy for the company, in respect of a director's conduct, is not unfettered. In substance, the right has been circumscribed by the courts by the application of criteria and the balancing of a number of matters. For instance, there appears to be a substantive requirement for the pursuer to give the company an opportunity to consider whether to ratify the alleged wrong or to raise the action;[37] effective ratification of the director's conduct bars a shareholder's action;[38] the court looks at whether the action is in the interests of the company in considering whether a shareholder's action is competent - and thus to permit an exception to the substantive rules of Scots law described above.[39]

33.   In substance, a similar practical result has been achieved to that applied for English law by the application of the rule in *Foss v Harbottle* and the qualifications/exceptions to that rule.

34.   As discussed above,[40] in some Scottish cases, these restrictions appear to have been applied expressly in reliance on the Foss principles, and so have been regarded by some as dependent on that case. The paucity of case law and the reference in the minority of cases to *Foss v Harbottle* lead to actual and potential confusion.

35.   Replacement of the existing common law right of action, therefore, with a new statutory right has the further additional benefit of enabling the difficulties and doubts to be laid to rest. The substantive criteria which the courts should apply, therefore in determining title to sue and the matters which should be balanced by the court could usefully be clarified and made accessible.

---

[36]   (1898) 1F 316: in particular the references to *Foss v Harbottle* and *Orr cit supra*.

[37]   See, eg, *Lee v Crawford* (1890) 17 R 1094; *Hannay v Muir* (1898) 1 F 306; and *Harris v A Harris Ltd* 1936 SC 183.

[38]   See the cases cited at n 37 above.

[39]   Para 9.

[40]   Para 9.

The appropriate legislative vehicle

36. The Law Commission explain[41] that in English law the derivative action is a procedural mechanism, that the conditions in which it may be brought are procedural matters, and that accordingly these can be set out in, and so in future changed also simply by, rules of court.

37. Under Scots law, title and interest to sue are matters of substantive law.[42] Before being allowed to enter on the merits of this case, a pursuer, if called on by the defender, must satisfy the court not only that he is the proper person to pursue that action, but also that he has a real interest in its result. In respect of title, he must satisfy the court that he has a formal legal right to pursue the action. He must have both title to sue at the date of raising the action and a continuing title to pursue the action to the final judgment.

38. In our view, it is not competent for substantive matters concerning title to sue to be dealt with by rules of court under cover of the provisions of section 5 of the Court of Session Act 1988 or section 32 of the Sheriff Court (Scotland) Act 1971. Substantive matters of title to sue are outwith the competence of those sections which enable, rather, procedural matters to be dealt with in rules made under them.

39. Significant problems could arise, however, if the relevant criteria and matters were enshrined in primary legislation. They would be crystallised, and the ability to change them in the future would be restricted - further primary legislation would be required. In contrast, for English law, changes to the rules of court would be a relatively simple matter, and could readily be made to keep abreast of the courts' application of and development of the relevant criteria and matters.[43]

40. In an area of law such as this, we consider it highly desirable that there should be consistency in policy between English law and Scots law. In order to achieve that consistency, where appropriate, it is important that, for Scots law, the relevant criteria and matters similarly can be changed to keep abreast of future developments.

41. One alternative means of stating the criteria and matters, therefore, would be for primary legislation to confer express power for the relevant criteria and matters to be prescribed by Act of Sederunt. The Lord President of the Court of Session has advised us that he would not be happy with any suggestion that the Court should be involved - even by way of the grant of a specific power, in making what would in effect be changes in substantive law. He has expressed the view that any necessary powers should lie in the hands of the Secretary of State.

---

[41] See paras 6.12 and 6.16-6.21 of the Report.

[42] See, Maxwell, *the Practice of the Court of Session* (1980) pp 147-150; Macphail, *Sheriff Court Practice* (1988) para 4-28.

[43] See, on this, the discussion at para 1.14 of the Report.

42. We agree with this view. Before discussing further our views as to the manner in which the Secretary of State's enabling powers should be set out in the legislation, it is appropriate to discuss what the relevant criteria and matters should be.

The relevant criteria and matters
Notice

43. As discussed above,[44] where a shareholder raises an action to protect the interests of his company, the Scottish courts have required that he has given the company an opportunity to consider the matter, to decide whether to put it right or alternatively to raise an action. Effectively, therefore, they have established a requirement of notice.

44. We consider that there should remain a requirement of notice. The flexibility of the current law should be retained by the court having power in appropriate circumstances, eg where urgency can be shown, to waive the requirement or to modify it - eg, by permitting a shorter period of notice. In relation, therefore, to the equivalent recommendation by the Law Commission,[45] as respects Scotland, we **recommend:**

> **(6) that, unless on cause shown the court orders otherwise, the applicant should be required to give the company notice of his intention to raise the action 28 days before the action is raised; and that the notice should specify the grounds of action and state that, if the company does not bring proceedings in respect of the cause of action, the applicant intends to raise the action (clause 1: new section 458B, subsections (3) to (5)).**

45. For Scotland, it is necessary to include the notice requirement expressly in primary legislation. To leave the requirement to be prescribed by the Secretary of State could give rise to problems of vires when the relevant statutory instrument falls to be made. As a matter of policy, it is necessary that the court should have power to dispense with or modify the requirement, but for the Secretary of State to confer that power on the court in a statutory instrument would amount to sub-delegation. To frame the Secretary of State's enabling power to confer express authority for this, in our view, would be not be a satisfactory approach. In our view, no flexibility is lost[46] by including the requirement of notice in primary legislation, given the express power which it can confer on the court to dispense with or modify the requirement.

Concept of leave to raise action

46. As discussed above,[47] at present, the Scottish courts both apply criteria and balance a number of matters. The criteria are generally determinative of whether

---

[44] Para 32.

[45] See the recommendations set out at paras 6.59 and 8.11(5), the related discussion at para 6.58 of the Report and rule 50.4 in Appendix B.

[46] See the discussion at paras 4 and 39-40 above.

[47] Para 32.

the action is competent. The matters, on the other hand, appear not to be determinative, but to be such as should be balanced. The court has and will continue to have to consider a number of factors at the outset, in addressing at that stage the question of title to sue. In our view, it is appropriate to deal with this by means of a requirement for the granting of leave to bring proceedings. The concept of leave in the field of company law is not something new for Scots law. Leave of the court is required to bring proceedings where an administrator or provisional liquidator has been appointed, where a winding up order has been made by the court or on the application of a liquidator in a voluntary winding up.[48] Accordingly, we **recommend:**[49]

> **(7) that leave of the court should be required to raise an action under the new statutory provision for Scotland (clause 1: new section 458B, subsection (1)).**

Matters relevant to grant of leave

47.   A number of matters will be relevant to the grant of leave. They will also of course be relevant to all other stages of an action if leave is granted. They are generally matters which the court will require to balance.

Court to consider all the relevant circumstances

48.   We agree with the view expressed by the Law Commission that it would be unsatisfactory to require the court to apply fixed or definitive criteria for the *granting* of leave.[50] It is essential that the court has flexibility to look at all of the relevant circumstances.

49.   Consultees for the Scottish interest supported a non-exhaustive list of matters which the court should be required to consider. We agree that this would be helpful and that it is consistent with our aim of seeking to clarify and make the law in this area more accessible. Such a list could then be developed in the future to take account, where appropriate, of developments in company law in both jurisdictions.

50.   Accordingly, as respects Scotland, we **recommend:**[51]

> **(8) that in considering whether to grant leave, the court should take account of all the relevant circumstances, without limit, and in particular, should take account of certain prescribed matters (clause 1: new section 458B, subsection (10)).**

---

[48]   See ss 11(3)(d), 113 and 130(2), Insolvency Act 1986.

[49]   The Law Commission discuss the issue of leave in the procedural context of English law at paras 6.66-6.69 of the report: see also rule 50.6 in Appendix B.

[50]   See the discussion at para 6.73 of the report. We do consider, however, that there should be certain fixed or definitive criteria for the refusal of leave - see paragraphs 61-64 below for a discussion of this matter.

[51]   The parallel recommendation by the Law Commission is set out at paras 6.73 and 8.11(8)-(11): see also the related discussion at paras 6.70-6.74 and rule 50.7(1) in Appendix B.

51. We now consider the specific matters of which we recommend the court should take account in considering whether to grant leave.

Applicant's good faith

52. We agree with the Law Commission's discussion of the matter of the applicant's good faith: this should be a matter to be taken account of by the court.[52] Consultees for the Scottish interest expressed a consistent view that the applicant's good faith should be a material consideration, but should not a pre-requisite in deciding whether to grant leave. They also expressed a consistent view that it was not possible satisfactorily to define the concept of good faith. We agree, and do not consider that the concept needs to be defined: it is a concept with which the Scottish courts are very familiar. Accordingly, as respects Scotland, we **recommend**:

> **(9) that the good faith of the applicant should be a specific matter to be taken account of by the court, but it should not be a pre-requisite; and that the concept of good faith should not be defined (clause 1: new section 458B, subsection (10)).**

Interests of the company

53. We agree with the Law Commission that the court should take into account the interests of the company, and in doing so, should have regard to the views of directors on commercial matters.[53] The concept of the interests of the company has been applied fully by the Scottish courts in the context of the shareholder's common law right of action - it is an inextricable part, eg, of ascertaining whether a purported ratification results from wrongdoer control of a majority of votes, etc.[54]

54. We agree that it is not appropriate to require the applicant to prove that the action is in the interests of the company in order to obtain leave. We agree also that if the court is satisfied that the action is not in the interests of the company, it should refuse leave - this matter is discussed further below in the context of the circumstances in which the court should be required to refuse leave.[55] Accordingly, as respects Scotland, we recommend:

> **(10) that the interests of the company should be a specific matter to be taken account of by the court, and in doing so, the court should have regard to the views of directors on commercial matters (clause 1: new section 458B, subsection (10)).**

---

[52] See the discussion at paras 6.75-6.76, the recommendation set out at paras 6.76 and 8.11(10)(i) of the Report and rule 50.7(2) in Appendix B.

[53] See the discussion at paras 6.77-6.79, recommendation set out at paras 6.79 and 8.11(10)(ii) of the Report and rule 50.7(2) in Appendix B.

[54] See, eg, *Lee v Crawford* 1890 17 R 1094; *Harris v A Harris Ltd* 1936 SC 183; 1936 SLT 227.

[55] See paras 61-64 below.

Authorisation and ratification

55. As for England and Wales,[56] under Scots law, if the director's conduct has been effectively ratified by the company (or if the company's claim against the director or third party - as appropriate - has been effectively waived), this will be a complete bar to an action by an individual shareholder or a minority of shareholders. There is clear authority that ratification (and similarly waiver) will not be effective if obtained by an interested majority or if the relevant majority was unfairly obtained.[57]

56. We agree with the Law Commission[58] that ratification (and waiver) should continue to be effective in the cases where they are effective at present to bar an action by a minority shareholder - where there has been *effective* ratification or waiver; but that otherwise the fact that the director's conduct is *ratifiable, or has purportedly been ratified*, or that the company may waive its claim or has *purportedly waived* its claim against the director or the third party, as the case may be, should be only factors of which the court should take account. So, for example, the fact that the director's conduct is ratifiable or indeed has purportedly been ratified in itself will not prevent a member from having title to raise an action under the new statutory provision for Scotland: rather, the court will take account of this in considering whether to grant leave. On the other hand, however, if the court is satisfied that there has been effective ratification (in the absence of wrongdoer control, etc) or waiver, then it should be required to refuse leave.[59] Accordingly, as respects Scotland, we **recommend**:[60]

> **(11) that the fact that the director's conduct has purportedly been, or may be, approved by the company in general meeting or that the company's claim against the director or the third party, as appropriate, has purportedly been, or may be, so waived by the company should be a specific matter to be taken account of by the court (clause 1: new section 458B, subsection (10)).**

57. The Law Commission discuss that it is open to a majority of members to resolve that no action should be taken in respect of a director's conduct, and that such a resolution, if made in good faith and what they consider to be for the benefit of the company, will bind the minority.[61] This is the case too under Scots law. In our

---

[56] See the discussion at paras 6.80-6.86 and para 6.87, n 125 of the Report.

[57] See, eg, *Lee v Crawford* (1890) 17 R 1094 ; *Hannay v Muir* (1898) 1 F 306; and *Harris v A Harris Ltd* 1936 SC 183.

[58] The Law Commission's recommendation is set out at paras 6.86 and 8.11(10)(iii) of the Report: see also para 6.87, n 125 and rule 50.7(2) of Appendix B.

[59] This matter is discussed at paras 63-64 below.

[60] We include waiver expressly in our recommendation because for Scotland the relevant matters will be set out in subordinate legislation, and not to include it might lead to difficulties of interpretation. The policy of the Law Commissions is the same; see the discussion at notes 123 and 125 to paras 6.86 and 6.87 of the Report.

[61] See para 6.87 of the Report, and in particular the discussion at n 125 of *Taylor v National Union of Mineworkers (Derbyshire Area)* [1985] BCLC 237 and of the position under English law generally.

view, in some cases such a resolution would amount to waiver, but in others it might not, eg, because the wording of the resolution might not amount to abandonment of a right. It may also be that it cannot be relied on - the party seeking to rely on it may not have conducted his affairs on the basis that the company had abandoned its right.[62] We agree that in both cases the fact that there has been such a resolution should be relevant and that this is a specific matter of which the court should take account in considering whether to grant leave.[63] Accordingly, as respects Scotland, we **recommend:**

> **(12) that the fact that the company in general meeting has resolved not to raise proceedings in respect of a director's conduct, against the director or third party, as appropriate, should be a specific matter to be taken account of by the court (clause 1: new section 458B, subsection (10)).**

Views of independent organ

58.   The concept of the views of an "independent organ" as applied under English law is discussed fully by the Law Commission.[64] As the Law Commission explain, even if there has been no approval (or purported approval) of the wrong, the court may be informed of commercial reasons why the shareholders (or a group of shareholders), or even the directors or a committee of directors, consider that the action should not proceed. The term "independent organ" is used to describe a group of persons within the company whose views would be taken into account for these purposes. These are persons whose votes would not be disregarded on the grounds that they had been (or would be) "cast with a view to supporting the defendants rather than securing benefit to the company, or [that] the situation of the person whose vote is considered is such that there is a substantial risk of that happening".[65]

59.   To date, this concept of an "independent organ" as such does not appear to have been established under Scots law. It seems more likely that this would be a general matter which would be considered by the court in ascertaining whether or not the action was in the interests of the company.[66] Consultation response for the Scottish interest on this point was mixed. Some consultees considered that the wishes of an "independent organ" should be conclusive. Others expressed concern that this would lead to the issue being pre-judged by the court. On balance, however, we think it is the case that Scottish courts would generally look at the matter - to assist them in ascertaining whether or not the action was in the interests of the company. We agree with the Law Commission[67] that the views of

---

[62]   See the discussion of the law of waiver in *Armia Ltd v Daejan Developments* 1979 SC (HL) 56; 1979 SLT.

[63]   The position where it amounts to effective waiver is discussed at paras 63-64 below.

[64]   See the discussion at paras 6.88-6.90 of the Report.

[65]   See para 6.88 of the Report and the discussion there of *Smith v Croft* (No 2) [1988] Ch 144.

[66]   For the discussion of that general matter, see paras 53-54 above.

[67]   See the recommendation set out at paras 6.90 and 8.11(10)(v) of the Report and rule 50.7(2) in Appendix B.

an "independent organ" should not be conclusive on the issue of whether or not leave should be granted. We also agree, however, that such views should be a factor to be taken account of by the court. Accordingly, as respects Scotland, we **recommend:**

> **(13) that the views (if any) of an independent organ that for commercial reasons the action should or should not be raised should be a specific matter to be taken account of by the court, but the views of the independent organ should not be conclusive on the issue of whether or not leave should be granted (clause 1: new section 458B, subsection (10)).**

Availability of alternative remedies

60. We agree with the Law Commission that the final matter which should be included in the list of matters of which the court should take account is the availability of other remedies.[68] Accordingly, as respects Scotland, we **recommend:**

> **(14) that the availability of alternative remedies should be a specific matter to be taken account of by the court, but that their availability should not necessarily be conclusive on the issue of whether or not leave should be granted (clause 1: new section 458B, subsection (10)).**

Criteria relevant to refusal of leave

61. We have explained above that we agree with the Law Commission that it would be unsatisfactory to require the court to apply fixed or definitive criteria for the *granting* of leave: rather, the court, as now, should take account of all relevant considerations. Consistent with the aim of seeking to clarify and make the law more accessible, however, there should be a list of certain specific matters falling within this head.[69]

62. We also indicated, however, that we considered it appropriate for there to be a requirement for the court to *refuse* leave in certain circumstances: on this, too, our policy is the same as that of the Law Commission.

63. The circumstances concerned are where the courts at present do not permit an action - the effect, therefore, being to deny title to sue. In short, the circumstances are where the court is satisfied that:

- the action is not in interests of the company;

- there has been effective ratification by the company in general meeting of the director's conduct, or effective waiver by the company in general

---

[68] See the discussion at paras 6.91-6.92, the related recommendation set out at paras 6.91 and 8.11(10)(vi) of the Report and rule 50.7(2) in Appendix B.

[69] See paras 48-51 above.

meeting of its claim against the director or the third party, as appropriate.[70]

64. Accordingly, as respects Scotland, we **recommend:**[71]

> **(15) that the court should refuse leave if satisfied that:**
>
> **(i) the action is not in the interests of the company; or**
>
> **(ii) there has been effective ratification by the company of the director's conduct or effective waiver by the company of its claim against the director or third party, as appropriate (clause 1: new section 458B, subsections (6) and (9)(b)).**

The manner in which the Secretary of State's enabling powers should be set out in the legislation

65. We have explained above our view that the requirements as to the matters of which the court should take account in considering the granting of leave and the criteria to be applied in relation to the refusal of leave should be set out by the Secretary of State by statutory instrument.[72]

66. We have given careful consideration to what should be the scope of the enabling power, and how that enabling power could properly be framed. It is not our intention that the Secretary of State should exercise his power in a manner which would stray into matters of procedure or which would derogate from the traditional power of the court to decide what is relevant within a framework of law laid down by Parliament.

67. To constrain the power, however, either positively, eg by specifying categories of criteria or matters which may be prescribed, or negatively by excluding certain categories, is not, in our view, an option. Either approach has potential for giving rise to significant problems in the future. In our view, at the very least, either approach would give rise to the possibility of at least doubtful vires and might result in there being no or inadequate vires to keep in step with developing case law and developments under English law in an area where it is desirable to be able to do so. We have explained above our view, and that of the Law Commission, that in substance this is an area where there should be consistency, as far as possible, in terms of policy between the jurisdictions.[73] This underlying policy aim was overwhelmingly supported on consultation.

68. We consider it essential, therefore, that the enabling power is not so constrained. We also consider it essential, however, that there is an adequate safeguard built

---

[70] See paras 32 and 56-57 above and the related discussion at paras 6.77-6.79 and 6.80-6.87 of the Report.

[71] The relevant recommendation by the Law Commission in respect of these matters is incorporated in the recommendations set out at paras 6.79, 6.86 and 8.11(9) and (10) of the Report: see also of rules 50.7 and 50.8 in Appendix B.

[72] Paras 39-42.

[73] Paras 4 and 40: see also the discussion at para 6.17 of the Report.

into the legislation to ensure that the Secretary of State does not so stray into matters which should be left to the courts. In our view, the appropriate safeguard is a requirement for the Secretary of State in exercising his power to consult with the Lord President of the Court of Session. The Lord President is content with such a requirement of consultation with him, and the Department of Trade and Industry is similarly content with this approach.

69. Accordingly, we **recommend**:

> **(16) that**
>
> **(a) express power should be conferred by statute on the Secretary of State to prescribe**
>
>> **(i) the matters (including the specific matters) of which the court must take account in reaching a decision as to whether to grant leave, and at any other stage in the action (clause 1: new section 458B, subsection (10)); and**
>>
>> **(ii) the criteria, any of which if shown to arise, should result in the court being required to refuse leave (clause 1: new section 458B, subsections (6) and (9)(b));**
>
> **(b) before exercising this power, the Secretary of State should be required to consult with the Lord President of the Court of Session; and that the Secretary of State's power should not be constrained otherwise than by this requirement of consultation (clause 1: new section 458B, subsections (9) and (10));**
>
> **(c) the court should take account of all relevant circumstances and such circumstances should, as at present, include the following matters**
>
> **- whether the applicant is acting in good faith in bringing the action,**
>
> **- whether the action is in the interests of the company, taking account of the views of the company's directors on commercial matters,**
>
> **- whether the director's conduct as a result of which the cause of action is alleged to arise may be approved by the company and (if it may be) whether it has purportedly been so approved,**
>
> **- whether the cause of action may be or has purportedly been waived by the company,**
>
> **- whether the company in general meeting has resolved not to raise proceedings in respect of the direcor's conduct against the director or the third party, as appropriate,**

- the opinion (if any) of an independent organ that for commercial reasons the action should or should not be pursued,

- whether an alternative remedy is available; and

(d) the criteria which should be prescribed, as at present, are:

- that the action is not in the interests of the company,

- that there has been effective ratification by the company of the director's conduct,

- that there has been effective waiver by the company of its claim against the director or third party, as appropriate.

Other relevant issues considered in Part 6 of Report

70.   The Law Commission consider a number of other issues in Part 6 of the Report in respect of the new derivative action recommended for English law. It is appropriate to discuss these also for Scotland.

Indemnity orders in relation to expenses

71.   The issue of costs indemnity orders relates to the derivative action under English law.[74] A similar issue, however, arises for Scotland. Under Scots law, as we have explained, the right of a shareholder to raise an action to protect the company's interests in respect of a director's breach of duty is not derived from the company. This has significant financial implications for applicants and potential applicants. Under Scots law, the court does not have a common law power to make an award of expenses against a person who is not a party to the cause unless he is the *dominus litis* or legal representative of the party.[75] The basis on which the action may be raised, and its purpose, is to protect the interests of the company and to obtain a remedy for the company. In our view, therefore, it is only right that the court should have power to grant an application by the shareholder for an indemnity out of the company's assets in respect of expenses incurred, or to be incurred, by him in relation to the action. This should not be confined to judicial expenses. The court should be able to make an award covering any and all expenses. Accordingly, as respects Scotland, we **recommend**:

> (17) that the court should have power to grant an application by the shareholder for an indemnity, out of the company's assets, in respect of expenses incurred or to be incurred by the member in relation to the action: this should not be confined to judicial expenses, but should be able to extend to all expenses incurred in relation to the action (clause 1: new section 458B, subsection (8)).

---

[74]   See para 6.104 and rule 50.13 in Appendix B to the Report.

[75]   *Meekison v Uniroyal Engelbert Tyres Ltd* 1995 SLT (Sh Ct) 63.

Court's power to appoint an independent expert

72.   The Law Commission do not consider that the court should have a special power to appoint an independent expert to investigate and advise on the action.[76] The consultation response for the Scottish interest was divided on this point. On balance, we agree with the views of the Law Commission.

Ability of member to seek remedy for himself under new statutory provision for Scotland

73.   The Law Commission have concluded that it should not be open to the court in a derivative action to make an order granting a personal benefit to a shareholder bringing that action, such as an order that the defendant wrongdoers buy the applicant's shares.[77] We agree that it would be inappropriate for a member raising an action under the new statutory provision we recommend for Scotland to be able to seek a remedy for himself in that action. We have explained above that, under Scots law at present, a member has a separate right of action to protect his own interests and to seek a remedy on his own behalf.[78] The new statutory provision recommended for Scotland is drawn explicitly to make clear that this right of action is preserved and not affected by the replacement of the existing common law right to raise an action to protect the interests of the company and to seek a remedy for the company by a new statutory right of action to do so.[79]

Multiple actions

74.   By multiple actions, in this context, we mean to refer to the discussion in the Report of whether a shareholder in a parent company should be able to bring an action under the new statutory provision for Scotland on behalf of a subsidiary or associated company within the group. The Law Commission conclude that there should be no express provision dealing with such actions.[80] The consultation response for the Scottish interest was divided on this point. On balance, we agree with the views expressed by the Law Commission.

Other matters

75.   Another matter discussed by the Law Commission in Part 6 of the Report is not, in our view, relevant as respects Scotland. The Law Commission discuss the question of the substitution of new plaintiffs to deal with conflict of interest situations making the initial plaintiff unsuitable to be a representative plaintiff.[81] This matter is not relevant for Scotland given the different background, namely that the member's right of action in Scotland is a direct right, and not derived from the company. He is not a "representative" applicant.

---

[76]   See para 6.99 of the Report.

[77]   See para 6.108 of the Report.

[78]   Paras 7 and 31.

[79]   See clause 1, new section 458B, subsection (12) set out in Appendix A to the Report.

[80]   For the discussion of this point, see paras 6.109-6.110 of the Report.

[81]   See paras 6.105-6.106 of the Report.

76. Other matters discussed by the Law Commission would constitute matters which, for Scotland, would appropriately be the subject of rules of court. Examples of such matters are whether it should be possible for a shareholder pursuer to be sisted into an action raised by the company but which the company fails to pursue diligently (in circumstances where this failure in itself is a breach of duty by the directors),[82] the sisting of an action on the ground that another action in respect of the same breach of duty is pending[83] and what are generally described as case management matters, eg, the power of the court to adjourn;[84] whether the company should be called as party to the action;[85] and discontinuance or compromise of actions.[86] As respects Scotland, the appropriate consultation would be carried out in the context of the relevant rules of court being drafted. Accordingly, we do not consider that these are matters on which it is appropriate for us to comment in this Appendix.

Summary of our recommendations as respects Scotland

77. In summary, as respects Scotland, **we recommend:**

> **(1) the right of a shareholder to raise an action to protect the interests of his company and to obtain a remedy on its behalf should be put on a clear statutory basis; (clause 1: new section 458B)**
>
> **(2) that a shareholder should be entitled to raise an action under the new statutory provision for Scotland if the cause of it arises as a result of an actual or threatened act or omission involving**
>
>> **(a) negligence, default, breach of duty or breach of trust by a director of the company, or**
>>
>> **(b) a director putting himself in a position where his personal interests conflict with his duties to the company; (clause 1: new section 458B, subsection (1)) and**
>
> **(3) that**
>
>> **(a) the action might be against the director or some other person, or both; (clause 1: new section 458B, subsection (2)) and**
>>
>> **(b) for the purposes of the new statutory provision, "director" should include a shadow director; (clause 1: new section 458B, subsection (9)(a))**

---

[82] See paras 6.60-6.65 of the Report.

[83] See para 6.94, n 139, of the Report.

[84] See paras 6.66-6.69 and 6.100-6.103 of the Report.

[85] See paras 6.94-6.96 of the Report.

[86] See para 6.107 of the Report.

(4) that the right of action under the new statutory provision for Scotland should be available only to members of the company; (clause 1: new section 458B, subsection (1))

(5) that the right of action under the new statutory provision for Scotland should replace the common law right of a shareholder to raise an action to protect the interests of the company and seek a remedy for the company in respect of a director's breach of duty; (clause 1: new section 458B)

(6) that, unless on cause shown the court orders otherwise, the applicant should be required to give the company notice of his intention to raise the action 28 days before the action is raised; and that the notice should specify the grounds of action and state that, if the company does not bring proceedings in respect of the cause of action, the applicant intends to raise the action; (clause 1: new section 458B, subsections (3) to (5))

(7) that leave of the court should be required to raise an action under the new statutory provision for Scotland; (clause 1: new section 458B, subsection (1))

(8) that in considering whether to grant leave, the court should take account of all the relevant circumstances, without limit, and in particular, should take account of certain prescribed matters; (clause 1: new section 458B, subsection (10))

(9) that the good faith of the applicant should be a specific matter to be taken account of by the court, but it should not be a pre-requisite; and that the concept of good faith should not be defined; (clause 1: new section 458B, subsection (10))

(10) that the interests of the company should be a specific matter to be taken account of by the court, and in doing so, the court should have regard to the views of directors on commercial matters; (clause 1: new section 458B, subsection (10))

(11) that the fact that the director's conduct has purportedly been, or may be, approved by the company in general meeting or that the company's claim against the director or the third party, as appropriate, has purportedly been, or may be, so waived by the company should be a specific matter to be taken account of by the court; (clause 1: new section 458B, subsection (10))

(12) that the fact that the company in general meeting has resolved not to raise proceedings in respect of a director's conduct, against the director or third party, as appropriate, should be a specific matter to be taken account of by the court (clause 1: new section 458B, subsection (10))

(13) that the views (if any) of an independent organ that for commercial reasons the action should or should not be raised should be a specific matter to be taken account of by the court, but the views of the independent organ should not be conclusive on the issue of whether or not leave should be granted; (clause 1: new section 458B, subsection (10))

(14) that the availability of alternative remedies should be a specific matter to be taken account of by the court, but that their availability should not necessarily be conclusive on the issue of whether or not leave should be granted; (clause 1: new section 458B, subsection (10))

(15) that the court should refuse leave if satisfied that:

(i) the action is not in the interests of the company; or

(ii) there has been effective ratification by the company of the director's conduct or effective waiver by the company of its claim against the director or third party, as appropriate; (clause 1: new section 458B, subsections (6) and (9)(b))

(16) that

(a) express power should be conferred by statute on the Secretary of State to prescribe

(i) the matters (including the specific matters) of which the court must take account in reaching a decision as to whether to grant leave, and at any other stage in the action; (clause 1: new section 458B, subsection (10)) and

(ii) the criteria, any of which if shown to arise, should result in the court being required to refuse leave; (clause 1: section 458B, subsections (6) and (9)(b))

(b) before exercising this power, the Secretary of State should be required to consult with the Lord President of the Court of Session; and that the Secretary of State's power should not constrained otherwise than by this requirement of consultation; (clause 1: new section 458B, subsections (9) and (10))

(c) the court should take account of all relevant circumstances and such circumstances should, as at present, include the following matters

- whether the applicant is acting in good faith in bringing the action,

- whether the action is in the interests of the company, taking account of the views of the company's directors on commercial matters,

- whether the director's conduct as a result of which the cause of action is alleged to arise may be approved by the company and (if it may be) whether it has purportedly been so approved,

- whether the cause of action may be or has purportedly been waived by the company,

- whether the company in general meeting has resolved not to raise proceedings in respect of the director's conduct against the director or third party, as appropriate,

- the opinion (if any) of an independent organ that for commercial reasons the action should or should not be pursued,

- whether an alternative remedy is available; and

(d) the criteria which should be prescribed, as at present, are:

- that the action is not in the interests of the company,

- that there has been effective ratification by the company of the director's conduct,

- that there has been effective waiver by the company of its claim against the director or third party, as appropriate;

(17) that the court should have power to grant an application by the shareholder for an indemnity, out of the company's assets, in respect of expenses incurred or to be incurred by the member in relation to the action: this should not be confined to judicial expenses, but should be able to extend to all expenses incurred in relation to the action; (clause 1: new section 458B, subsection (8)).

APPENDIX E

Relevant extracts from the Companies Act 1985 (including proposed amendments)

Section 14

(1)   Subject to the provisions of this Act, the memorandum and articles, when registered, bind the company and its members to the same extent as if they respectively had been signed and sealed by each member, and contained covenants on the part of each member to observe all the provisions of the memorandum and of the articles.

...

Section 458A

(1)   A derivative action is an action by a member of a company where the cause of action is vested in the company and relief is sought on its behalf.

(2)   A derivative action may be brought if and only if the cause of action arises as a result of an actual or proposed act or omission involving—

> *(a)   negligence, default, breach of duty or breach of trust by a director of the company, or*

> *(b)   a director putting himself in a position where his personal interests conflict with his duties to the company.*

(3)   The cause of action may be against the director or another person (or both).

(4)   Subsections (1) to (3) do not affect the court's power to make an order under section 461(2)(c) or anything done under such an order.

(5)   References in this section to a director include references to a shadow director.

(6)   This section does not apply to Scotland.

Section 458B

(1)   In Scotland, to protect the interests of a company and obtain a remedy on its behalf, a member of the company is, with leave of the court and subject to subsections (3) to (5), entitled to raise under this section an action the cause of which arises as a result of an actual or proposed act or omission involving—

> *(a)   negligence, default, breach of duty or breach of trust by a director of the company, or*

> *(b)   a director putting himself in a position where his personal interests conflict with his duties to the company.*

(2)   The action may be against the director or another person (or both).

(3)   Subject to subsection (5), the member shall serve notice on the company that, unless within the period of 28 days beginning with the day of service the company raises an action as respects the actual or proposed act or omission, he intends to raise such an action under this section; and it shall not be competent for the member to raise it until that period has elapsed.

(4)   The notice shall specify the cause of action and shall include a summary of the facts on which the action is based.

(5)   The court may on cause shown disapply, or modify the application of, the provisions of subsections (3) and (4) in any case.

(6)   Leave of the court shall be refused for the purposes of subsection (1) if any of the relevant criteria is shown to arise.

(7)   Subsections (1) to (6) do not affect the court's power to make an order under section 461(2)(c) or anything done under such an order.

(8)   In an action raised under this section the court may, on such terms as it thinks fit, grant an application by the member for an indemnity, out of the company's assets, in respect of expenses incurred, or to be incurred, by him in or in relation to the action.

(9)   References in this section—

> *(a)   to a director, include a shadow director; and*

> *(b)   to relevant criteria, are to such criteria as may be prescribed for the purposes of this section after consultation with the Lord President of the Court of Session.*

(10)   There may also be prescribed, after such consultation, matters to which the court shall have regard in reaching a decision—

> *(a)   at any stage, in an action raised under this section; or*

> *(b)   as to whether to grant leave for the purposes of subsection (1).*

(11)   A statutory instrument made by virtue of subsection (9)(b) or (10) shall be subject to annulment in pursuance of a resolution of either House of Parliament.

(12)   This section is without prejudice to the right of a member of a company to raise an action to protect his own interests and to obtain a remedy on his own behalf.

Section 459

(1)   A member of a company may apply to the court by petition for an order under this Part on the ground that the company's affairs are being or have been conducted in a manner which is unfairly prejudicial to the interests of its members generally or of some part of its members (including at least himself) or that any actual or proposed act or omission of the company (including an act or omission on its behalf) is or would be so prejudicial.

(1A) A petition for an order under this Part may include an application to the court to order the winding up of the company, but only if the court gives leave for it to include such an application.

(2)   The provisions of this Part apply to a person who is not a member of a company but to whom shares in the company have been transferred or transmitted by operation of law, as those provisions apply to a member of the company; and references to a member or members are to be construed accordingly.

(3)   In this section (and so far as applicable for the purposes of this section, in section 461(2)) "company" means any company within the meaning of this Act or any company which is not such a company but is a statutory water company within the meaning of the Statutory Water Companies Act 1991.

Section 459A

(1)   This section applies if—

> *(a)   a member of a private company limited by shares petitions under section 459(1) for an order under this Part,*
>
> *(b)   it is shown that the member has been removed as a director or has been prevented from carrying out all (or substantially all) his functions as a director,*
>
> *(c)   immediately before the removal or prevention mentioned in paragraph (b) the member held at least 10 per cent of the voting rights in the company, and*
>
> *(d)   immediately before the removal or prevention mentioned in paragraph (b) all (or substantially all) the members of the company fulfilled the director condition set out in subsection (3).*

(2)   Unless the contrary is shown, it must be presumed that because of the removal or prevention mentioned in subsection (1)(b) the company's affairs have been conducted in a manner which is unfairly prejudicial to the interests of the petitioner.

(3)   A member fulfils the director condition at the time concerned if he is then a director of the company.

(4)   Nothing in this section affects the operation of section 459 apart from this section.

Section 459B(1)   *The reference in section 459A(1)(c) to the voting rights in the company is to the rights conferred on shareholders in respect of their shares to vote at general meetings of the company on all (or substantially all) matters.*

(2)   For the purposes of section 459A(1)(c) rights of the member must be taken into account only if they are rights as sole holder of shares.

(3)   For the purposes of section 459A(1)(c) rights which are exercisable only in certain circumstances must be taken into account only—

(a) *when the circumstances have arisen, and for so long as they continue to obtain, or*

(b) *when the circumstances are within the control of the person who has the rights.*

(4) *For the purposes of section 459A(1)(c) rights which are normally exercisable but are temporarily incapable of exercise must continue to be taken into account.*

(5) *The following rules apply for the purposes of section 459A(1)(d) if at the time concerned a share is held by persons jointly—*

(a) *if at least one of the holders is a director of the company, the director whose name appears first in the company's register of members must be taken to be the only member by virtue of the share;*

(b) *in any other case, the holder whose name appears first in the company's register of members must be taken to be the only member by virtue of the share.*

...

Section 461

(1) If the court is satisfied that a petition under this Part is well founded, it may make such order as it thinks fit for giving relief in respect of the matters complained of.

(2) Without prejudice to the generality of subsection (1), the court's order may—

(a) regulate the conduct of the company's affairs in the future,

(b) require the company to refrain from doing or continuing an act complained of by the petitioner or to do an act which the petitioner has complained it has omitted to do,

(c) authorise civil proceedings to be brought in the name and on behalf of the company by such person or persons and on such terms as the court may direct,

(d) provide for the purchase of the shares of any members of the company by other members or by the company itself and, in the case of a purchase by the company itself, the reduction of the company's capital accordingly,

(e) *provide for the company to be wound up.*

(2A) *However, the court may not provide for the company to be wound up unless the petition includes an application to the court to order its winding up.*

(3) If an order under this Part requires the company not to make any, or any specified, alteration in the memorandum or articles, the company does not then have power without leave of the court to make any such alteration in breach of that requirement.

(4)   Any alteration in the company's memorandum or articles made by virtue of an order under this Part is of the same effect as if duly made by resolution of the company, and the provisions of this Act apply to the memorandum or articles as so altered accordingly.

(5)   An office copy of an order under this Part altering, or giving leave to alter, a company's memorandum or articles shall, within 14 days from the making of the order or such longer period as the court may allow, be delivered by the company to the registrar of companies for registration; and if a company makes default in complying with this subsection, the company and every officer of it who is in default is liable to a fine and, for continued contravention, to a daily default fine.

(6)   The power under section 411 of the Insolvency Act to make rules shall, so far as it relates to a winding-up petition, apply for the purposes of a petition under this Part.

Section 461A

(1)   This section applies if—

> *(a)   by virtue of section 459A the presumption there mentioned applies and the contrary is not shown, and*

> *(b)   the court decides to make an order under this Part providing for the purchase of the petitioner's shares.*

(2)   It must be presumed that the order should provide for—

> *(a)   the purchase to be for a price which represents for each share of a particular class a rateable proportion of the market value of all the company's shares of that class;*

> *(b)   that market value to be found by assuming a sale by a willing seller to a willing buyer of all the company's issued share capital.*

(3)   The presumption mentioned in subsection (2) is displaced if the court orders it to be displaced.

Section 461B

(1)   The provisions of the Insolvency Act 1986 about winding up on the application of a contributory (except for sections 122, 124 and 125) apply in a case where an application for the winding up of a company is included in a petition under section 459(1) by virtue of section 459(1A).

(2)   Subsection (3) has effect if a member of a company petitions under section 459(1) for an order under this Part and the petition is amended so as—

> *(a)   to include an application for the winding up of the company by virtue of section 459(1A), or*

(b)   to include an application for the winding up of the company under section 122(1)(g) of the Insolvency Act 1986 (the just and equitable ground).

(3)   In such a case section 129(2) of the Insolvency Act 1986 (winding up deemed to commence at time of presentation of petition) applies as if the reference to the presentation of the petition for winding up were to the making of the amendment of the petition.

APPENDIX F

Relevant extracts from the Insolvency Act 1986 (including proposed amendments)

Section 122

(1)   A company may be wound up by the court if—

(a)   the company has by special resolution resolved that the company be wound up by the court,

(b)   being a public company which was registered as such on its original incorporation, the company has not been issued with a certificate under section 117 of the Companies Act (public company share capital requirements) and more than a year has expired since it was so registered,

(c)   it is an old public company, within the meaning of the Consequential Provisions Act,

(d)   the company does not commence its business within a year from its incorporation or suspends its business for a whole year,

(e)   except in the case of a private company limited by shares or by guarantee, the number of members is reduced below 2,

(f)   the company is unable to pay its debts,

(g)   the court is of the opinion that it is just and equitable that the company should be wound up.

...

Section 124

(1)   Subject to the provisions of this section, an application to the court for the winding up of a company shall be by petition presented either by the company, or the directors, or by any creditor or creditors (including any contingent or prospective creditor or creditors), contributory or contributories or by the clerk of a magistrates' court in the exercise of the power conferred by section 87A of the Magistrates' Courts Act 1980 (enforcement of fines imposed on companies), or by all or any of those parties, together or separately.

(2)   Except as mention below, a contributory is not entitled to present a winding-up petition unless either—

(a)   the number of members is reduced below 2, or

(b)   the shares in respect of which he is a contributory, or some of them, either were originally allotted to him, or have been held by him and registered in his name, for at least 6 months during the 18 months before the commencement of the winding up, or have devolved on him through the death of a former holder.

(3)   A person who is liable under section 76 to contribute to a company's assets in the event of its being wound up may petition on either of the grounds set out in section 122(1)(f) and (g), and subsection (2) above does not then apply; but unless the person is a contributory otherwise than under section 76, he may not in his character as contributory petition on any other ground.

This subsection is deemed included in Chapter VII of Part V of the Companies Act (redeemable shares; purchase by a company of its own shares) for the purposes of the Secretary of State's power to make regulations under section 179 of that Act.

(4)   A winding-up petition may be presented by the Secretary of State—

      (a)   if the ground of the petition is that in section 122(1)(b) or (c), or

      (b)   in a case falling within section 124A below.

(5)   Where a company is being wound voluntarily in England and Wales, a winding-up petition may be presented by the official receiver attached to the court as well as by any other person authorised in that behalf under the other provisions of this section; but the court shall not make a winding-up order on the petition unless it is satisfied that the voluntary winding up cannot be continued with due regard to the interests of the creditors or contributories.

...

Section 124AA

(1)   Unless he has the court's leave, a member of a company may not—

      (a)   apply to wind it up under section 122(1)(g) when he makes or while he is pursuing a section 459 application with regard to it;

      (b)   pursue an application to wind it up under section 122(1)(g) if, having made the application, he makes a section 459 application with regard to it.

(2)   A section 459 application is an application under section 459 of the Companies Act 1985 (unfair prejudice).

Section 125

(2)   If the petition is presented by members of the company as contributories on the ground that it is just and equitable that the company should be wound up, the court, if it is of opinion—

      (a) that the petitioners are entitled to relief either by winding up the company or by some other means, and

      (b)   that in the absence of any other remedy it would be just and equitable that the company should be wound up, shall make a winding-up order; but this does not apply if the court is also of the opinion both that some other remedy is available to the petitioners and that they are acting unreasonably in seeking to have the company wound up instead of pursuing that other remedy.

...

Section 127

In a winding up by the court, any disposition of the company's property, and any transfer of shares, or alteration in the status of the company's members, made after the commencement of the winding up is, unless the court otherwise orders, void.

...

Section 129

(1)   If, before the presentation of a petition for the winding up of a company by the court, a resolution has been passed by the company for voluntary winding up, the winding up of the company is deemed to have commenced at the time of the passing of the resolution; and unless the court, on proof of fraud or mistake, directs otherwise, all proceedings taken in the voluntary winding up are deemed to have been validly taken.

(2)   In any other case, the winding up of a company by the court is deemed to commence at the time of the presentation of the petition for winding up.

APPENDIX G
1990 Practice Direction (Ch D) (Companies Court: Contributory's Petition)

1. Practitioners' attention is drawn to the undesirability of including as a matter of course a prayer for winding up as an alternative to an order under section 459 of the Companies Act 1985. It should be included only if that is the relief which the petitioner prefers or if it is considered that it may be the only relief to which he is entitled.

2. Whenever a prayer for winding up is included in a contributory's petition, the petition shall include a statement whether the petitioner consents or objects to an order under section 127 of the Insolvency Act 1986 in the standard form, and if he objects the affidavit in support shall contain a short statement of his reasons.

3. If the petitioner objects to a section 127 order in the standard form but consents to such an order in a modified form, the petition shall set out the form of order to which he consents, and the affidavit in support shall contain a short statement of his reasons for seeking the modification.

4. If the petition contains a statement that the petitioner consents to a section 127 order, whether in the standard or a modified form, but the petitioner changes his mind before the first hearing of the petition, he shall notify the respondents and may apply on notice to a judge for an order directing that no section 127 order or a modified order only (as the case may be) shall be made by the registrar, but validating dispositions made without notice of the order made by the judge.

5. If the petition contains a statement that the petitioner consents to a section 127 order, whether in the standard or a modified form, the registrar shall without further inquiry make an order in such form at the first hearing unless an order to the contrary has been made by the judge in the mean time.

6. If the petition contains a statement that the petitioner objects to a section 127 order in the standard form, the company may apply (in cases of urgency ex parte) to the judge for an order.

SECTION 127 ORDER
STANDARD FORM

"ORDER that notwithstanding the presentation of the said petition

> (1) payments made into or out of the bank accounts of the company in the ordinary course of the business of the company and

> (2) dispositions of the property of the company made in the ordinary course of its business for proper value

between the date of presentation of the petition and the date of judgment on the petition or further order in the mean time shall not be void by virtue of the provisions of section 127 of the Insolvency Act 1986 in the event of an order for the winding up of the company being made on the said petition."

By direction of the Vice-Chancellor
22 February 1990

APPENDIX H
Companies (Unfair Prejudice Applications) Proceedings Rules 1986

Citation, commencement and interpretation

1 (1) These Rules may be cited as the Companies (Unfair Prejudice Applications) Proceedings Rules 1986 and shall come into force on 29th December 1986.

(2) In these Rules "the Act" means the Companies Act 1985.

Preliminary

2 (1) These Rules apply in relation to petitions presented to the court on or after 29th December 1986 under Part XVII of the Act (protection of company's members against unfair prejudice) by a member of a company under section 459(1), by a person treated as a member under section 459(2) or by the Secretary of State under section 460.

(2) Except so far as inconsistent with the Act and these Rules, the Rules of the Supreme Court and the practice of the High Court apply to proceedings under Part XVII of the Act in the High Court, and the Rules and practice of the County Court apply to such proceedings in a county court, with any necessary modifications.

Presentation of petition

3 (1) The petition shall be in the form set out in the Schedule to these Rules, with such variations, if any, as the circumstances may require.

(2) The petition shall specify the grounds on which it is presented and the nature of the relief which is sought by the petitioner, and shall be delivered to the court for filing with sufficient copies for service under Rule 4.

(3) The court shall fix a hearing for a day ("the return day") on which, unless the court otherwise directs, the petitioner and any respondent (including the company) shall attend before the registrar in chambers for directions to be given in relation to the procedure on the petition.

(4) On fixing the return day, the court shall return to the petitioner sealed copies of the petition for service, each endorsed with the return day and the time of hearing.

Service of petition

4 (1) The petitioner shall, at least 14 days before the return day, serve a sealed copy of the petition on the company.

(2) In the case of a petition based upon section 459 of the Act, the petitioner shall also, at least 14 days before the return day, serve a sealed copy of the petition on every respondent named in the petition.

Return of petition

5 On the return day, or at any time after it, the court shall give such directions as it thinks appropriate with respect to the following matters—

(a)   service of the petition on any person, whether in connection with the time, date and place of a further hearing, or for any other purpose;

(b)   whether particulars of claim and defence are to be delivered, and generally as to the procedure on the petition;

(c)   whether, and if so by what means, the petition is to be advertised;

(d)   the manner in which any evidence is to be adduced at any hearing before the judge and in particular (but without prejudice to the generality of the above) as to-

      (i)   the taking of evidence wholly or in part by affidavit or orally;
      (ii)   the cross-examination of any deponents to affidavits;
      (iii)   the matters to be dealt with in evidence;

(e)   any other matter affecting the procedure on the petition or in connection with the hearing and disposal of the petition.

Settlement and advertisement of the order

6 (1) When an order has been made by the court under Part XVII of the Act, the petitioner and every other person who has appeared on the hearing of the petition shall, not later than the business day following that on which the order is made, leave at the court all the documents required for enabling the order to be completed forthwith.

(2) It is not necessary for the court to appoint a time, date and place for any person to attend to settle the order, unless in any particular case the special circumstances make an appointment necessary.

(3) If the court considers that the order should be advertised, it shall give directions as to the manner and time of advertisement.

APPENDIX I
Relevant extracts from the Draft Civil Proceedings Rules

The overriding objective

1.1   (1)   The overriding objective of these Rules is to enable the court to deal with cases justly.

(2)   The court must apply the Rules so as to further the overriding objective.

(3)   Dealing with a case justly includes-

(a)   ensuring, so far as is practicable, that the parties are on an equal footing;

(b)   saving expense;

(c)   dealing with the case in ways which are proportionate-

(i)   to the amount of money involved;

(ii)   to the importance of the case;

(iii)   to the complexity of the issues; and

(iv)   to the parties' financial position;

(d)   ensuring that it is dealt with expeditiously; and

(e)   allotting to it an appropriate share of the court's resources, while taking into account the need to allot resources to other cases.

Duty of the parties

1.2   The parties must help the court to further the overriding objective.

Court's duty to manage cases

1.3   The court must further the overriding objective by actively managing cases, and in particular-

(a)   by identifying the issues at an early stage;

(b)   by deciding, as soon as is practicable after they have been identified, which issues need full investigation and trial and accordingly disposing summarily of the others;

(c)   by encouraging the parties to use alternative dispute resolution procedure if the court considers that appropriate and by facilitating their use of such procedure;

(d)   by helping the parties to settle the whole or part of the case;

(e)   by deciding the order in which issues are to be resolved;

(f)   by fixing timetables or otherwise controlling the progress of the case;

(g)   by considering whether the likely benefits of taking a particular step will justify the cost of taking it;

(h)   by dealing with as many aspects of the case as is practicable on the same occasion;

(i)   by dealing with the case, where it appears appropriate to do so, without the parties needing to attend at court; and

(j)   by the appropriate use of technology.

...

Scope of this Part

14.1   This Part sets out a procedure by which the court may decide a case or part of a case without a trial.

Grounds for summary judgment

14.2   The court may give summary judgment on the whole of a claim or on a particular issue if-

(a)   it considers that-

(i)   the claimant has no realistic prospect of success on the claim or issue; or

(ii)   the defendant has no realistic prospect of success on his defence to the claim or issue; and

(b)   there is no other reason why the case or issue should be disposed of at a trial.

Types of proceedings in which summary judgment is available

14.3   The court may give summary judgment in any type of proceedings except-

(a)   proceedings which have been allocated to the small claims track;

(b)   proceedings for possession of residential premises against a tenant or a person holding over after the end of his tenancy; and

(c)   proceedings for-

(i)   malicious prosecution;

          (ii)   false imprisonment; or

          (iii)   libel or slander.

Procedure

14.4   (1)   The court may give summary judgment on or without an application.

        (2)   Where a summary judgment hearing is fixed, the respondent (or the parties where the hearing is fixed without an application) must be given at least 7 days' notice of-

          (a)   the date fixed for the hearing; and

          (b)   the issues which the court is proposed to decide at the hearing.

        (3)   Where a defendant applies for summary judgment before filing a defence, the application must be supported by evidence.

        (4)   If a party wishes to rely on evidence which was not set out in or attached to a statement of case, he must-

          (a)   file the evidence; and

          (b)   serve copies on any other party,

        at least 3 days before the summary judgment hearing.

        (Part 10 contains the general rules about how to make an application.)

    …

Duty of court to control evidence

28.1   It is the duty of the court to control the evidence by deciding-

          (a)   the issues on which it requires evidence;

          (b)   the nature of the evidence which it requires; and

          (c)   the way in which any matter is to be proved.

Evidence at trial - general rule

28.2   (1)   The general rule is that any fact which needs to be proved at a trial by the evidence of witnesses is to be proved by their oral evidence given in public.

        (2)   This is subject-

(a)   to any provision to the contrary contained in these Rules or elsewhere; and

(b)   to any order of the court.

Evidence by video link or other means

28.3   Where a witness would give his evidence orally, the court may allow the witness to give evidence without attending through a video link or by other means.

Witness statements

28.4   Subject to any order of the court, a witness statement is admissible as evidence of any fact which needs to be proved.

APPENDIX J
Statistics relating to the filing of section 459 petitions

The court files relating to petitions presented to the Companies Court at the Royal Courts of Justice between January 1994 and December 1996 seeking relief under section 459 of the Companies Act 1985 were inspected with the leave of Mr Registrar Buckley. A total of 254 section 459 petitions were recorded as presented during the relevant period. A total of 233 section 459 petitions were inspected.

		of 233	%
Petitioner	minority shareholder/s	164	70.4
	50% shareholder	56	24.0
	majority shareholder	6	2.6
	personal representative	5	2.1
	unknown	2	0.9
Sections	459 alone	144	61.8
	459 and 122(1)(g)*	88	37.8
	54† (in addition to any of above)	1	0.4
	371† (in addition to any of above)	2	0.9
Type of company	private	225	96.6
	public	8	3.4
No of shareholders	2	79	33.9
	3 - 5	112	48.1
	6 - 10	25	10.7
	over 10	10	4.3
	not known	7	3.0
Pre-existing partnership	no partnership	211	90.6
	partnership of		
	up to 3 years	6	2.6
	over 3 years	6	2.6
	unknown length	10	4.3
Involvement in management	all/most of shareholders involved		
	joint venture	30	12.9
	family company	33	14.2
	other cases where all/most involved	113	48.5
	not mostly involved/unclear	57	24.5
Ebrahimi considerations pleaded‡	mutual trust and confidence	83	35.6
	continued participation	84	36.1
	restriction on transfer of shares	3	1.3
Specific reference to quasi-partnership		71	30.5
Legitimate expectation pleaded♠		123	52.8
Time span of allegations	up to 1 year	84	36.1
	1 - 2 years	32	13.7
	2 - 5 years	71	30.5
	5 - 10 years	19	8.2
	over 10 years	7	3.0
	not given/applicable	26	11.2
Average: **2.75** **years**			

Allegations pleaded♥	exclusion from management	150	64.4
	failure to provide information	93	39.9
	mismanagement	64	27.5
	misappropriation of assets	93	39.9
	excessive remuneration	36	15.5
	failure to remunerate/pay dividend	53	22.7
	improper allotment/unfair increase in capital	27	11.6
	unfair offer for shares/failure to purchase	15	6.4
	failure to register	4	1.7
	breach of statute	49	21.0
	breach of articles	26	11.2
	breach of agreement	60	25.8
	other breach of fiduciary duty	70	30.0
	deadlock	35	15.0
	other	57	24.5
Relief sought under s 461♦	purchase of P's shares	162	69.5
	sale of R's shares	55	23.6
	purchase or sale of shares in related co	3	1.3
	injunction	54	23.2
	declaration	31	13.3
	regulation of co affairs	25	10.7
	461(2)(c)	27	11.6
	duty to account	35	15.0
	compensatory damages	17	7.3
	interest	7	3.0
	rectification	12	5.2
	appointment of receiver	7	3.0
	other	19	8.2
Relief under 122(1)(g)		87	37.3
Other statutory relief♣		10	4.3
Rule 5 hearing	points of claim ordered	52	22.3
	petition to stand as points of claim	84	36.1
	no order made as to pleadings	97	41.6
	order preventing advertisement	62	26.6
	pre-trial hearing ordered	1	0.4
Strike out	applied for	46	19.7
	successful (including in part)	14	30.4
	failing completely	9	19.6
	no order made	23	50.0

179

Outcome	ongoing	89	38.2
	settlement	44	18.9
	struck out entirely	17	7.3
	full hearing	10	4.3
	adjourned generally/stayed	39	16.7
	dormant	34	14.6
Time for disposal of first instance proceedings	up to 3 months	26	11.2
	3 - 6 months	20	8.6
	6 - 12 months	14	6.0
	over 12 months	7	3.0
	not disposed of	172	73.8
Average: **4.71 months**			
Legally aided petitioner		46	19.7

NOTES

*   Of the Insolvency Act 1986.

†   Of the Companies Act 1985.

‡   Note that any given petition may include reference to one or more of these considerations.

♠   Including reliance on agreement, without necessarily specific reference to legitimate expectations.

♥   Note that any given petition may include reference to one or more of these allegations.

♦   Note that any given petition may include reference to one or more of these forms of relief.

♣   Under sections 54, 359 or 371 of the Companies Act 1985, or statutory interest under section 35A of the Supreme Court Act 1981.

APPENDIX K
List of persons and organisations who commented on Consultation Paper No 142

The following list includes not only those who responded to the consultation paper, but also those who assisted subsequently.

Judges

Judge Paul Baker QC (retired)

Judge John Behrens

Mr Registrar Buckley

Lord Justice Chadwick

Mr Justice Colman

Judge George

Judge Howarth

District Judge G A Needham

Lord Penrose, Scottish Court of Session

Mr Justice Rattee

District Judge J B Rawkins

Lord Rodger of Earlsferry, the Lord President of the Scottish Court of Session

Sir Richard Scott V-C

Lord Justice Staughton

Lord Justice Robert Walker

Barristers (including barristers' organisations)

Richard Adkins QC (3/4 South Square, Gray's Inn)

James H Allen QC (Chancery House Chambers, Leeds)

George Bompas QC (4 Stone Buildings, Lincoln's Inn)

Michael Briggs QC (Thirteen Old Square, Lincoln's Inn)

Chancery Bar Association

The Commercial Bar Association

Michael Crystal QC and Simon Mortimore QC (3/4 South Square, Gray's Inn)

Anthony Elleray QC (St James's Chambers, Manchester)

Erskine Chambers

The Faculty of Advocates

Peter Griffiths (4 Stone Buildings, Lincoln's Inn)

Victor Joffe (13 Old Square, Lincoln's Inn)

Law Reform Committee, General Council of the Bar

Ian Leeming QC (St John Street, Manchester)

N F Riddle (14 Castle Street, Liverpool)

Catherine Roberts (Erskine Chambers)

R A Sterling (St James Chambers, Manchester)

Sir Thomas Stockdale (Erskine Chambers)

Andrew Thompson (Erskine Chambers)

Bernard Weatherill QC (3 New Square, Lincoln's Inn)

Robert Wright QC (Erskine Chambers)

Solicitors (including solicitors' organisations)

Burness Solicitors

Colin Bamford (Financial Law Panel)

Susan Biddle (Biddle & Co)

Bournemouth & District Law Society

British Association of Lawyer Mediators

City of Westminster Law Society (Company/Commercial Law Committee)

David Doyle⊕ (Dickinson, Cruickshank & Co)

D J Freeman

Dundas & Wilson Solicitors

Frere Cholmeley Bischoff

Christopher Gibbons (Stephenson Harwood)

Belinda Gibson (Mallesons Stephen Jaques)

Anthony Gubbins (Wedlake Bell)

Daniel Harris (Quin & Hampson)②

Hertfordshire Law Society (Property & Commercial Committee)

J C Hill (Shoosmiths & Harrison)

The Law Society Commerce and Industry Group

The Law Society Company Law Committee

The Law Society of Scotland

London Solicitors Litigation Association

Lovell White Durrant

Mark Mattison (Eversheds)

Peter Mount (Leeds Day)

Nicholson Graham & Jones

Northamptonshire Law Society (Non-Contentious Business Sub Committee)

Rochdale Law Association

William Knight (Simmons & Simmons)

Suffolk & North Essex Law Society

Surrey Law Society (Commercial Sub Committee)

Sussex Law Society

Keith Wallace (Richards Butler)

John Wylde (Davies Arnold Cooper)

Academic Lawyers

Colin Baxter (University of Hull Law School)

Professor A J Boyle (Queen Mary and Westfield College)

Stephen Copp (Bournemouth University)

Simon Deakin (ESRC Centre for Business Research, University of Cambridge)

Professor Deborah A Demott (Duke University School of Law, North Carolina)

Professor Janet Dine (University of Essex)

Professor John Farrar (Bond University, Queensland, Australia)

Professor Nigel Fury (University of Bristol)

N J M Grier (Napier University, Edinburgh)

Stephen Griffin (University of Wales)

Professor J Henning (University of the Orange Free State)

Andrew Hicks (University of Exeter)

Michael Lower (Liverpool, John Moores University)

Masumi Matsushima (Meiji University)

Dr Leslie Moran (Lancaster University)

Professor G K Morse (University of Nottingham)

Dr Hans-Friedrich Muller (University of Mainz)

Professor D A Oesterle (University of Colorado)

Professor J E Parkinson (University of Bristol)

Ben Pettet (University College, London)

Dr Sven Reckewerth (British Institute of International and Comparative Law)

Professor William M Rees (Institute of Advanced Legal Studies)

C A Riley (University of Hull Law School)

Professor L S Sealy (Cambridge University)

Professor David Sugarman (Lancaster University)

G R Sullivan (University of Durham)

Accountants (including accountants' organisations)

John P Allday (Ernst & Young)

Association of Chartered Certified Accountants

Bruce Sutherland & Co

Angela M Hennesy

Institute of Chartered Accountants in England and Wales

Small Practitioners Association

Chris Swinson (BDO Stoy Hayward)

Companies and commercial organisations

ANZ Bank

Barclays Group

Centre for Dispute Resolution

City Disputes Panel

Guardian Asset Management

Institute of Business Ethics

Hambros Group Investments Ltd

HSBC Holdings plc

Hugh J Osburn (American Appraisal (UK) Ltd)

Jim Lowe and Company

Kelvin King (Corporate Valuations)

Mercury Asset Management

Natwest Group

Portman Building Society

West of England Trust Ltd (Jordans)

Representative bodies (other than legal and accountancy organisations)

The Academy of Experts

The Association of Registration Agents Ltd

The Chartered Institute of Arbitrators

Confederation of British Industry

The Institute of Chartered Secretaries

The Institute of Directors

The National Association of Pension Funds Limited

The Small Business Bureau

UK Shareholders Association

Government and regulatory bodies

Companies House

The Court Service

Department of Trade and Industry

The Insolvency Service

London Stock Exchange

Lord Chancellor's Department

Securities and Investments Board

Individuals

Leon Curzon

Derek French

Ewan MacIntyre

John Pickering

I G C Stratton

①Barristers and Attorneys at Law.

⊕ Advocate, Isle of Man.

Printed in the UK for The Stationery Office Limited on behalf of the
Controller of Her Majesty's Stationery Office
Dd 5067730, 10/97, 39462, Job No 27947